Power in Education

WE DEDICATE THESE PAGES
TO
GEORGE AND LOUISE SPINDLER
GEORGE DEVOS
AND
PAULO FREIRE
IN RECOGNITION OF THEIR THEORETICAL
CONTRIBUTIONS TO EDUCATIONAL RESEARCH
AND
AS A TOKEN OF OUR PERSONAL GRATITUDE

Power in Education
The Case of Miao University Students and its Significance for American Culture

Henry T. Trueba
Yali Zou

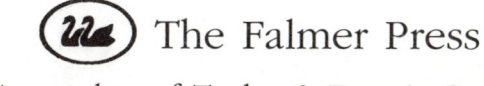 The Falmer Press

(A member of Taylor & Francis Group)
Washington, DC • London

UK   The Falmer Press, 4 John Street, London WC1N 2ET
USA   The Falmer Press, Taylor & Francis Inc., 1900 Frost Road, Suite 101, Bristol, PA 19007

© H.T. Trueba and Y. Zou 1994

All rights reserved. No part of this publication may be reproduced, stored in a retrieval system, or transmitted in any form or by any means, electronic, mechanical, photocopying, recording or otherwise, without permission in writing from the Publisher.

First published in 1994

A catalogue record for this book is available from the British Library

Library of Congress Cataloging-in-Publication Data are available on request

ISBN 0 7507 0322 9 cased
ISBN 0 7507 0323 7 paper

Jacket design by Caroline Archer

Typeset in 10/12pt Garamond and printed by Graphicraft Typesetters Ltd., Hong Kong

Contents

Dedication	ii
List of Plates, Tables, Maps and Figure	viii
Acknowledgments	x
Foreword	xi

Chapter 1. Education, Ethnicity and Empowerment:
The Authors' Perspectives — 1
- Statement by Yali Zou — 7
- Statement by Henry Trueba — 9
- Social and Economic Status of Minorities — 13
- Ethnic and Social Identification Processes — 17
- Empowerment Processes — 20
- References — 25

Chapter 2. Educational Ethnography: Research Design — 31
- Educational Ethnography — 31
- Types of Ethnographic Research — 36
- The Concept of Culture — 39
- Culture and Ethnicity — 42
- Research Design — 45
- References — 48

Chapter 3. The Miao Among Chinese Nationalities — 53
- New China's Territorial Organization — 54
- Han Hegemony — 57
- Ethnic Diversity and Political Complexity — 59
- Political Organization of Modern China — 61
- Contemporary Ethnic Minority Groups or Nationalities — 66
  - The Five Largest Minority Groups: — 71
  - The Zhuang Nationality — 72
  - The Manchu Nationality — 72
  - The Hui Nationality — 73
  - The Uygur Nationality — 73

Contents

The Miao Nationality ... 74
References ... 82

Chapter 4. Miao Students Reflect on their Lives:
The Painful Journey from Home to School ... 83

Village Life among the Miao ... 84
Testimonies of Central University for Nationalities (CUN) Students ... 88
- Text #1 by Wang Daqing ... 88
- Text #2 by Long Jianhua ... 92
- Text #3 by Du Xiaobo ... 93
- Text #4 by Tian Zhenmin ... 94
- Text #5 by Wang Zhongmin ... 95
- Text #6 by Yang Dexin ... 96
- Text #7 by Xiong Qiang ... 97

Testimonies of Guizhou Institute for Nationalities (GIN) Students ... 98
- Text #8 by Tao Xiaoping ... 98
- Text #9 by Yang Li ... 99
- Text #10 by Xiong Jinliang ... 99
- Text #11 by Wang Bingzhong ... 100
- Text #12 by Yang Yuxi ... 100
- Text #13 by Li Maohong ... 101
- Text #14 by Tao Wencen ... 101

Context for Students' Testimonies ... 102
References ... 108

Chapter 5. Miao Students' Experience at the University ... 109

Selected Students' Characteristics ... 110
Bond with Family and Community ... 115
Best Experiences at the University ... 119
Worst Experience at the University ... 120
Sharing the Best and Worst Experiences ... 121
Change in Values ... 123
Social Status Change ... 125
Instructors' Treatment ... 127
Future Goals ... 128
References ... 129

Chapter 6. Social Identification and Achievement
Motivation among the Miao University Students ... 130

The Process of Social Identification for Achievement ... 130
Towards a Theory of Social Identification ... 137
The Inner Miao Self ... 140
My Life History by Professor Wu Dekun ... 143

A Miao Cosmology: Comments on Professor Wu Dekun's Statement	145
Conclusion	146
References	148

Chapter 7. Early Socialization, Social Identification and Empowerment — 150
Is Cultural Ecology Applicable to the Miao?	156
Poverty and Disempowerment	158
References	167

Chapter 8. The Mediating Role of Language and Culture in Social Identification — 170
Language in Ethnic Identification and Achievement	170
Peer Socialization through Gangs	178
Self-Concept and Prejudice in American Schools and Society	181
References	189

Chapter 9. The Basis of Empowerment: Cultural Therapy and Critical Theory — 192
Culture Therapy	196
Critical Theory	201
Conclusion	206
References	208

Chapter 10. Implications for Research and Educational Reform in the United States — 211
New Intellectual Leaders and Educational Reform	211
Selective Approaches to Educational Reform	214
Basic Reform in Academia	217
Role of Universities in Democratic Reform of Schools	218
Educational Problems in North America	218
Survival and Elitism in North America and China	220
References	223

Index	224

List of Plates, Tables, Maps and Figure

Plate 1:	Miao students, professors and Yali Zou in the Guizhou Institute for Nationalities. November 1, 1992.	108
Plate 2:	Henry Trueba with Chinese students at the Great Wall. October 24, 1992.	108
Plate 3:	Pupils of an elementary school on a field trip to the Great Wall. October 24, 1992.	108
Plate 4:	A Miao girl selling Miao clothing in Guizhou Province. November 2, 1992.	108
Plate 5:	Student dormitory of Guizhou Institute for Nationalities. November 1, 1992.	108
Plate 6:	Henry Trueba with the professors of the history department of the Central University for Nationalities, Yan Yingjun, Gu Jiehua and Huang Xiuyi. October 20, 1992.	108
Plate 7:	Yali Zou with two anthropologists, Lin Yaohua and Chen Yongling, in the Central University for Nationalities in Beijing. October 19, 1992.	108
Plate 8:	Henry Trueba and Yali Zou with the President of the Guizhou Institute for Nationalities, Mr. Wu Zhiguo in front of the administration building of the Guizhou Institute for Nationalities. October 31, 1992.	108
Table 1:	The Fify-Five Ethnic Minority Groups of China	67
Table 2:	Ethnic Groups by Region and Population	68
Table 3:	Largest Ethnic Groups in China	68
Table 4:	Miao Students in Study	111
Table 5:	Categories of Basic Interpersonal Concerns from Text	142
Map 1:	Provinces and Autonomous Regions of China	63
Map 2:	Largest Ethnic Groups in China	69
Figure 1:	Questionnaire	116

Henry Trueba and Yali Zou in Miao clothing standing by Huangguoshu Pubu in Guizhou Province. November 2, 1992.

Acknowledgments

Throughout our academic careers we have received much inspiration from professors, colleagues and friends. In the course of designing and pursuing the project that resulted in this book we also became indebted to many people in the United States and in China. Unable to recognize every one of them, we want to thank those most closely associated with our efforts. First of all, we are deeply grateful to Jackie Captain whose support from the beginning made possible the organization of our efforts, the pursuit of the research in China, the organization of the manuscript, the production of tables and the various detailed editing that she so wisely and patiently did for us. She has proven that team efforts with non-native writers of English can make it possible to write correctly and clearly, even if the writing is about complex cultural phenomena occurring in an entirely different setting. We also want to thank Carolyn Hackler for the continued support, her assistance to both of us during the many other tasks assigned to us, and her wisdom in facilitating our scholarly efforts even when we had to work 2500 miles apart (Yali Zou in Davis, California, and Henry Trueba in Madison, Wisconsin).

    We want to recognize the theoretical contributions of professors, colleagues and friends whose writings helped us conceptualize the research project, gather significant data and analyze it in meaningful ways. In the United States, we thank George and Louise Spindler, George DeVos, and Marcelo Suárez-Orozco; in Brazil, Paulo Freire, and in China, Dekun Wu and Dingzhi Pan whose intimate knowledge of the Miao people enlightened and redirected our study. We want to express our appreciation to the numerous persons who helped us both in China and in the United States to resolve the many problems we faced in the process of gathering and analyzing the data. Finally, our most sincere and deeply-felt gratitude goes to the Miao university students from the Central University for Nationalities in Beijing and those from the Guizhou Central Institute for Nationalities, who trusted us and shared with us their struggles and most intimate moments.

Foreword

This book joins three dimensions of sociocultural and pedagogical reconstruction ordinarily left apart: critical theory, as expressed in Paulo Friere's conscientization; cultural therapy as expressed in the work of George and Louise Spindler and associates; and empowerment, as expressed in the works of many contemporary forefront scholars. All three of these dimensions are forces for constructive change in the present articulation of power, class, culture, ethnicity, and education. The outstanding virtue of this book is that these forces for change are interpretively interrelated — not as replications of each other — but as overlapping in content and process but with quite different structural endpoints. The interpretive analysis of these interrelationships causes one to perceive and think about needed reform in education and society differently. Anything that does that is worth serious attention.

The approach taken by Henry Trueba and Yali Zou is intellectually eclectic and pays little heed to disciplinary hegemony. Big problems require strategically formulated approaches from many positions. It is to the authors' credit that their wide scholarship and experience enables them to mount these strategic approaches. Trueba's penchant is anthropology, with strong experience in education and religion. Zou's is education, with strong experience in anthropology and its pedagogical applications.

As important as Zou's professional training is her cultural background as Chinese. Her cultural and linguistic skills have been critical in the study of and gathering of data on Miao ethnicity and the relationships between the Miao and the Chinese 'mainstream'. This study of the Miao, done in remarkably short term, given the extent and relevance of the information collected, gives this volume an international perspective that has been notably lacking in the works of scholars directed at our schools and the struggles of ethnic minorities in them in the USA.

The location of the Miao and the attention directed to them is almost incidental, despite its bulk, to the thrust of this book as a *tour de force* in the foundations of educational criticism and reform. The Miao and their situation in modern China is of importance, however, since so little is known in the west outside of relatively narrow academic circles about ethnic minorities in China. It is probably correct to say that most Americans, even educated ones, think of the overseas Chinese as being one great glob of undifferentiated

Foreword

humanity, 'over there', facing few of our problems as cast up by our heterogeneous ethnicity and class structure.

The combination of strong conceptualization about a most significant arena of human affairs and original data on a major power and population make this volume well worth the reading.

George Spindler, Stanford University

Chapter 1

Education, Ethnicity and Empowerment: the Authors' Perspectives

This book is the result of a research project in China conducted by two immigrants to the United States, a Mexican immigrant and a Chinese immigrant. The project was originally conceived as the continuation of the study of the Hmong, the Indochinese people hired by the CIA to help in the Vietnam War who from 1976 to the present became refugees in the United States. This group, today approximating 200,000 in the United States, was the focus of a study conducted by Trueba, Jacobs and Kirton and discussed in a book entitled *Cultural Conflict and Adaptation: The Case of Hmong Children in American Society* (1990). During the research among the Hmong we realized that there was little or no original information about the ancestors of the Hmong in China, that is, about the Miao. Communication with Chinese scholars by mail, the previous experience of living in China by one of the authors and a visit to China by both authors and their assistants gave these authors the opportunity to get first hand information and original research from Chinese scholars on the Miao of China. Focusing on the Miao students at the Beijing University for Nationalities and at the Guizhou Institute for Nationalities was the most decisive step towards finding substantial data. When we first began to make inquiries in the United States, to request written materials and to call various scholars, we could not anticipate the central theme of our research. The interviews with students and faculty in China made the difference. We realized then we had some important information and data, comparable to other data discussed in both European and American research literature on ethnic minority groups.

This study was finally pulled together around the data analysis which took place while the research team was still in China and the interview data were fresh in our minds. The focus was ethnic identity and its empowering role in motivating Miao students to achieve success in the university. Behind the issues of ethnic identity, the question of the nature of that identity and what possible contradictions were involved in a humble, low-income Miao village boy or girl becoming a member of the select university student group was more complicated. The process of ethnic identification does not take place in a vacuum, it is an ongoing process anchored in the experiences of people attempting to function effectively in their own learning and working environments. This process of self-identification is part of becoming a functional adult and active member of a society. For the Miao students, socialization to become good Miao peasants was not the best preparation to become good university students. Indeed, changing schools in their early years, and leaving their Miao language schools to enter higher level larger schools in which Mandarin was the language of instruction and prestige was a considerable shock. Being conspicuously different as Miao children among their Han peers who were unaccepting and prejudiced was not easy. Having to move again to even larger and more distant senior high schools entailed much more difficult adaptation and physical stamina. A Miao student had to travel a great deal (as much as 20 or 30 miles one way) to go home and bring food provisions several times each month, or wait for some money from home to buy food at school. It is clear that these are determined individuals, fully committed to become educated, who successfully passed difficult examinations. Why? Where did they get their motivation? How did they support themselves in case of need? What was the impact of their life as students, especially at the university, that permitted them to remain loyal to their ethnic group, and to maintain their language and culture? These and other intriguing questions guided the research team and the co-authors throughout the entire project.

The research team consisted of the two co-authors, Henry Trueba, and his then doctoral student Yali Zou, with a research assistant from the University of Wisconsin-Madison, Jackie Captain, and a number of professors and students from China. These people are mentioned in more detail in Chapter 2, within the discussion of the design. Suffice it to say that the support and care of our Chinese colleagues, their genuine scholarship and their original research was most inspiring, although much of the documentation they made available to us was not specific enough or covered areas that required a great deal more knowledge of the local folklore. Their recommendations and their support to reach Miao students and other faculty was most useful. The Beijing professors, historians, anthropologists, linguists and folklorists all insisted that we needed to go to the Guizhou Institute for Nationalities. We went there and obtained extremely useful data in the interviews with students and professors, and later on some valuable data from two of the professors who had written about the history of migrations of the Miao (part of it is used in Chapter 3). Very quickly, the communication between the Miao students, Miao professors and our team became clearly focused on issues of importance for both teams; they taught us more about their culture and the meaning of being a Miao in China, and in turn, we discussed with them issues of ethnic minorities around the world, including Europe and the United States.

Implied in the title, *Power in Education: The Case of Miao University Students and its Significance for American Culture*, is the notion that education is instrumental to empowerment which is understood to be the capacity to function effectively in a given social setting, with active participation in the cultural, political and economic institutions, and the possession of full rights and obligations enjoyed by other members of society. The Miao people, the fourth largest ethnic minority group (if we consider the Han as mainstream society and not as a minority nationality), have had a history of oppression since the fourteenth century (see Chapter 3), and have struggled and migrated consistently for the last four hundred years, therefore to speak of ethnic identity is already problematic. All people, especially people on the move, change, intermarry, adapt to new ecologies and social environments, accept new cultural values that enhance their survival and go on in life. What would make us think that the Miao — after centuries of migration from Guizhou, Hunan, Yunnan and Sichuan to Indochina, to Vietnam, Laos, Burma and Thailand, and from there to France, Canada, Australia, and the United States — have retained an ethnic identity, a sense of peoplehood, of belonging to a single nation? And if this is so, what does such an identity mean or what is it based on? As if dealing with ethnic identity was not enough, why would we want to deal with the empowerment of the Miao? What does it mean for the Miao to become empowered? The more questions we asked about the Miao ethnic identity, and the more we observed and analyzed students and the content of their testimonies, the more we became aware of the profound link between ethnic identity and the Miao students' ability to participate fully in academic activities, and to function effectively as students. Education was not only the result of their commitment to honor their ethnic group and families, it became the main instrument to pursue that commitment with more determination and to become more aware of the value of their cultural heritage. Therefore, the relationships between ethnic identity, education and empowerment are increasingly more salient in the testimonies of Miao students and professors. Indeed, the recognition of this triple relationship of ethnic identity to education and empowerment was the best way for the Miao student to resolve the inherent conflict in drastic social and cultural change, the change involved in leaving one's village and life as a peasant to become a scholar.

The book, therefore, deals with these topics in a gradual fashion. Chapter 1 introduces the researchers and provides the theoretical perspectives from social scientists interested in these topics, especially from those involved in cross-cultural research, and with the difficulties inherent in the application of Western concepts to the study of Chinese phenomena, such as the existence of *nationalities*. What are the similarities and differences between nationalities and ethnic minority groups? What is the status of ethnic minorities in China as compared with minorities in the United States or Europe? What is the role of education for minorities, and to what extent does public policy reflect views on the education of minorities? This chapter also focuses on the key questions of the relationship of ethnic identity and academic achievement, the mediating role of the home language and culture in the process of ethnic identification, and in the implications of both ethnic identity and the home language and culture for the empowerment of minorities. Because the book deals with an ethnic group in a Communist country with a presumed Marxist economic and educational philosophy, it is important to discuss the implications of Chinese policies for the participation of minorities in university programs.

American and European scholarship (especially of educational sociologists and anthropologists) is used to analyze issues of social and economic status of ethnic minorities in Western countries and the contrasts found in China. Finally, the literature on the process of ethnic identification (early socialization processes) known in Western countries is discussed here with the hope of identifying some parameters for comparative analysis of the materials gathered in China. The theoretical developments of anthropologists dealing with cultural therapy, and of psychologists and critical pedagogues dealing with critical theory and psychopedagogy are briefly mentioned in Chapter 1, and fully developed in the final chapters.

Chapter 2 describes in detail the research design and methodology of the study. It offers an ethnohistorical account of American educational ethnographic developments with its debates and assets. This chapter answers questions about the nature of quality ethnographic research, its focus on cultural explanations of behavior and its basic requirements. The historic relationship between method and theory is discussed in some detail in the context of the different types of ethnographic research as conducted by various social scientists, ethnohistorians, ethnographers of communication, cultural anthropologists and psychological ethnographers. Because of the importance of the concept of culture and its role in ethnic identification and empowerment processes, it is discussed at some length, especially with reference to contrasts with other concepts, such as that of race or ethnicity. Finally, the research design is presented briefly. This chapter, in summary, offers an appropriate historical context for the use of ethnographic research methods which are central in the present study.

Chapters 3, 4, 5, and 6 form a section with a close internal relationship. Chapter 3 offers a historical framework for the study of the Miao. First, it lists all the ethnic minority groups with their populations, general characteristics, and regional distribution; second, it discusses in some detail the five largest ethnic groups: the Zhuang, Manchu, Hui, Miao and Uygur; the chapter presents a summary of the history of the Miao, their migrations and cultural characteristics. This chapter also provides a necessary context for the presentation of Chapters 4, 5 and 6, which offer the data configuration on Miao students' experience at the university, their personal life experiences and struggles in their efforts to get an education, and the analysis of the data to understand better the process of social identification and achievement motivation. These last three chapters constitute the most original part of the research project and are pivotal in the conception of the study. All other chapters surround the main findings discussed in these three chapters. Chapter 4 provides some information about the students' own sociocultural characteristics and summarizes the result of a detailed questionnaire filled out by Miao students after our visit to China in 1992 — for example, details of the income of students' families, or their parents' education, or other information that helps us to understand the change in the lifestyles of these students going to the university. Their statements of deep commitment to their families and communities are most eloquent and clearly lead to discussions in later chapters. Chapter 5 has very touching stories of students going through trauma and deprivation in order to get a better education. Their life histories make the reader respect them and admire their determination. In turn, Chapter 6 is grounded ethnographic analysis, that is, an analysis anchored in the findings from the previous two chapters and takes text to its logical consequences in terms of ethnic identification and the self-definition of students.

The following chapters are linked by parallel theoretical concerns; both attempt to reconcile existing research in Europe and the United States with the findings presented in the study. Thus, for example, Chapter 7 is a theoretical discussion of the relationship between ethnic identification and empowerment, in light of the contrast between Western research and the findings obtained in China from Miao students; Chapter 8 offers an alternative approach to appreciate the significance of the findings in China, that is, the use of Neo-Vygotskian and Bakhtinian approaches focusing on the mediating role of language and culture in social identification. The theoretical import of these chapters may be of great interest to scholars and other interested parties familiar with American and European research on ethnic minorities.

The last two chapters offer a concluding section that attempts to apply to daily pedagogical practice some of the theoretical principles discussed in previous chapters. Chapter 9 revisits the issues of empowerment and presents two basic requirements to facilitate the process of empowerment: 1) *cultural therapy*, or the necessary healing from psychological injuries caused by racism and oppression, and 2) *critical theory*, the embedded need to become conscious of the role of education, and the need to capitalize on the linguistic and cultural resources of children to strengthen their self-identity and give them a chance to become empowered. Their interrelationships and their function as foundations for empowerment are discussed in some detail. Finally, Chapter 10 brings back the discussion of the research project to deal with implications for research and educational reform in the United States. What are the lessons learned in China that can help us in the Western educational system, especially in America? What can we learn about the education of ethnic groups in China that can help us deal with the problems in Eastern Europe or with the ethnic hatred in other European countries?

This book does not really provide many answers, but gives opportunities to reflect on the context of research focused on other settings and cultural groups. It is by making the familiar strange, and the strange familiar that we learn how to appreciate multiculturalism and the need to respect ethnic identities and cultural differences. The intent of this book was to bring some hope, to discover the light that Paulo Freire has recently called '*pedagogia da esperança*' or 'pedagogy of hope' as a new encounter with the pedagogy of the oppressed (Freire 1993). Documenting the failure of oppressed populations has only demonstrated the obvious, and has not opened the way to a better future for the children of the next generation. In the context of the assassination of street children and the abuse of the working classes by the rich, Freire points out the fact that if people are angry and protest there is hope:

> The people yell in protest against testimonies of insolence. Public squares are once more filled up. There is hope, it does not matter that it is not smart, in the corners of streets, in the body of each one of us. It is as if the majority of the nation was taken by an unstoppable need of vomiting in the face of such shameful events. On the other hand, without wanting to be able to deny the despair (*desesperançao*) as something concrete, and not ignoring the historical, economic and social reasons that explain it, I cannot understand human existence and the necessary struggle to improve it, without hopes and dreams. Hope is an ontological need; despair is a hope that, losing its direction, turns into a distortion of the ontological need. As a program [for action], lack of hope paralyses us and makes us fall into fatalism where it is impossible to muster the necessary strength in order to fight for recreation of the world. I am not hopeful out of stubbornness, but because of the existential and historical imperative. I do not want to say, however, that because I have hope, I attribute to my hope the power of transforming reality, or, thus persuaded, I engage in the struggle without taking into consideration the concrete and pragmatic facts, insisting that my hope is enough. Hope alone cannot win a struggle, but without hope we will be weak and hesitate in the struggle. We need critical hope, in the same way that a fish needs clean water.
> (Freire 1993:10. Translation by Henry T. Trueba)

In a very vivid way the substance of this book deals with the ontological need to hope that warms the hearts of many young Miao who want to learn and who dream of becoming university students. Without those dreams and the motivation to achieve them, the poor peasants from Yunnan and Guizhou would never have passed the tough examinations used to screen potential senior high school candidates and potential college students. In a genuine sense, this book is the story of empowerment of a Chinese minority with a very low status and a history of oppression and ignorance. Their learning the word and the world became possible only after they learned the painful history of their ancestors who fought for centuries to retain their independence, and who happily joined Chairman Mao in the Revolution that resulted in the 1949 reform.

A book is better understood when the readers know something about the authors. What the authors have in common is that both came as immigrants to the United States in their thirties, both acquired English as a second language, and both are deeply grateful and appreciative of American democracy, freedom and quality of life.

The Authors' Perspectives

Statement by Yali Zou

I was born on November 11, 1949, in Beijing, China, the year that New China was founded, and I remained there until December 1988 when I came to the United States. As many people have remarked, my pulse jumps together with that of the Peoples' Republic of China (PRC). Yes, I am a person who is the same age as the PRC. Therefore, I have experienced all social, ideological, economic and political changes and movements that have happened in the last four decades in China. I attended elementary school and high school in Jilin City which is located in the northeast part of China. I was in senior high in 1966 when The Cultural Revolution began. All students started to 'make revolution' instead of studying, until 1968 when all junior and senior high school students were sent to the countryside to 'Receive reeducation from peasants' which was Chairman Mao's call. I was sent to a small village which belongs to Tian Feng people's commune of Yong Ji county, Jilin Province, located in Northeast China. I lived and worked in the field with the peasants for two years. These two years helped me to know and understand Chinese peasant life in nearly primitive conditions without any modern conveniences, such as electricity, running water or heat. They had nothing but what they grew in the field.

In 1970, some plants and factories began to recruit 'educated youth' from the countryside. I was lucky to be chosen by Jilin Iron and Steel Plant, the largest iron and steel plant in China, providing more than 60 per cent of the materials needed by China for making steel. It has more than 8000 workers. I worked in the central laboratory as a quality analyst and had a lot of time to talk to the workers, technicians, and cadres and made a lot of friends. After a year and a half I was sent to Shanghai Metallurgical Mechanical College to learn the Albanian language because the former Premier Zhou Enlai signed an agreement to support Albania by establishing the Albashang Steel Combination Company. After two-and-a-half years, I began to work as an interpreter for the Shanghai Government. At that time I was working intensively with Albanian engineers and met many Albanian leaders. Through this experience, I acquired some translation skills and an understanding of the role of language in communication.

In 1976, I was asked to go to Changchun Film Studio (China's first and biggest film studio) to translate imported Albanian films. When I worked there I met a number of famous Chinese writers, poets, musicians and film directors, who became my good friends. From that time on I began to understand Chinese intellectuals' life, their work and their concerns. In 1978, I entered the English Department of Jilin University where I studied English and Chinese literature, while at the same time I began to teach in the Changchun Architectural Engineering College which belongs to the Metallurgical Ministry of the PRC. My students came from twenty-four provinces and several autonomous regions, often from rural and remote places. After they graduated from the college, they worked for the plants and factories which belong to the Ministry. Most of those plants are located in the mountain areas near the mineral resources. During my ten years in Changchun, I taught thousands of students from different social and economic levels. This experience helped me to get a deep understanding of Chinese students' philosophy, values, beliefs, lifestyles, struggles, goals, personalities, etc.

In 1988, with a strong desire to study Western theories of philosophy and a profound commitment to democratic education, I came to the United States. At the University of California, Davis, I received more than four years of intensive study and strict professional training. I met a number of outstanding scholars whose works deeply influenced me and helped me to understand the educational foundations of American democracy, western philosophy, and western educational theories. While attending several classes on educational anthropology, I had the chance to become familiar with the research literature on ethnic minorities, refugees and immigrants, not only in the United States, but in Europe and Asia, and received intensive training in how to conduct ethnographic research. Later I was lucky enough to become a member of an ethnographic research team involved in the study of Woodland, California, which culminated in our publication: *Healing Multicultural America: Mexican Immigrants Rise to Power in Northern California* (Trueba, Rodríguez, Zou and Cintrón 1993). I greatly benefited from this research project because I became aware of the important role that Spanish language and culture had played in the educational and political success of the Latinos in Woodland, and I learned how to do ethnographic interviews and participant observations, how to keep journals, and how to do audio-tape analysis. This work also inspired me to plan a research project on Chinese minority groups.

As a Chinese, and more in particular as a member of the Han majority group, I grew up in a middle-class family and spent my childhood in Jilin city. This is a naturally beautiful small town surrounded by mountains on three sides. The Songhuajiang River goes through the middle of the town. I have sweet memories of my home town, but whenever I recall my elementary school, I am bothered. When I was four, my family moved from Beijing to Jilin city; my father had been transferred to the Jilin Railway Bureau, which is located in the northeast part of China. Jilin city is a small town with more than ten ethnic groups. There I had the chance to associate with children from different social and economic levels. At that time the Jilin Railway Bureau had just been founded — there were seven bureaus in the whole country at that time, each bureau was in charge of transportation in three provinces. The rank of the director of the bureau equals that of governor. The elementary school and high school which I attended were attached to the bureau. The students of these school were the children of the cadres, workers and temporary workers of the Bureau. Some of my classmates were from high rank cadres' families, and some from very poor temporary workers' families. In the cold winter you could recognize immediately those who were from poor families. Those children wore *mian ao* and *miao ku* (cotton-padded clothes) with many holes through which you could see the cotton coming out. They did not have warm hats, scarves, and shoes. Their faces were always dirty in the cold weather because they shed tears and then they used their hands to clean them up, thus leaving many traces on their faces. The teachers openly showed their dislike for these children. Sometimes in front of the class they loudly ordered them to go home to wash their faces. When the teacher found that these children made some mistakes, or they talked without permission in the class, or played with papers or notebooks and did not finish their homework, the teacher would punish them by asking them to stand in front of the class the whole day. But the kids from the cadres' families seldom had this experience. These phenomena were quite popular at that time and became acceptable teacher's behavior. Even in the late 1980s the same thing still happened. At that time my daughter was attending primary school in China — she is now a junior high school student in the United States. Every time she returned from school, the first thing she would tell me was who had received physical punishment because they talked with other students in class, or because they did not finish their homework. Whenever I heard this I felt very sympathetic towards those children and felt bad for those teachers. I was always thinking that one day I would do something to change that situation.

Statement by Henry Trueba

I was born in a small town called Mixcoac, south of downtown Mexico City on October 29, 1931. I was the tenth child in a family of twelve children (seven boys and five girls). My parents, from Basque ancestry, lived briefly in New York, but were unhappy with the way Spanish-speaking immigrants were treated, and thus decided to go south where all of us were born. The Great Depression years in Mexico were much worse than in the United States, and I recall how we all were crowded in a small rented house, sharing clothes (passed down from older brothers and sisters) and sleeping in very small beds with our feet sticking out from the knee on. The pressures on my father to make ends meet and the tears of my mother are still very vivid in my memory. Eventually, having attended a Jesuit high school, it seemed that a good way out of the crowded family quarters was to get good grades and enter the seminary. I became a Jesuit on December 31, 1947, and followed the entire career — two years of novitiate (dedicated to spiritual exercises alone), four years of juniorate (dedicated to the study of humanities), three years of philosophy, three years of teaching in a college, and five years of Theology which I finished in 1964 — until December 31, 1965, eighteen long years of my life that left a clear mark on my thinking, my daily habits and my work ethic.

As a Jesuit I had to study the Latin and Greek classics, to memorize Latin poetry, participate in Greek plays, speak Latin all day (except during recreation times) and engage in a serious three year full-time study of Thomistic Philosophy. At the end (with the equivalent of an MA in Philosophy), at the age of twenty-five, I had to teach in the Jesuit schools, at the elementary level, but more so at the college level. All during my years of philosophy, I had requested permission to study Tzeltal, a Mayan language spoken by a group of Indians living in Bachajon, Chiapas State, Mexico. I also had obtained permission to be trained as a paramedical missionary in the Red Cross in Mexico City. I wanted to be a missionary with the Indians all my life, and was finally granted permission to work in Chiapas. Over a period of several years, even after I had entered the United States, I worked intermittently in Chiapas, learned the Tzeltal language well enough to function, and travelled throughout the Indian villages curing people and seeing many of them, especially children, die. This was the most difficult period of my life. I began to wonder if being a Jesuit was the best thing for me. These doubts motivated my superiors and me to ask for a transfer to the United States where I would study Theology. Apparently, my exams in philosophy had been satisfactory.

In September of 1961 I flew to Maryland to start my studies in the Jesuit Seminary of Woodstock (a remodelled World War II concentration camp built in a beautiful area of the state). The experience was intense and difficult, because I did not know English and my professors did not understand my Latin (pronunciation of Latin in Spanish-speaking countries is very different). A first hand exposure to a large American seminary with the usual drinking problems and the psychological crises of many theologians ready to be ordained intensified my doubts about becoming an ordained priest. But the following year came too fast and I had no way to tell my mother and the entire family that I did not want to be ordained! So, I went through the ceremonies, only to start actively requesting dispensation of celibacy and the other vows to become a regular person out of the priesthood. It was going to take a very long time and many letters to get that permission. When I finally obtained it I was already studying at Stanford, while at the same time I was the Associate Pastor for the Stanford Newman Center. I left, never to regret it. My short experiences as a special confessor for priests had revealed to me many additional reasons why some should have never become priests and should be free to leave in good conscience. My main argument to the Catholic powers was that a child of 14 or 15 years of age cannot make a decision for life, especially if misguided by the early rigorous discipline of the Jesuits.

Because one of the requirements from the church to give me permission to leave the priesthood was that I did not live where I had practiced as a priest, I had to promise to leave Stanford and seek another institution to continue my graduate work in Anthropology. I was fortunate to receive a teaching assistantship first, and later an Andrew Mellon Fellowship to study at Pittsburgh University. My MA in Anthropology from Stanford left a bad taste in my mouth because of the crises I faced in those days and the elitism of American students that made me feel isolated. Pittsburgh was very different and provided a much broader training in structural and social anthropology, linguistics, archaeology and physical anthropology. It was a wonderful academic opportunity that permitted me to use my knowledge of Spanish and my contacts among Nahuat Indians in Puebla, Mexico to do my dissertation research. My

The Authors' Perspectives

research among the Nahuat of Puebla opened the door to future work with Spanish-speaking people in the United States. The similarity of power relationships between the landowners in Puebla with the growers in California and the treatment of the lower-class agricultural laborers was remarkable. Once back in the United States, while I was teaching in Sacramento, California, I found myself working with migrant and Chicano populations in the community and surrounding areas.

My interests in language minority populations, in their education and historical struggles to achieve equity, led me to examine the struggles of other ethnic populations in the United States and in Europe. I was teaching at the University of California, Santa Barbara, when I realized that in our own backyard, within a mile from the campus, a Hmong community was suffering prejudice and racism, even in the form of well-intentioned efforts from school personnel who had already classified many Hmong children as 'learning disabled'. Several colleagues and I collected data and wrote the book entitled *Cultural Conflict and Adaptation: The Case of Hmong Children in American Society* (1990). This book is a continuation of my interest in the study of ethnic minorities, especially in those minorities whose ancestors are far away, because this study raises important questions about the significance of ethnic cultures that continue to impact peoples' lives thousands of miles and centuries away from those ancestors. Ethnic cultures can be a powerful force which can be either constructive in enriching other peoples' cultures and lives, or destructive in the form of hatred and genocide. There is much to learn from the Chinese ethnic minorities, especially the Miao.

My work since the 1980s has remained consistently focused on issues of race, ethnicity and adaptation. More recently, I have focused on the mediating role that language and culture have on learning processes, and on processes of ethnic identification. Because of administrative duties since 1989, data collection and analyses have been slow and fragmented. Yet, thanks to the support of the various institutions I worked in, especially the University of Wisconsin-Madison, I have been able to continue my intellectual endeavors. I feel that over the years I have developed some sensitivity to issues related to children's intellectual development and have paid special attention to their needs. It is my hope that, as a result of the efforts reflected in this book and other similar efforts, we can learn something about saving the next generations, and can become aware that our decisions today relative to ethnicity, race and peace have consequences for children more than for any other group of people in the world. And, since China is the country that has the largest number of children, we ought to be more knowledgeable about Chinese ethnic minority children.

Social sciences are facing a number of difficult theoretical issues whose implications go well beyond theory and affect everyday life for millions of people — issues of ethnic and racial relations in a world increasingly more divided. Equally complex is the study of minority education in Western societies. But the most serious challenge involves efforts at understanding the rapid changes in power and knowledge affecting ethnic groups. This chapter will focus on the research behind the study of ethnicity, education and the empowerment of minorities.

One of the most difficult challenges of cross-cultural research is to identify the appropriate theoretical structure to provide an adequate framework for a research design. When the comparison of data and analyses involves countries as different as the United States, Europe and the Peoples' Republic of China, then this challenge requires a great deal of reflection and accommodation. There are relatively few sources in Chinese to deal with social theory about the nature of ethnicity or ethnic differences, or about the changes in status from pre-Mao Revolution in 1949 to after Mao's Revolution. There is almost nothing specifically dealing with class and status differences among the various nationalities or minority groups in China, because one of the most important principles (an ideal) in Communist philosophy is equality for all. The search, therefore, must be reduced to historical and folklore documents that, by implication, speak to these issues. Indeed, part of the information presented in this study is taken from recent writings of Chinese scholars and their perception of issues related to ethnicity and empowerment. Their very concept of empowerment is framed by the assumption that after 1949 all minority nationalities were empowered to participate in public life as much as economics and technical know-how would permit. On the other hand, professors and students who belong to minority groups confess that they see great differences between the lifestyles of their fellow members of ethnic minorities and mainstream society. In a parallel situation with some of the minorities in the United States, in China all minorities are *de jure* first class citizens, but not *de facto*. The liberation movement and the ambition of minority scholars and university students is to make a difference in the speed of transition from being *de jure* to becoming *de facto* first class citizens, by changing the economy of their peoples, bringing progress to their villages and a bolstering a new sense of belonging in the great country of China. Education sociologists offer important insights into the differential status of class groups, also applicable to those ethnic and linguistic minorities who tend to fall into the low-income groups. Bowls and Gintis state:

> Education in the United States plays a dual role in the social process whereby surplus value, i.e., profit, is created and expropriated. On the one hand, by imparting technical and social skills and appropriate motivations, education increases the productive capacity of workers. On the other hand, education helps diffuse and depoliticize the potentially explosive class relations of the production process, and thus serves to perpetuate the social, political, and economic conditions through which a portion of the product of labor is expropriated in the form of profits.
>
> (Bowls and Gintis 1976:11)

While these authors and other social scientists agree that schools attempt and may seem to be genuinely committed to democratic ends, actually they achieve the opposite, they disempower some students, while they prepare others for success. More recently the work of Apple (1992, 1993) and Popkewitz (1993) focuses on issues of inequality that shape the content of the curriculum and the nature of instruction under the general pressures of societal biases. Thus, for example, teachers are not prepared to work with linguistically or culturally different students or with economically disadvantaged students, because they carry cultural blinders and cannot see the impact of their teaching as negating the contributions (and even the existence) of other ethnic groups. In fact, it seems that some social scientists in the United States establish the theoretical foundations of multicultural education on the premise that many teachers, principals and other school personnel, while they project racial and class biases, seem to be color blind when they try to remedy inequities; they do not know how to recognize students' different ethnic and social identities (see Skutnabb-Kangas 1984; Sleeter and Grant 1987; Secada 1989; Sleeter 1991, 1992; Banks and McGee-Banks 1989; and Trueba 1989, 1993).

The central theoretical questions guiding this study are the following: What is the relationship of social/ethnic identification processes to the emergence of power in minority groups? As subparts of this question, we are asking:

1. What is the relationship of ethnic identification to academic achievement?
2. What is the nature of the mediating role of the home language and culture in the acquisition of knowledge?
3. How do the home language and culture affect education?
4. What is the role of education on empowerment?

These questions are asked in the context of the Miao people, and in particular of the Miao university students whose life histories and background were studied via personal interviews, analysis of their written materials and analysis of detailed questionnaires. These questions are asked in the larger context of the history of minorities in China since 1949. The study focuses on these questions in the light of studies conducted in the United States, Europe and Asian countries. The review of the theoretical literature guiding this study is divided into three parts:

1. social and economic status of minorities in Europe and the United States;
2. ethnic and social identification processes, and explanations for their differential status and academic success;
3. implications of ethnic identification for processes of empowerment and disempowerment.

Social and Economic Status of Minorities

The differential impact that schools have on the status of students and their ability to move up in society, both with respect to the actual acquisition of knowledge and to their overall socialization into professions and careers, has been a primary concern of many social scientists in the last two decades. They have talked about the reproduction of the social order, the need for critical thinking, of the role of schools in creating social strata and maintaining them, social epistemology, etc. In fact, the work by educational sociologists, philosophers and critical pedagogues, such as Apple 1982, 1990; Popkewitz 1991, 1993; Aronowitz and Giroux 1985, 1991; McLaren 1989, 1991; Banks and McGee-Banks 1989; and others has sharpened the focus on these issues and produced significant contributions to our understanding of social epistemology. For example, Popkewitz states:

> I use the phrase *social epistemology* as a means of making the knowledge of schooling as a social practice accessible to sociological inquiry; it is intended to emphasize the relational and social embeddedness of knowledge in the practices and issues of power. In this sense, I accept the pragmatic philosophical tradition and reject the notion of epistemology as concerned with universal knowledge claims about the nature, origin, and limits of knowledge . . .
> (Popkewitz 1991:15)

The significance of epistemologies, such as those held by Bowls and Gintis (1976) and Bernstein (1977) impacted Apple's conception of social class and culture and assisted him in understanding the dynamic mechanisms of schooling in shaping class and culture, and how class and culture excluded certain individuals from upward social mobility. Apple (1982, 1985, 1989, 1990, 1992, and 1993) rejects the interpretation that schools function as equalizers of social status and power in capitalist democratic societies, and feels that while the schools may seem to be genuinely committed to democratic ends, they actually achieve the opposite. Schools are meant to reproduce the social order, perpetuate power relationships and prepare laborers for jobs in industry; in the end, the reproduction of the social order is then rationalized with cultural norms that have social support and legitimacy (Apple 1985, 1989, 1992). Apple also explores the relationship between culture and economy and argues from a neo-Marxism position that education is a political act and that knowledge is inextricably linked to power. Schools, as social and cultural institutions, distribute ideological values and knowledge and also help to produce the type of knowledge that is needed to maintain, legitimate, and replicate dominant economic, political, and cultural arrangements. Schools are agents of cultural and ideological hegemony and agents of selective tradition and cultural incorporation. Apple argues against the notion that education is a neutral activity and insists that 'social and economic values are embedded in the design of the institutions we work in, in the "formal corpus of school knowledge" preserved in the curriculum, in our modes of teaching, and in our principles, standards and forms of evaluation' (Apple 1990:8–9).

Apple maintains that schools replicate the unequal social and economic

The Authors' Perspectives

conditions of a late-industrial capitalist society by reproducing class relations. Capitalism, as both an economic and a cultural system, permeates the depths of the collective psyche (what Apple refers to as the bottom of our brains) and penetrates what we think of as commonsensical knowledge. We thus see the world through culturally capitalistic eyes, and hegemonic capitalism informs everything we do. Apple argues that there is both an overt and a hidden curriculum, each of which contributes to the reproduction of the social division of labor. 'The overt and covert knowledge found within school settings, and the principles of selection, organization, and evaluation of this knowledge, are value-governed selections from a much larger universe of possible knowledge and selection principles' (Apple 1990:45). Much of the curriculum is rooted in social control and historically, schools were used as the primary agency for the inculcation of values to create an 'American community'. In brief, throughout his work, Apple explores how a system of unequal power in society is maintained and recreated by the transmission of culture. In some way, according to Apple, schools are related to other more powerful institutions and combined with them to generate structural inequalities of power and differential access to resources. In different ways these inequalities are reinforced, at least partially, by schools. It is precisely through the curriculum and the instructional process in general that schools play a significant role in either preserving or generating such inequalities. Along with many other mechanisms for social and cultural preservation, schools contribute to the cultural reproduction of class relations in industrial societies (Apple, 1990:64).

The work of educational sociologists, such as Apple, has had a profound impact on the work of educational researchers and educational anthropologists who are deeply concerned about the mechanisms used by schools to perpetuate the social order. For example, the work by ethnographers, sociolinguists, cultural ecologists, social epistemologists and critical pedagogues, enlightens these mechanisms. The replication by schools of the social and economic order was shown by Rist's two-and-a half years study (Rist, 1970). Teachers in the kindergarten and elementary schools placed children in reading groups according to their socio-economic background. In doing so the teachers displayed different attitudes towards different groups of students. Teachers' expectations of richer students were much higher. Teachers permitted low-income students to be ridiculed and stereotyped by their richer peers. Rist concluded that, 'the school strongly shares in the complicity of maintaining the organizational perpetuation of poverty and unequal opportunity, this, of course, is in contrast to the formal doctrine of education in this country to ameliorate rather than aggravate the conditions of the poor' (Rist 1970:447). In Rist's opinion schools never have worked very well towards equipping lower-class students and preparing them for mobility within the social and economic realms in American society (Rist 1973:4). Other anthropologists agree with Rist and raise important issues regarding the role of schools in working with low-status children.

Watson-Gegeo (1990) and Watson-Gegeo and D. Gegeo (1992), in a discussion of schooling, knowledge and power, present an ethnohistory of socialization in the Solomon Islands and the difficult transition from the traditional system existing before Europeans arrived (a fairly equalitarian system based on sharing) to a competitive society ruled by new values acquired from Christian missionaries. With the colonization and missionization of the islands, the lifestyle changed dramatically and the style of education changed. Acquiring knowledge and skills that change one's status in society (either up or down) requires a deeper understanding of the relationship between schooling and social stratification; this is the central concern of social epistemology. One of the important contributions made by Karen Watson-Gegeo to our understanding of the role that schools have in ascribing different status to different students (that is, in perpetuating the status differences among students) was her study of the Kamehameha schools in Hawaii, and the significance of native discourse patterns in the acquisition of reading skills by children (Au and Jordan 1981; Boggs 1985). The significance of her 'talk story' findings is that language and culture are intimately united in the context of learning, and that if the home language and culture is ignored, children cannot process information as effectively and cannot develop a high level of motivation to achieve reading skills. The implication was that teachers ought to capitalize on the children's cultural and linguistic resources to maximize teaching effectiveness and children's mental development and school achievement.

Beyond the studies in Hawaii that focused on the role of discourse (as a linguistic and cultural instrument in the acquisition of knowledge), Watson-Gegeo and Gegeo studied historically, and observed systematically, the behavior of children in the Solomon Island schools, and concluded with a forceful argument related to the impact of schools on local children:

> The first major impact of the pattern of schooling in the Solomons has been to support a growing class division among islanders and a growing inequity between urban and rural areas. The second major impact of schooling has been to undermine traditional forms of knowledge and teaching.
> (Watson-Gegeo and Gegeo 1992:28–9)

The erosion of the native Solomon cultures and the increasing social and economic gap between rural and urban life is, according to these authors, clearly related to the curriculum and instructional patterns used in public schools. Both Watson-Gegeo and Rist emphasize the nature of classroom interaction and the importance of understanding the social and linguistic classroom system. Watson-Gegeo's original work in Hawaii with the Kamehameha Schools is often associated with the distribution of children in reading groups, but groups in which their culturally-determined discourse patterns are used to advance children's comprehension in classroom interactions. Rist's study shows another organization of groups, but this time a sort of tracking system. Teachers in the kindergarten and elementary school years placed children according to their socioeconomic status, and treated them differently. For example, teachers spent more class time with upper-class students, they spent less time disciplining them, and held them up as models for the rest, thus reinforcing their self-confidence with statements about 'how special' they were.

In conclusion, the studies by Watson-Gegeo, Watson-Gegeo and Gegeo, and Rist, among others, raise important questions that have troubled anthropologists, especially those called 'cultural ecologists'. Indeed, cultural ecology is one of the most salient recent theoretical developments (Ogbu 1974, 1978, 1982, 1983, 1987a, 1987b, 1989; Gibson and Ogbu 1991; and Suárez-Orozco 1987, 1989). Because John Ogbu and his associates represent the most visible position on cultural ecology, I will discuss his contributions and some of the limitations of cultural ecology.

Ethnic and Social Identification Processes

The process of adaptation of entire social groups to new linguistic and cultural settings, as well as the process of adjustment of individuals to such settings has preoccupied psychological and cultural anthropologists for several decades. The seminal work by Spindler and Spindler (1971) on Menomini adaptation to cultural contact with European and American cultures, and George Spindler's discussion of cultural change and continuity in values (1955) were two important contributions that dealt with social identification and acculturation. The well-known volume edited by George Spindler (1978) entitled *The Making of Psychological Anthropology*, includes a most interesting chapter on the psychology of culture change and urbanization by Louise Spindler (pp. 187–95). Furthermore, Louise Spindler's book *Culture Change and Modernization: Mini-models and Case Studies* (1984) contains references to 64 case studies. Both of the Spindlers eventually moved on to a more profound analysis of psychological processes of adaptation and change, relying primarily on ethnographic research and less on projective techniques. A number of significant pieces were published in their volume entitled Interpretive Ethnography of Education (1987a), and their original methodology based on ethnographic research produced important contributions such as the Instrumental Activities Inventory (Spindler and Spindler 1965) and comparative cross-cultural approaches as in their study of Schoenhausen and Roseville (Spindler and Spindler 1987b).

The theory of early socialization and psychological processes of ethnic and social identification have been developed by George DeVos, a psychological anthropologist with extensive fieldwork in Japan and the United States. His study of psychological determinants of caste was developed during the study of the Burakumin — Japan's autochthonous outcasts — and of Japanese from Korean background (1967). DeVos expanded his study of the Burakumin and developed a theory of oppression whereby he explored the role of cultural factors in the response of some groups to social oppression (1973b). His main concern was to emphasize that class considerations did not explain the psychological response of some groups to oppression. In DeVos' opinion, degradation incidents — systematic oppressive interactions emphasizing the low-status of some groups — and the collective response of low-status groups to systematic racism in Japan had created several caste-like groups. This contribution was going to become the centerpiece of John Ogbu's theory of cultural ecology which he used to explain differential adaptation and performance of minority groups, especially in the United States.

DeVos pursued significant concepts and offered important insights into the psychodynamics of personality formation and the formation of ethnic identities among minorities (1983). His main point was that the unique psycho-cultural considerations that explained self-identification (ethnic and social) among minority groups in Japan and the United States reflected well-patterned adaptive strategies, as outlined by his previous work (1980, 1982). Then DeVos (1978, 1992) began to compare data obtained from projective techniques (especially from the Thematic Aperception Test, or TAT) about the same ethnic group, the Korean, both in Japan and the United States. He discovered that the two different cultures in the host countries had resulted in different responses from people who share the same home culture. The outlook on life, the higher achievement of Koreans in the US, and their different self-concepts suggested that the process of self-identification and the resulting ethnic identity was impacted by both the home culture and the host culture. This research also played a key role in Ogbu's theoretical discussions of *cultural inversion* (the development of oppositional ethnic identities, i.e. in contrast with the perceived cultural values and characteristics of the host culture), and secondary discontinuities (those resulting from the cultural contact in the host country, in contrast with the primary discontinuities which are brought from the experience of oppression in the home country).

DeVos continued to explore, over a period of twenty-five years, the relationships between psychological processes linked to cultural values and adaptive strategies in the face of demands to function in a different cultural environment. His work with Romanucci-Ross, *Ethnic Identity: Cultural Continuities and Change* (1982) is crucial to our understanding of the formation of self-identity. With Wagatsuma (DeVos and Wagatsuma 1966) he has written about the prejudice in Japan (which they call *invisible race*) against groups that are physically identical, but from recognized lower-status ethnic groups. This work, and further comparative analysis of data from around the world, has resulted in two additional volumes: *Status Inequality: The Self in Culture* (DeVos and Suárez-Orozco 1990) and *Social Cohesion and Alienation: Minorities in the United States and Japan* (DeVos 1992).

Building on the influential work of his professor, George DeVos, John Ogbu has become one of the best known anthropologists of education who studies ethnic identification and adaptive strategies. His work started with an ethnographic study of low-income and minority populations in Stockton, California, and resulted in his first major publication, *The Next Generation: An Ethnography of Education in an Urban Neighborhood* (1974). In this study, Ogbu applies DeVos' concept of caste to urban California. His central idea was that there was a qualitative cultural difference between those groups who had adjusted well in American society and those who had not. The former had, after several generations, succeeded educationally, and consequently had become full citizens and active participants in social institutions. The latter were unable to respond to the demands and the oppression in the United States and remained in their misery. He used the *castelike* concept, along the lines of DeVos' original concept, and developed a typology of minority groups, essentially separating those who were castelike from the others. His work in the following years further developed these concepts. Thus, his second major book, *Minority Education and Caste: The American System in Cross-Cultural Perspective* (Ogbu 1978) was a major leap into a cross-cultural comparison of oppressed castelike groups who behaved as those in the United States, that is, failed to adapt and succeed. The central part of his theory was identical; home cultural patterns determine peoples' responses to oppressive conditions, and consequently, those ethnic groups who succeed must be culturally different from those who fail in the same cultural setting. In this sense, he was revisiting the theories presented by George DeVos, but he had added some power to the typology of minorities and had spelled out some of the peculiar behavioral mechanisms.

Ogbu, an African and a scholar coming from a strong sociology of education tradition in which macro-sociological structural conditions — such as job ceiling and discrimination — had a direct impact on peoples' failures, is forceful in pronouncing an indictment against colonialist Western societies. His more detailed discussions of how and why diverse ethnic groups vary in their ability to succeed and why some of them conspicuously fail developed further his initial perspectives (1987a, 1987b, 1989, 1991a, 1991b, and 1992). Because many of his theoretical contributions will be discussed in great detail in the context of the analysis of the data collected, I will not elaborate any further on his ideas. Suffice it to say that, while many of his contributions have been widely accepted, there are limitations that must be pointed out. Ogbu's summary of his original Stockton study (1974, 1978) has been recently enriched, not so much with new data, as with additional analytical observations:

> The central thesis of this chapter is that the relatively poor school performance of blacks in Stockton, in spite of their wish to succeed, is rooted in their history of involuntary incorporation into American society and the subsequent discriminatory treatment of them in a system of racial castes. The economic and other positions assigned to blacks under this system did not require, promote or reward school success for many generations... For their part, blacks contributed to the problem of lower school performance by the nature of their coping responses. They developed a folk theory of success in which school credentials play an ambiguous role, survival strategies compete with or detract from schooling, a cultural frame of reference and identity system make it difficult to cross cultural boundaries in school learning,

and a deep distrust does not encourage school learning or following school norms.

(Ogbu 1991b:283)

Efforts by other cultural ecologists to pursue these ideas cross-culturally have been made by Ogbu and Matute-Bianchi (1986); Gibson (1987a, 1987b, 1987c, 1988); Suárez-Orozco (1987, 1989, 1991a, 1991b, 1991c); Gibson and Ogbu (1991). Overall, Ogbu's contribution has been very positive and is welcomed as a reaction against biological and psychological determinism that presumed to explain differential achievement between mainstream and ethnic minorities in the United States and Europe. However, more recently cultural ecologists have been viewed by some and criticized as rather rigid and mired in terminological and theoretical problems (Trueba 1988a, 1988b, 1991, 1993; Foley, 1991).

As we strive to explain academic success when failure is expected, we must deal not only with the disempowerment of some, but with the process of empowerment and the mechanisms used by some ethnic groups to gain access to mainstream societal benefits. In this context, the study of the Miao can help offer an alternative interpretation of the role of ethnic identity and the possibility of using the home language and culture as mediating forces in adapting to new cultural values. In other words, rather than looking for qualitative cultural differences in comparing ethnic groups who succeed with those that fail, we must take DeVos' contributions (especially his most recent) and apply them to the case of the Miao. The reason why Koreans or the Miao may succeed in one setting and fail in another is not explained by the cultural differences in the home culture, but by the incentives for adaptation and success jointly constructed by the host culture and the ethnic culture. In the end, after a detailed analysis of the materials presented, we find that the work by DeVos, enriched by insights from Vygotsky and Bakhtin, can best help us understand how the Miao construct their new social identity as university students without abandoning their commitment to their ethnic culture. Thus, the discussion of empowerment processes becomes a central part of this book, but in the context of a socio-historical approach.

Empowerment Processes

The three major bodies of literature that form the foundations of empowerment as a process that can be studied and followed up are: *cultural therapy*, *early socialization* (from both anthropological and psychological perspectives, including psychopedagogics), and *critical theory*. The concept of cultural therapy will be discussed in detail and is central to the theoretical explanations of the data presented here. Essentially, however, George and Louise Spindler in their general writings discussed earlier, and in their more recent volume entitled *Pathways to Awareness: Cultural Therapy with Teachers and Students* (1994) present the notion that cultural therapy is a necessary condition for democracy and peaceful living. Many of the wounds and suffering associated with the pain humans caused each other are rooted in a profound ethnocentrism and lack of understanding not only of other people's cultures, but of their own. It is only through cross-cultural comparisons that we understand prejudice and mistreatment, as well as the important cultural values we hold dear to our hearts. Unless we heal from these wounds, empowerment is impossible. Therefore, to start the empowerment process, there has to be some healing.

The notions of empowerment and disempowerment as applied to educational research (especially ethnographic research) were presented by Trueba in Delgado-Gaitan and Trueba (1991) and draw heavily on research by educational sociologists such as Apple, Bowls and Gintis, Giroux, and others, as presented earlier in this chapter. What Trueba has added is the notion that the theory of empowerment as a process to gain control of one's own life, individually and collectively, must go beyond the rhetoric of empowerment. Consequently, the study of empowerment should not be narrowly conceived as an epistemological frivolous discussion among esoteric groups of critical pedagogues and critical theory experts. Empowerment and disempowerment must be approached in ways such that the consequences of these processes can be touched and seen. For Trueba, this is not merely an academic abstract discussion, but one which needs to be validated by concrete results. For example, the projects generated by Trueba since the early 1980s have focused on these issues, such as his study of adjustment problems of Mexican-American children in school (1983), his discussion of academic success or failure (1987a) and his work on literacy acquisition among Mexican children and youth (1987b, 1988a, 1988b, 1988c). More recently, however, he and his colleagues have made substantial efforts to document the process of empowerment and the mediating of role of the home language and culture in empowerment; see for example, *Cultural Conflict and Adaptation: The Case of Hmong Children in American Society* (with L. Jacobs, and E. Kirton, 1990); *Healing Multicultural America: Mexican Immigrants Rise to Power in Rural California* (with C. Rodríguez, Y. Zou, and J. Cintrón, 1993); *Myth or Reality: Adaptive Strategies of Asian Americans in California* (with L. Cheng and K. Ima, 1993); and *Language and Culture in Learning: Teaching Spanish to Native Speakers of Spanish* (B. Merino, H. Trueba, and F. Samaniego, 1994). What Trueba and his associates have done is to move away from major macro-sociological or macro-anthropological theories of successful adaptation or of failure and examine in specific cases the role that language and culture have in preparing ethnic persons and groups to deal with racial, social or ethnic prejudice, with the challenges of forming new self-identities, and with the serious problems of socializing children facing rapid cultural change.

In this context, the work of psychologists and anthropologists is important and has central relevance to adaptive approaches in institutions tending to disempower minority children. What are the appropriate conditions for children to learn behaviors that will lead them to academic and social success?

What is the role of adults in this task? What kinds of mentoring relationships and processes of teaching/learning must be developed to provide effective instruction and to teach children the values that will bring success to their lives? This concept is compatible and complementary to the studies of enculturation or culture acquisition in anthropology (see George and Louise Spindler 1987a and 1987b; and G. Spindler 1988; see also the work by G. DeVos mentioned earlier, especially his work on socialization, 1973b). Both of these anthropological approaches emphasize the acquisition of knowledge and values necessary to function effectively as an adult in society, and both stress the need for conscious, organized and intentional tasks that children must voluntarily engage in, experience and live through in order to learn.

The linkage between learning and experiencing is called *psychopedagogics* because it requires the work of the mind; the child is socialized through his/her higher mental functions to understand and internalize cultural values and symbols leading to motivation to act and to achieve. There is another important connection between anthropology and psychopedagogics: action is linked to a cultural value system that provides the rationale, the motivation, while at the same time a cultural value generates actions. There is a symbiotic relationship between acting and thinking and between the cultural value embedded in action and the willingness to act. George and Louise Spindler in their recent *American Cultural Dialogue and its Transmission* (1990) establish this relationship and elaborate on its consequences for our understanding of differential adaptation processes of persons under acculturation. The global view of the many relationships between educating or socializing children to become empowered, and the kind of schooling needed to retain a positive ethnic identification are an increasing part of the literature addressed by Trueba. Teachers' assumptions about children's academic potential determine the nature of academic socialization and future academic success or failure. These assumptions do not have be overt and conscious; in fact, often they are part of the hidden curriculum, or unintended set of messages given to children. This hidden curriculum may go on unnoticed along with the regular curriculum and quietly but forcefully send negative messages to some students and thus perpetuate social strata in the future generations. The perception of differential potentials on the part of teachers has a cost in children's self-concept. American schools, and Chinese schools for that matter, are not really equalitarian; some are more equal than others.

The study of these differential messages by anthropologists such as Watson-Gegeo has helped us understand better the role of schools during early child socialization. According to Watson-Gegeo, for example, schools perpetuate social strata and the social order or the power hierarchy among students (Watson-Gegeo 1990; Watson-Gegeo and Gegeo 1992). Some children are guided into taking subservient roles in society, while others are taught to lead society and join the powerful and the rich. The use of sociolinguistic analysis in this type of research reinforces the sentiment of Neo-Vygotskians who stress the importance of language (Wertsch, 1991).

The Authors' Perspectives

Empowerment research has emphasized language and culture and a crosscultural perspective, in the hope to understand the ethnocentrism of human social groups which tend to perpetuate mythical notions about other groups in order to retain internal ethnic cohesiveness in their own group. The notion of group boundaries has been emphasized by Barth (1969:10–12) and DeVos and Suárez-Orozco (1990:104). While boundaries and competition among ethnic groups are seen as essential for the existence of these groups, competition in industrial societies translates into social and political forces often aligned along ethnic boundaries. The implications of this statement means that ethnic affiliation can mean peace or war, as we have learned recently from the conflicts in Bosnia, Croatia and Serbia, and from the incredible abuses committed against underclass ethnics in these countries, the former Soviet Union, and even in European countries such as Germany, Belgium, and France. That cultural myths were invented to rationalize abuse of power is nothing new in history; colonialism illustrated that fact many times in Africa and Latin America. (See Roosens 1989a, 1989b, 1993; Boos-Nunning and Hohmann 1989; Tomlinson 1989, 1991; Eldering and Kloprogge 1989; and Suárez-Orozco 1991a, 1991b).

The study of empowerment is embedded in the study of cultural conflict, injustice and hatred, as well as in the study of ethnic boundaries, myths about inferiority of some races and the superiority of one, the white Aryan race. The world has taken notice of the Jewish Holocaust and the systematic disempowerment of Jewish and other low-status people that preceded their destruction by the Hitler machinery. The study of disempowerment among certain ethnic groups is of international interest, and so is the new empowerment of traditionally underclass groups (as in the case in China with the Miao and other groups). This interest is selfish in many cases, for example, in Europe now under the threat of an 'immigrant invasion' by peoples of color; the subsequent mixture of cultures and races frightens many Europeans. The public discourse of 'racial purity' (or 'ethnic cleansing') is euphemistically addressed as 'cultural purity' in the news. As will be seen in the final chapters, the implications of this theoretical approach to the interpretation of the data presented here shows the need for more proactive and consistent empowerment policies for all ethnic groups. While China has taken drastic measures and used enforcement methods disliked in Western societies to assure equality of groups since 1949 with Chairman Mao's Revolution, Western societies have maintained institutional inequalities and the mistreatment of minorities in ways that would not happen in China. Perhaps we can learn some lessons from the Chinese history of minority empowerment. Systematic discrimination, deprivation of civil rights, policies of violence and overt abuses against minorities in Europe have a high price for all humanity, because they violate the rights of all of us and perpetuate an exploited underclass. Empowerment studies are truly needed. The suffering of the next generations with the conspicuous rituals of degradation of ethnic minorities will leave a permanent mark on all children's minds.

As the social sciences mature, and as they revise previous theoretical frameworks, there is clear progress, but we must continue to strive to keep this momentum. Empowerment research represents one of the most positive trends in the efforts of scholars across nations. It is only sixty years since Margaret Mead, Alfred Kroeber, Solon T. Kimball, Cora Dubois, Jules Henry and the young George Spindler began to discuss the fate of children (especially immigrant children) exposed to drastic social and cultural changes and the dangers of ethnocentrism. They preached cross-cultural research, particularly ethnographic, and it took us half a century to learn the lessons they taught us (G. Spindler 1955). During these sixty years of American anthropological research we have attempted to move away from biological and psychological determinist explanations of behavior, and we have followed the intellectual leaders such as Franz Boas, Edward Sapir, Melville Herskovits, and Ruth Benedict who, having experienced oppression and racism, warned us about pseudo-scientific racism and simplistic notions of cultural unilineal evolution (Suárez-Orozco 1993:1–2).

In the end, castification or disempowerment (first shown in terms of temporary marginalization of ethnic groups) turns out to rob people of their human status and takes away from them the opportunity to share their talents with the other members of the human race. In order to create adequate interventions to prevent trends of disempowerment evident in social neglect of children because of their color, religion or other excuses, we must emphasize the unity of all mankind. The study presented here is an effort in that direction. The application of the theories of the role of language and culture in cognitive development presented by Bakhtin (1981, 1986) and Vygotsky (1962, 1978) have been advanced by Neo-Vygotskians (Wertsch 1981, 1985a, 1985b, 1991; Cole and Scribner 1974; Cole 1985; Tharp and Gallimore 1989; Moll 1990). With these ideas of Bakhtin and Vygotsky we can redirect the attention of scholars not only to the intermediate agencies (and away from macro-sociological and economic factors), but to the intra-psychological elements as affected by the home language and culture, under the rubric of *mediated action* (Wertsch 1991). Mediated action theory as applied to cognitive development and learning environments is a fairly productive approach, especially when it is combined with ethnographic approaches in the study of ethnic communities (Moll and Diaz 1987; Moll 1990). There are other approaches to the study of empowerment which focus on teacher education for diversity by scholars who use ethnographic research methods as a means to socialize teachers into a reflective mode of teaching. These scholars view language and culture as a mediating instrument for transferring knowledge and communicating effectively. Their analysis of this *reflective teaching* and *inquiry-oriented* teacher education has been discussed in the recent literature (Tabachnick and Zeichner 1991; Zeichner 1990, 1991, 1992; Zeichner and Gore 1990). An understanding of the mediating process leads to instructional decisions that help construct better learning environments at home and in school. This study does not focus on teacher education *per se*, but it explores ways to identify processes of empowerment among members of the Miao group, and it searches for more adequate explanations

The Authors' Perspectives

of their academic success. The role of students' home language and culture in mediating their achievement underlies the study.

References

APPLE, M. (1982) *Cultural and Economic Reproduction in Education*, New York, NY: Macmillan.
APPLE, M. (1985) *Education and Power*, Boston, MA: Ark Paperbacks. (First published in 1982).
APPLE, M. (1989) *Teachers and Texts: A Political Economy of Class and Gender Relations in Education*, New York, NY: Routledge. (First published in 1986).
APPLE, M. (1990) *Ideology and Curriculum*, London, England: Routledge & Kegan Paul. (First published in 1979).
APPLE, M. (1992) 'Do the standards go far enough? Power, policy, and practices in mathematics education', *Journal for Research in Mathematics Education*, **23**(5), pp. 412–31.
APPLE, M. (1993) *Official Knowledge: Democratic Education in a Conservative Age*, New York, NY: Routledge.
ARONOWITZ, S. and GIROUX, H.A. (1985) *Education Under Siege*, South Hadley, MA: Bergin & Garvey.
ARONOWITZ, S. and GIROUX, H. (1991) *Postmodern Education: Politics, Culture and Social Criticism*, Minneapolis, MN: University of Minnesota Press.
AU, K.H. and JORDAN, C. (1981) 'Teaching reading to Hawaiian children: Finding a culturally appropriate solution', in TRUEBA, H. GUTHRIE, G. and AU, K. (Eds) *Culture and the Bilingual Classroom: Studies in Classroom Ethnography*, Rowley, MA: Newbury House Publishers, Inc., pp. 139–52.
BAKHTIN, M.M. (1981) *The Dialogic Imagination: Four Essays by M.M. Bakhtin*, HOLQUIST, M. (Ed) HOLQUIST, C. and M. (translator) Austin, TX: University of Texas Press.
BAKHTIN, M.M. (1986) *Speech Genres and Other Late Essays*, EMERSON, C. and HOLQUIST, M. (Eds) and McGEE, V.W. (translator), Austin, TX: University of Texas Press.
BANKS, J.A. and McGEE-BANKS, C.A. (Eds) (1989) *Multicultural Education: Issues and Perspectives*, London, England: Allyn and Bacon Publishers.
BARTH, F. (1969) *Ethnic Groups and Boundaries*, Boston, MA: Little, Brown.
BERNSTEIN, B. (1977) *Class, Codes and Control: Towards a Theory of Educational Transmissions*, Vol. 3, Second edition, London, England: Routledge & Kegan Paul.
BOGGS, S.T. (1985) *Speaking, Relating, and Learning: A Study of Hawaiian Children at Home and at School*, Norwood, NJ: Ablex Publishing Corp.
BOOS-NUNNING, U. and HOHMANN, M. (1989) 'The educational situation of migrant workers' children in the Federal Republic of Germany', in ELDERING, L. and KLOPROGGE, J. (Eds) *Different Cultures Same School: Ethnic Minority Children in Europe*, Amsterdam, The Netherlands: Swets & Zeitlinger, pp. 39–59.
BOWLS, S. and GINTIS, H. (1976) *Schooling in Capitalist America: Education Reform and the Contradictions of Economic Life*, New York, NY: Basic Books.
COLE, M. (1985) 'The zone of proximal development: Where culture and cognition create each other', in WERTSCH, J.V. (Ed) *Culture, Communication and Cognition: Vygotskian Perspectives*, Cambridge, MA: Cambridge University Press, pp. 146–61.
COLE, M. and SCRIBNER, S. (1974) *Culture and Thought: A Psychological Introduction*, New York, NY: Basic Books.

DELGADO-GAITAN, C. and TRUEBA, H. (1991) *Crossing Cultural Borders: Education for Immigrant Families in America*, London, England: Falmer Press.

DEVOS, G. (1967) 'Essential elements of caste: Psychological determinants in structural theory', in DEVOS, A. and WAGATSUMA, H. (Eds) *Japan's Invisible Race: Caste in Culture and Personality*, Berkeley, CA: University of California Press, pp. 332–84.

DEVOS, G. (1973a) 'Japan's outcastes: The problem of the Burakumin' in WHITAKER, B. (Ed) *The Fourth World: Victims of Group Oppression*, New York, NY: Schocken Books, pp. 307–27.

DEVOS, G. (Ed) (1973b) *Socialization for Achievement: Essays on the Cultural Psychology of the Japanese*, Berkeley, CA: University of California Press.

DEVOS, G. (1978) 'Selective permeability and reference groups sanctioning: Psychocultural continuities in role degradation', in YINGER, M. (Ed), *Major Social Issues: A Multicommunity View*, Glencoe, IL: Free Press, pp. 9–14.

DEVOS, G. (1980) 'Ethnic adaptation and minority status', *Journal of Cross-Cultural Psychology*, **11**, pp. 101–24.

DEVOS, G. (1982) 'Adaptive strategies in US minorities', in JONES, E.E. and KORCHIN, S.J. (Eds) *Minority Mental Health*, New York, NY: Praeger, pp. 74–117.

DEVOS, G. (1983) 'Ethnic identity and minority status: Some psycho-cultural considerations', in JACOBSON-WIDDING, A. (Ed) *Identity: Personal and Socio-cultural*, Uppsala, Sweden: Almquist & Wiksell Tryckeri AB, pp. 90–113.

DEVOS, G. (1992) *Social Cohesion and Alienation: Minorities in the United States and Japan*, San Francisco, CA: Westview Press.

DEVOS, G. and ROMANUCCI-ROSS, L. (Eds) (1982) *Ethnic Identity: Cultural Continuities and Change*, (Second Edition) Chicago, IL: The University of Chicago Press. (First edition) (1975) by The Wenner-Gren Foundation for Anthropological Research, Inc.).

DEVOS, G. and SUÁREZ-OROZCO, M.M. (1990) *Status Inequality: The Self in Culture*, Newbury Park, CA: Sage Publications.

DEVOS, G. and WAGATSUMA, H. (1966) *Japan's Invisible Race: Caste in Culture and Personality*, Berkeley, CA: University of California Press.

ELDERING, L. and KLOPROGGE, J. (Eds) (1989) *Different Cultures Same School: Ethnic Minority Children in Europe*, Amsterdam, The Netherlands: Swets & Zeitlinger.

FOLEY, D. (1991) 'Reconsidering anthropological explanations of ethnic school failure', *Anthropology and Education Quarterly*, **22**(1), pp. 60–86.

FREIRE, P. (1993) *Pedagogia da Esperança: Um reencontro com a pedagogia do oprimido*, São Paulo, Brazil: Editora Paz e Terra, S.A.

GIBSON, M. (1987a) 'Playing by the rules', in SPINDLER, G. (Ed) *Education and cultural process: Anthropological Approaches*, Second Edition, Prospect Heights, IL: Waveland Press, Inc., pp. 274–83.

GIBSON, M. (1987b) 'The school performance of immigrant minorities: A comparative view', *Anthropology and Education Quarterly*, **18**(4), pp. 262–75.

GIBSON, M. (1987c) 'Punjabi immigrants in an American high school', in SPINDLER, G. and L. (Eds) *Interpretive Ethnography of Education: At Home and Abroad*, Hillsdale, NJ: Lawrence Erlbaum Associates, Publishers, pp. 281–310.

GIBSON, M. (1988) *Accommodation Without Assimilation: Sikh Immigrants in an American High School*, Ithaca, NY: Cornell University Press.

GIBSON, M. and OGBU, J. (Eds) (1991) *Minority Status and Schooling: A Comparative Study of Immigrant and Involuntary Minorities*, New York, NY: Garland Publishing Inc.

McLaren, P. (1989) *Life in Schools*, New York, NY: Longman.
McLaren, P. (Ed) (1991) *Postmodernism, Postcolonialism and Pedagogy*, Victoria, Australia: James Nicholas Publishers.
Merino, B., Trueba, H.T. and Samaniego, F. (1994) *Language and Culture in Learning: Teaching Spanish to Native Speakers of Spanish*, London, England: Falmer Press.
Moll, L. (1990) *Vygotsky and Education: Instructional Implications and Applications of Sociohistorical Psychology*, Cambridge, MA: Cambridge University Press.
Moll, L. and Diaz, E. (1987) 'Change as the goal of educational research', *Anthropology and Education Quarterly*, **18**(4), pp. 300–11.
Ogbu, J. (1974) *The Next Generation: An Ethnography of Education in an Urban Neighborhood*, New York, NY: Academic Press.
Ogbu, J. (1978) *Minority Education and Caste: The American System in Cross-Cultural Perspective*, New York, NY: Academic Press.
Ogbu, J. (1982) 'Cultural discontinuities and schooling', *Anthropology and Education Quarterly*, **13**(4), pp. 290–307.
Ogbu, J. (1983) 'Minority status and schooling in plural societies', *Comparative Education Review*, **27**(2), pp. 168–90.
Ogbu, J. (1987a) 'Variability in minority responses to schooling: Nonimmigrants vs. immigrants', in Spindler, G. and L. (Eds) *Interpretive Ethnography of Education: At Home and Abroad*, Hillsdale, NJ: Lawrence Erlbaum Associates, Publishers, pp. 255–78.
Ogbu, J. (1987b) 'Variability in minority school performance: A problem in search of an explanation', *Anthropology and Education Quarterly*, **18**(4), pp. 312–34.
Ogbu, J. (1989) 'The individual in collective adaptation: A framework for focusing on academic underperformance and dropping out among involuntary minorities', in Weis, L., Farrar, E. and Petrie, H. (Eds) *Dropouts from School: Issues, Dilemmas, and Solutions*, Albany, NY: State University of New York Press, pp. 181–204.
Ogbu, J. (1991a) 'Immigrant and involuntary minorities in comparative perspective', in Gibson, M. and Ogbu, J. (Eds) *Minority Status and Schooling: A Comparative Study of Immigrant and Involuntary Minorities*, New York, NY: Garland Publishing, Inc., pp. 3–33.
Ogbu, J. (1991b) 'Low school performance as an adaptation: The case of blacks in Stockton, California', in Gibson, M. and Ogbu, J. (Eds) *Minority Status and Schooling: A Comparative Study of Immigrant and Involuntary Minorities*, New York, NY: Garland Publishing, Inc., pp. 249–85.
Ogbu, J. (1992) 'Understanding cultural diversity', *Educational Researcher*, **21**(8), pp. 5–24.
Ogbu, J. and Matute-Bianchi, M.E. (1986) 'Understanding sociocultural factors: Knowledge, identity and school adjustment', in *Beyond Language: Social and Cultural Factors in Schooling Language Minority Students*, Sacramento, CA: Bilingual Education Office, California State Department of Education, pp. 73–142.
Popkewitz, T.S. (1991) *A Political Sociology of Educational Reform: Power/Knowledge in Teaching, Teacher Education and Research*, New York, NY: Teachers College, Columbia University.
Popkewitz, T.S. (Ed) (1993) *Changing Patterns of Power: Social Regulation and Teacher Education Reform*, New York, NY: State University of New York Press.
Rist, R.C. (1970) 'Student social class and teacher expectations: The self-fulfilling prophecy in education', *Harvard Educational Review*, **40**(3), pp. 411–51.

RIST, R.C. (1973) *Urban Schools: A Factory for Failure*, Cambridge, MA: Massachusetts Institute of Technology Press.

ROOSENS, E. (1989a) 'Cultural ecology and achievement motivation: Ethnic minority youngsters in the Belgian system', in ELDERING, L. and KLOPROGGE, J. (Eds) *Different Cultures Same School: Ethnic Minority Children in Europe*, Amsterdam, The Netherlands: Swets & Zeitlinger, pp. 85–106.

ROOSENS, E. (1989b) *Creating Ethnicity: The Process of Ethnogenesis*, in BERNARD, H.B. (Series Editor) *Frontiers of Anthropology, Volume 5*, Newbury Park, CA: Sage Publications.

ROOSENS, E. (Ed) (1993) *The Insertion of Allochthonous Youngsters in Belgian society*, Special Issue of *Migration*, sponsored by the Verlagsabteilun des Berliner Instituts für Vergleichende Sozialforschung, erscheint vierteljährl. Berlin, Germany: Edition Parabolis.

SECADA, W. (Ed) (1989) *Equity in Education*. London, England: Falmer Press.

SKUTNABB-KANGAS, T. (1984) *Bilingualism or Not: The Education of Minorities*, Clevendon, England: Multilingual Matters.

SLEETER, C. (Ed) (1991) *Empowerment Through Multicultural Education*, Albany, NY: State University of New York Press.

SLEETER, C. (1992) *Keepers of the American Dream: A Study of Staff Development and Multicultural Education*, London, England: Falmer Press.

SLEETER, C. and GRANT, C. (1987) 'An analysis of multicultural education in the US, *Harvard Educational Review*, **57**(4), pp. 421–44.

SPINDLER, G. (Ed) (1955) *Anthropology and Education*, Stanford, CA: Stanford University Press.

SPINDLER, G. (with SPINDLER, L.) (1971) *Dreamers Without Power: The Menomini Indians*, New York, NY: Holt, Rinehart and Winston. (Republished by Waveland Press in 1984).

SPINDLER, G. (Ed) (1988) *Doing the Ethnography of Schooling: Educational Anthropology in Action*, Prospects Heights, IL: Waveland Press, Inc.

SPINDLER, G. and SPINDLER, L. (1965) 'The Instrumental Activities Inventory: A technique for the study of the psychology of acculturation', *Southwestern Journal of Anthropology* **21**(1) pp. 1–23.

SPINDLER, G. and SPINDLER, L. (Eds) (1977) *Native North American Cultures: Four Cases*, New York, NY: Holt, Rinehart & Winston.

SPINDLER, G. and SPINDLER, L. (Eds) (1987a) *The Interpretive Ethnography of Education: At Home and Abroad*, Hillsdale, NJ: Lawrence Erlbaum Assoc.

SPINDLER, G. and SPINDLER, L. (1987b) 'Cultural dialogue and schooling in Schoenhausen and Roseville: A comparative analysis', *Anthropology and Education Quarterly*, **18**(1), pp. 3–16.

SPINDLER, G. and SPINDLER, L., with TRUEBA, H. and WILLIAMS, M. (1990) *The American Cultural Dialogue and its Transmission*, London, England: Falmer Press.

SPINDLER, G. and SPINDLER, L. (Eds) (1994) *Pathways to Awareness: Cultural Therapy with Teachers and Students*, Newbury Park, CA: Corwin Press.

SPINDLER, L. (1978) 'Researching the psychology of culture change and urbanization', in SPINDLER, G. (Ed) *The Making of Psychological Anthropology*, Berkeley, CA: University of California Press, pp. 187–95.

SPINDLER, L. (1984) *Culture Change and Modernization: Mini-models and Case Studies*, Prospect Heights, IL: Waveland Press, Inc.

SUÁREZ-OROZCO, M.M. (1987) 'Towards a psychosocial understanding of Hispanic adaptation to American schooling', in TRUEBA, H. (Ed) *Success or Failure: Linguistic Minority Children at Home and in School*, New York, NY: Harper & Row, pp. 156–68.

SUÁREZ-OROZCO, M.M. (1989) *Central American Refugees and US High Schools: A Psychosocial Study of Motivation and Achievement*, Stanford, CA: Stanford University Press.

SUÁREZ-OROZCO, M.M. (1991a) 'Dialogue and the transmission of culture: The Spindlers and the making of American anthropology', *Anthropology and Education Quarterly*, **22**(3), pp. 281–91.

SUÁREZ-OROZCO, M.M. (1991b) 'Migration, minority status, and education: European dilemmas and responses in the 1990s', *Anthropology and Education Quarterly*, **22**(2), pp. 99–120.

SUÁREZ-OROZCO, M.M. (1991c) 'Immigrant adaptation to schooling: A Hispanic case', in GIBSON, M. and OGBU, J. (Eds) *Minority Status and Schooling: A Comparative Study of Immigrant and Involuntary Minorities*, New York, NY: Garland Publishing, Inc., pp. 37–61.

SUÁREZ-OROZCO, M.M. (1993) 'Three generations in the reshaping of psychological anthropology', unpublished Manuscript, Center for Advanced Study in the Behavioral Sciences. Stanford University, Stanford, CA.

TABACHNICK, R. and ZEICHNER, K. (Eds) (1991) *Issues and Practices in Inquiry-oriented Teacher Education*, (The Wisconsin Series of Teacher Education). London, England: Falmer Press.

THARP, R. and GALLIMORE, R. (1989) *Rousing Minds to Life: Teaching, Learning and Schooling in Social Context*, Cambridge, MA: Cambridge University Press.

TOMLINSON, S. (1989) 'Ethnicity and educational achievement in Britain', in ELDERING, L. and KLOPROGGE, J. (Eds) *Different Cultures, Same School: Ethnic and Minority Children in Europe*, Amsterdam, The Netherlands: Swets & Zeitlinger, pp. 15–37.

TOMLINSON, S. (1991) 'Ethnicity and educational attainment in England — An overview', *Anthropology and Education Quarterly*, **22**(2), pp. 121–39.

TRUEBA, H.T. (1983) 'Adjustment problems of Mexican-American school children: An anthropological study', *Learning Disability Quarterly*, **4**(4), pp. 395–415.

TRUEBA, H.T. (Ed) (1987a) *Success or Failure: Linguistic Minority Children at Home and in School*, New York, NY: Harper & Row.

TRUEBA, H.T. (1987b) 'Organizing classroom instruction in specific sociocultural contexts: Teaching Mexican youth to write in English', in GOLDMAN, S. and TRUEBA, H.T. (1987b) *Becoming Literate in English as a Second Language*, Norwood, NJ: Ablex Corporation, pp. 235–52.

TRUEBA, H.T. (1988a) 'English literacy acquisition: From cultural trauma to learning disabilities in minority students', *Journal of Linguistics and Education*, **1**, pp. 125–52.

TRUEBA, H.T. (1988b) 'Culturally-based explanations of minority students' academic achievement', *Anthropology and Education Quarterly*, **19**(3), pp. 270–87.

TRUEBA, H.T. (1989) *Raising Silent Voices: Educating Linguistic Minorities for the Twenty-first century*, New York, NY: Harper & Row.

TRUEBA, H.T. (1991) Comments on Foley's 'Reconsidering anthropological explanations . . .', *Anthropology and Education Quarterly*, **22**(1) pp. 87–94.

TRUEBA, H.T. (1993) 'Many groups, one people: The meaning and significance of multicultural education in modern America', *Bilingual Research Journal*, **16**(3), and (4) pp. 83–107.

TRUEBA, H.T., JACOBS, L. and KIRTON, E. (1990) *Cultural Conflict and Adaptation: The Case of the Hmong Children in American Society*, London, England: Falmer Press.
TRUEBA, H.T., RODRÍUEZ, C., ZOU, Y. and CINTRÓN, J. (1993) *Healing Multicultural America: Mexican Immigrants Rise to Power in Rural California*, London, England: Falmer Press.
TRUEBA, H.T., CHENG, L. and IMA, K. (1993) *Myth or Reality: Adaptive Strategies of Asian Americans in California*, London, England: Falmer Press.
VYGOTSKY, L.S. (1962) *Thought and Language*, Cambridge, MA: Massachusetts Institute of Technology Press.
VYGOTSKY, L.S. (1978) *Mind in Society: The Development of Higher Psychological Processes*, COLE, M., JOHN-TEINER, V., SCRIBNER, S. and SOUBERMAN, E. (Eds) Cambridge, MA: Harvard University Press.
WATSON-GEGEO, K. (1990) 'The social transfer of cognitive skills in Kwara'ae', *Quarterly Newsletter of the Laboratory for Comparative Human Cognition*, **12**(2), pp. 86–90.
WATSON-GEGEO, K. and GEGEO, D. (1992) 'Schooling, knowledge, and power', *Anthropology and Education Quarterly*, **23**(1), pp. 10–29.
WERTSCH, J. (1981) *The Concept of Activity in Soviet Psychology*, New York, NY: M.E. Sharpe, Inc.
WERTSCH, J. (1985a) *Vygotsky and the Social Formation of Mind*, Cambridge, MA: Harvard University Press.
WERTSCH, J. (Ed) (1985b) *Culture, Communication, and Cognition: Vygotskian Perspectives*, Cambridge, MA: Cambridge University Press.
WERTSCH, J. (1991) *Voices of the Mind: A Sociolcultural Approach to Mediated Action*, Cambridge, MA: Harvard University Press.
ZEICHNER, K. (1990) 'Preparing teachers for democratic schools', *Action in Teacher Education*, **11**(1), pp. 5–10.
ZEICHNER, K. (1991) 'Contradictions and tensions in the professionalization of teaching and the democratization of schools', *Teachers College Record*, **92**(2), pp. 363–79.
ZEICHNER, K. (1992) 'Educating teachers for cultural diversity', unpublished manuscript, Wisconsin Center for Educational Research, School of Education, University of Wisconsin-Madison.
ZEICHNER, K. and GORE, J. (1990) 'Teacher socialization', in HOUSTON, W.R. (Ed) *Handbook of Research on Teacher Education*, New York, NY: Macmillan, pp. 329–48.

Chapter 2

Educational Ethnography: Research Design

Educational ethnographers are frequently trained by social scientists other than cultural anthropologists. The methodological rigors learned from seasoned ethnographers in long-term research among exotic aborigines are now learned in misleadingly 'familiar' urban settings. The mystique of ethnography as a powerful instrument that provides profound insights into the lives of others, has been traded for the pedestrian reality of deceivingly simple, theoretically fragmented, and often unsafe urban ethnography.

Educational Ethnography

Modern ethnographic work has become a rather practical tool among other instruments pragmatically chosen to conduct certain kinds of research, on certain topics and with focuses that are expected to bring new light to urban problems. Consequently, ethnographic work is extremely diversified and can be framed from many different theoretical perspectives. As such, educational ethnographic studies can be versatile, eclectic or opportunistic.

Educational ethnographers trained by cultural anthropologists observe with some anxiety the new popularity of qualitative research methods — particularly ethnography — and the proliferation of research designs that include an 'ethnographic component'. They would like to see ethnographic projects of higher quality, long-term and well organized; that is, structured to pursue systematically the cohesive answers to questions that have cross-cultural comparability and relevance. Indeed, there are varying degrees of sophistication in the practice of ethnographic research.

Experienced ethnographers insist that in the study of behavior the focus and emphasis is on *culture*, or culture acquisition, cultural transmission, cultural conflict, etc. Because culture means different things to different people, the methodological debate becomes a theoretical one. Furthermore, experienced ethnographers do not demonstrate great enthusiasm for technological advances in the collection and analysis of data — such as the use of software to classify and compare information categories. For them the research instrument is the ethnographer, and the quality of an ethnographic study depends on the wisdom and ability of those who conduct it.

The debate is healthy and forces reflection: Is ethnography, traditionally used to make sense of behavior, compatible with evaluative judgments of 'good' or 'bad' performance? Can the purposes of evaluation be reconciled with those of ethnography? In a comparable scenario, can ethnography be used to study equity practices? Is advocacy compatible with the presumed neutrality of scientific research? It is unlikely that modern social scientists escape the responsibility that accompanies the study of social phenomena (as, for example, in current research on ethnic, immigrant and refugee minorities). Qualitative approaches are suitable for the study of inequity, oppression, differential access to resources, school failure, racial prejudice, the nature of decision-making as it relates to upward mobility of women and ethnic groups, etc. These topics are not neutral. The awareness that research must also serve functions other than the accumulation of scientific knowledge for science's sake has been emphasized with the increasing participation of researchers who belong to ethnic and racial groups traditionally underrepresented in the research community.

The birth of educational anthropology is also the birth of educational ethnography, and it is traced back to the early 1950s when scholars around the country, especially in New York and California, began to show concern for the effectiveness of schools and the needs of teachers working with culturally different children. George and Louise Spindler were originally affiliated with organizations pursuing what was then called, and still is psychological anthropology. For them the connection between psychological anthropology and education was a natural one. In fact, George, with Louise, convoked the first significant conference on educational anthropology in the early 1950s which resulted in one of his first volumes, *Anthropology and Education* (1955) in which Spindler presents the papers of the experts of that time: Alfred Kroeber, Cora Dubois, Margaret Mead, Jules Henry, Solon T. Kimball, C.W.M. Hart and others. What is remarkable is that these outstanding anthropologists were also recognized ethnographers, with long time experience in data gathering and analysis. From this time on, we see the development of programs, books and traditions which form a very substantial body of literature today in educational anthropology and education that continues to maintain method and theory together. George and Louise Spindler, for example, along with their study of schools, continued to work for many years among the Menominee of Wisconsin and the Blood of Alberta to pursue issues on acculturation, cultural conflict and personality structure.

George and Louise Spindler authored *Dreamers Without Power: The Menomini Indians* (1971), and George Spindler edited *Education and Cultural Process: Anthropological Approaches* (a classic source for educators), with a second edition published in 1987, in which George and Louise Spindler had several important contributions. George and Louise Spindler edited another important volume *The Interpretive Ethnography of Education: At Home and*

Abroad (1987a). The central assumption of many ethnographers is that culture acquisition and cultural transmission are an integral part of learning processes, because, in their minds, culture mediates learning. The Spindlers, however, emphasize cultural transmission as an essential instrument to communicate knowledge and to assign meaning to it. Their book on American culture, written with H. Trueba and M. Williams, *The American Cultural Dialogue and Its Transmission* (1990) describes a holistic model of American culture. Here once more, the method, ethnography, is an essential mechanism to get into the study of culture. The assumption is that no study of culture, cultural values, behavior, content, transmission, loss, etc., was possible without ethnographic research. On the other hand, ethnographic research was not perceived as being only qualitative, because indeed many of the anthropologists using ethnography were also gathering large amounts of quantitative data. George and Louise Spindler provided not only the general philosophy of ethnographic research, but specific ideas, instruments, criteria and insights.

The readers can examine the following sources: *Being an Anthropologist: Fieldwork in Eleven Cultures* (edited by G. Spindler, with a joint chapter by G. and L. Spindler on their Menomini research, 1970); *Doing the Ethnography of Schooling: Educational Anthropology in Action* (second edition, G. Spindler (Ed) 1988); and *Interpretive Ethnography of Education: At Home and Abroad* (1987a, mentioned earlier). In this last book they elaborate on the nature of ethnographic research and its requirements, one of which is precisely that ethnography is quintessentially interpretive and systematic, and consequently impacts the design in an ongoing research project extending through time. In these volumes, as well as other journals (including *Education and Cultural Process*) the Spindlers include their own work (see, for example, G. Spindler and L. Spindler, 1987b, 1987c) as well as the work of other scholars.

The Spindlers also published hundreds of case studies, and journal articles, especially in the *Anthropology and Education Quarterly*. Ethnographers of education writing on research methodology are relatively few and most of them are connected with its original designers, especially with the Spindlers who have trained over thirty generations of researchers and taught over 40,000 students at Stanford, the University of Wisconsin-Madison, and the University of California, Santa Barbara (1991, personal communication). What follows is a brief discussion of some other ethnographers of education and their major contributions.

One of the most insightful ethnographers of education who has written important articles on methodology is Frederick Erickson (1982, 1984, 1986). Some of his articles have become classic, for example, 'Some approaches to inquiry in school/community ethnography' (1977), and his 'School literacy, reasoning, and civility: An anthropologist's perspective' (1984). The fundamental contributions Erickson made to our understanding of the interpretive process, and the way we use context to make inferences about the meaning of interactions, exchanges and messages, was greatly enriched by his knowledge of sociolinguistics and his keen observational powers. His *micro-ethnographic* studies of day-to-day interactions resulted in important observations about participation structures of students and teachers. One of his most substantive contributions is entitled 'Qualitative methods in research on teaching' (1986). Erickson, who also has trained many generations of school ethnographers, continues to make significant methodological contributions that attempt to respond to current methodological demands and problems faced in urban settings. His skills in analyzing audio and video-tapes have become a science.

Another methodologist who has distinguished himself for the depth of his analysis of text and interpersonal interaction, particularly through the use of videotapes, is Ray McDermott (1977; 1987). His major hypothesis was that school failure did not occur by chance, but that it was 'accomplished' and required systematic efforts on the part of school personnel and students; consequently, he argued, school failure was not the child's failure, but rather a system failure possibly engineered for ulterior reasons. Later on, as he engaged in the study of Vygotsky and Neo-Vygotskians he worked on the nature of interactional support systems helping children achieve (see Goldman and McDermott, 1987). The ethnographic detail of daily observations and the testimonies of students make the study very powerful.

The work by Ogbu cited in Chapter One, which will later be discussed in detail, is an example of another type of ethnographic research focused not so much on personal face-to-face interaction, but on the collection of massive data about a community, the study of power distribution among community organizations, and the relationship between minority communities and schools. While some studies have remained relatively focused on specific themes or issues, others have attempted to provide a broad ethnohistorical base as a context for specific data. In this category, the work by Trueba and associates (mentioned in the previous chapter and the final chapters) is a clear example. As a student first, and now a colleague of the Spindlers, Trueba has made an effort to present a historical context of the antecedents of the current ethnography of a school, or of the children under study. Other ethnographers of education have made efforts to distinguish proper ethnographic studies from other qualitative studies with an ethnographic component (see the work by Harry Wolcott 1987, 1988). Above and beyond anthropologically-trained persons there are many who continue to use ethnographic methods very effectively, and who write about ethnographic methodology (see, for example, LeCompte and Goetz 1984). Many other scholars in the United States have worked abroad and used ethnographic methods (Suárez-Orozco 1987, 1989, 1990, 1991a, and 1991b; DeVos, whose work is discussed in detail throughout this study, especially his work in Japan and the United States, 1973a, 1973b, 1983; and DeVos and Wagatsuma 1966). Among international scholars who have conducted systematic ethnographic research among minorities and have obtained broad recognition are Roosens in Belgium (1989a, 1989b, 1993); Boos-Nunning and Hohmann in Holland (1989); Tomlinson (1989, 1991); and Au in Hawaii (1980, 1981), among many others.

To discuss methodological tools (modern ethnography) in a political or theoretical vacuum, that is, in the absence of appropriate socio-political and theoretical contexts and frameworks, is impossible. Research designs are meaningful, useful, dangerous, irrelevant, or stimulating, and significant precisely because of their contribution to the historically defined theoretical, political and social contexts of the research. Academia (the culture of the academy), and ethnographers within it, share specific values and behavioral norms. Thus, for example, part of those values requires the monitoring of the proliferation of articles, presentations and books that discuss *qualitative research* in general, and *ethnographic research* in particular, without pointing clearly at their context, basic intent, common denominator, purpose and usefulness. The broad variety of studies included in those categories is a cause for alarm.

First of all, it is important to distinguish methodological techniques from research approaches. Techniques can accompany different types of approaches; thus, for example, techniques such as interviews, video-taping, audio-taping, photography, life histories, case studies, vignettes, journals, participant observations, unobtrusive observations, note-taking, linguistic text analysis, historical accounts, archival documents, and others can be very instrumental in a number of different designs and research approaches. Often, a modern ethnography is selectively built with a variety of approaches, depending on its purpose and focus. Most modern ethnographies, however, do attempt to make explicit their focus, central thrust and purposes. The Spindlers wrote a chapter in their *Interpretive Ethnography of Education: At Home and Abroad* (1987c:17–33) in which they describe ethnography, spell out the criteria for a good ethnography, and discuss the practical ways of conducting ethnographic research.

The Spindlers list ten criteria for a good ethnography (1987c:18–20) which require contextualization of observations of behavior beyond the immediate interactional setting, development of hypotheses to explain observed behavior grounded not just on the observations made, but on serious theoretical research of a problem, systematic gathering of data, efforts to arrive at an emic view of events (that is, from the perspective of the people under study), efforts to elicit socio-cultural knowledge in interaction participants, the use of instruments, questionnaires, interviews and other inquiries (perhaps including historical — archival, and prehistorical evidence where relevant and possible), the use of *transcultural* comparative perspectives, efforts to make explicit what seems to be implicit, efforts not to overimpose one's own views and theoretical frameworks on the people studied, and the use of appropriate technology in order to facilitate data collection (such as cameras, audio- and video-tape equipment, computers, field-based instruments, etc.). These criteria are necessary but not sufficient to produce a good ethnography. The interpretation of data, the inferences made, the ability of ethnographers to keep their own personal views away and to see the world through the lenses of the people under observations are the most difficult requirements. Because there are many different ways of interpreting behavior and many different theoretical approaches to study behavior, it follows that ethnographic studies vary a great deal according to the relationship between disciplinary perspectives and the method.

Types of Ethnographic Research

It would be useful to mention a few of the types of ethnographic research approaches that share some characteristics and can be used as complementary methods. There are not discrete categories and some types may involve aspects or techniques used in others. A general typology (partially based on Trueba's discussion of the Spindlers as ethnographers, 1992:77–78) and a discussion of the differences and similarities may help. There are five basic types: ethnohistorical ethnography, ethnography of communication, ethnomethodological ethnography, socio-cultural ethnography and psychological ethnography.

1. *Ethnohistorical* ethnography requires approaches used to reconstruct historical periods as part of the social and cultural context of behavior. Often historical reconstruction depends on oral accounts, newspaper articles, study of archaeological and contemporary sites (cemeteries, public places, etc.), and face-to-face interviews with people whose version of events have been ignored.
2. *Ethnography of communication*, established by early sociolinguists such as Gumperz and Hymes (see Gumperz and Hymes 1964, 1972; Hymes 1964; Gumperz 1982, 1986) advocates as its most fundamental principle the need to use language in order to understand behavioral intent and basic meaning in interpersonal interaction. It also requires that the researcher respect peoples' views, taxonomies, and language domains.
3. *Anthropological ethnography* encompasses the more traditional anthropological type of studies such as the case studies (Chavez 1992) on undocumented Mexican workers, and holistic ethnographies covering themes such as the setting, methodology, social organization of the group, family, residence, religion, kinship system, marriage patterns, economy, values, rites of passage and life cycle events.
4. *Psychological Ethnography*, one of the most recent methodological approaches, is based on the socio-historical school of psychology led by Vygotsky (1962, 1978) and Bakhtin (1981, 1986) as used by Russian, European and American Neo-Vygotskians and Bakhtinians (Cole and D'Andrade 1982; Wertsch 1981, 1985a, 1985b, 1991) to provide a theoretical framework for the study of cognitive development in specific social and cultural settings.

There are continuously emerging new approaches that utilize ethnographic methods of research, and combinations between the above types and scholars involved in critical theory or critical pedagogy. While the beginnings of new ethnographic approaches are eclectic and not yet fully developed into a body of literature, it seems that ethnographic research continues to be an extremely vital part of modern social science research across disciplines and fields.

Research Design

A particular common denominator to most ethnographic studies, regardless of disciplinary origin, is an attempt to describe in an objective way the reality observed in its social context and to provide an interpretation of behavior that is consistent with that context. Many ethnographies are intended to present a cohesive, comprehensive, holistic description of human behavior from a particular theoretical perspective. But, of course, different disciplines provide different direction to modern ethnographies, because not every aspect of human behavior is equally important to all social sciences.

It is precisely the methodological and theoretical plasticity that makes ethnography compatible across disciplines and extremely useful for diverse theoretical foci. Indeed, ethnographic research has been a preferred method in the study of race, ethnicity, equity and differential performance of minority groups, as we have seen in the previous chapter. While the many and complex dimensions of behavior in pluralistic societies are accessible from a variety of qualitative approaches, modern ethnography has provided unique insights because it offers a cross-cultural comparative approach. Among the criteria for a good ethnography, the Spindlers emphasized this aspect of cross-cultural comparison (1987c:18–21). In brief, because ethnographic approaches remain a genuine long-term, interpretive, historically grounded, systematic approach to making sense of socially-shared values as expressed in observable behavior, socio-cultural ethnographic research methods were the primary instrument for data gathering in this study. And because the main tool in ethnography is the ethnographer, the authors accept the responsibility for the limitations of the study. It was our judgment that led us to interpret data in certain ways. We discussed our backgrounds in the introduction. In general, however, because Yali Zou was born and raised in China, we felt confident that we understood and interpreted sufficiently well the data gathered; her familiarity with the social, cultural and economic contexts of Chinese society and its nationalities was essential to interpret the statements made by Miao students in the interviews and written materials.

We realized that, as we proceeded in the data collection and analysis, new and more comprehensive hypotheses of the observed behavior and reported responses had to be explored. The full picture of the process of ethnic identification, and the significance of the family values, did not occur until the last stage of the data analysis. After reading the materials collected many times and asking ourselves fundamental questions about why Miao students persist in their commitment to academia, in spite of poverty and deprivation of food, sleep and even moral support at times, we realized that the notion of 'honor' and 'commitment to the family and the Miao group' was translated into commitment to high achievement in academia. This realization was also important to resolve apparent conflicts of self-redefinition and changes in self-identity occurring during the university training. In other words, the apparent ambivalence of students in seeing themselves both as 'poor peasants' and, in contrast, also as 'members of the elite of university students' could not be resolved without understanding the relationship of academic achievement to family values. That is, one can remain a Miao peasant, fully committed to the home village, community and family by demonstrating one's commitment to honor family and community via academic excellence.

The ethnographic approach to inquire about these apparent contradictions was instrumental in finding a way to resolve the problem. It became clear that the reason why the ethnographic approach is so productive and creative is precisely because the actual data gathered continuously has an impact on the research hypotheses and allows the ethnographer to restructure the inquiry with the help of information obtained. New questions must be asked to get to the bottom of explanations or of configuration of new data, and consequently, new goals must be constructed as relevant to the new line of inquiry that promises to be emically significant; that is, functionally relevant to the ethnographer's understanding of the culture and behavior of the people under study.

The reason why ethnographic research — in spite of the challenges involved in conducting it in urban settings, because it demands long-term and intensive efforts, good judgment to pursue interpretive analysis, flexibility, etc. — continues to attract large numbers of scholars, is that researchers are frustrated with simplistic answers to intriguing behavioral questions. Take questions associated with the study of human behavior in drug addiction, rape, verbal or physical abuse, teenage suicide, teenage pregnancies, child abuse, and pornography, just to mention a few examples. Individual differences, family, peer groups, voluntary associations, church, politics, health, a combination of factors beyond the control of people along with those close to his/her sphere of influence, result in very complex human phenomena. A deeper understanding of race, ethnicity and class in the formation of self-identity and the ability to compete successfully in academia is also often compounded by the phenomena alluded to above. Ethnographic research helps us search for contextual information and socio-cultural explanations to make sense of observed behaviors from the perspective of cultural values. Indeed, at the bottom of ethnographic research we seek to understand the role of language and culture in the production of observed behaviors. For this reason, some specific conditions for quality ethnographic research should be understood better after the discussion of the concept of culture that follows. In the final analysis, the ethnographer is the weakest link in the ethnographic inquiry. The context may be accessible, rich and pointing clearly in some direction. Yet, the ethnographer may be blind, biased, unable or unwilling to make certain interpretations as linked to contextual factors. In this case, at the very least, other ethnographers should be able to get access to the original data and make their own interpretations. This is where cross-cultural comparisons are very useful to disclose personal biases. We are more willing to make interpretations that affect other peoples with whom we are not associated. The data gathered and analyzed here have been discussed with other scholars precisely to help us identify our own biases.

The Concept of Culture

The latitude used by researchers using the term *culture*, and especially by contributors to current education journals, would suggest that culture is some sort of amorphous, reified, static entity that causes people to behave in certain ways, to express and exhibit certain values, beliefs and practices, but an entity that can be packaged and transferred from one generation to the next with relatively few changes. To some social scientists, culture is simply a lifestyle manifested in interactional events, and shared with members of the same social or ethnic group. For example, members of the same church, military unit, government bureaucracy, public health system, industrial complex, etc., do share etiquette and patterns of behavior. Even casual and superficial observations of ethnic groups, for example, of Mexicans in some parts of Sacramento, may lead to the conclusion that Mexicans attend public parks and Catholic churches in family units, or that they shop in certain grocery stores only, and that they speak Spanish, using certain intonation patterns and voice pitch in contrast both with English-speaking and Chinese-speaking persons, or that they eat peculiar foods (tortillas, salsa), or they laugh and play in ways contrasting with those of Chinese families. How much of the Mexican culture can we understand by making these observations in contrast with the mainstream American culture and Chinese cultures? What is culture in this context?

Certainly, culture is not an appendix attached to the groups of people exhibiting different public behavior, but part of their value system, their traditions and their world view. We talk, for example, about the culture of academia, the culture of schools, the culture of poverty, and the drug culture. Do these groups of professors, poor people and drug addicts also have a world view and a set of values that explains their behavior? If we apply the concept of culture to the Miao students, can we say that the culture of the Miao peasants is identical to the culture of the Miao students? Are the Miao students members of the culture of the university, or members of the Miao village culture, or both? This is where the problem exists. The definition of culture is one of the most difficult tasks in anthropology. Goodenough stated that culture 'is made up of the concepts, beliefs, and principles of action and organization' (1976:5). Anthropologists have agreed that sharing a given culture means being able to function effectively in the socio-cultural environment also shared with members of the same group. In contemporary societies, however, there is a great deal of mobility from country to country, and within countries. As economic crises occur, or as economic opportunities appear, individuals take their families in search of survival and a better life. The result of waves of immigration and change, of attempts to adapt to different countries with a new language and culture, is ethnic pluralism, and as such goes beyond the presence of a mosaic of ethnic and linguistic groups, and becomes an international crisis affecting mainly European countries and the United States.

To complicate matters more in the attempt to define culture, ethnographic studies of ethnic pluralism, multilingualism and multiculturalism suggest complex relationships between culture, race, class and ethnicity. In the United States, for example, how is Chicano, African American, Native American, Asian, or Hmong culture, different from Chicano ethnicity, African American ethnicity, etc.? What is the role of class and race in the construction of each of these 'ethnic' cultures? Some of the ethnic groups may be composed of a variety of racial groups, and others may be racially homogeneous. Some ethnic groups may belong primarily to a single social or economic class (low-income, for example), while others (those in the United States who have been in the country longer and have been successful, Jewish immigrants, for example) may belong primarily to the middle and upper classes. We know that at different times in history *culture* has had various definitions in the social sciences, and has been applied to a variety of contexts and settings. In the specific context of educational research some of the concepts of culture have enjoyed significant continuity and consistency. This book raises issues about the risk of overextending this concept to a point that it becomes meaningless. We will argue for a notion of culture that may be instrumental in the study of dynamic and complex educational phenomena, and, consequently, more functional and constructive in educational research.

A cultural system cannot be described adequately unless it is compared and contrasted with other systems. It is only in the contrast of facing other cultural norms, codes of behavior, and cognitive approaches that we realize what our own culture is all about, and what culture is. Cross-cultural comparisons have been most insightful in anthropology. Being in another culture and observing the behavior of other peoples is not as difficult as analyzing that culture. The problem is not 'to state what someone did but to specify the conditions under which it is culturally appropriate to anticipate that he, or persons occupying his role, will render an equivalent performance' (Frake 1964:112). Knowing another culture is being able to anticipate peoples' observed behaviors; this requires cultural knowledge and an understanding of their cultural values. Yet, the understanding of ongoing cultural changes, processes of adaptation in cultural contact, and adaptive strategies (see Trueba, Cheng and Ima 1993) requires a better understanding of the process of culture acquisition and transmission. Sophisticated scholars, on one extreme, and common immigrants and refugees on the other, continue to ask themselves questions such as the following: What is American culture? What is the essence of American democracy? Who determines cultural values? What is the role of schools in determining cultural values? Do the schools have a culture of their own? Do age groups have a culture of their own? Do the homeless, drug addicts, and minorities have a culture of their own? How do you define culture in these diverse contexts? These questions transcend any one culture in particular. Cultural contrasts and cultural change underline the unique nature of Western cultures in industrial societies, especially those like the United States facing the flow of large numbers of immigrants and refugees.

George Spindler in his *Education and Cultural Process* (1987:303–34) discusses the nature of cultural transmission and suggests that in order to understand the concept of culture it is essential to view it as a dynamic process that is an integral part of the social transaction called *cultural transmission*. That is, as a dynamic transactional process through which the meaning of values and their normative forces are reinterpreted and recreated by the members of the socio-cultural group as they pass cultural traditions on from one generation to the next. Culture, in the Spindlers' minds, is not an abstract concept of cognitive codes which result in complex interrelationships between observed behavior and conceptual systems. Nor is culture a cumbersome and somewhat amorphous sum total of cultural values and traditions presumed to be shared by members of the same society. What culture is and what it becomes is understood as an internal, dynamic force produced by actual tangible transactions of day-to-day life taking place in different contexts. Because culture is a powerful force driving people to the pursuit of actions that reflect socially shared values, culture is revealed to us in what people do and what they do not do. If we observe actions, we should be able interpret the reasons why people do whatever they do. There is an intimate relationship between action and culture, as well as between motivation to act and cultural values (G. Spindler 1959, 1977; and G. Spindler and L. Spindler 1983, 1987b, 1987c; Trueba, Spindler and Spindler, 1989). In brief, ideally ethnographic research should be systematic, ethnohistorically grounded, long-term, cross-cultural, comparative, aiming at understanding human behavior from the perspective of the people under study, descriptive of behaviors in their appropriate contexts, often aided by the use of instruments, codes, schedules, questionnaires, interviews, etc., focused on actions and communicative interactional phenomena, interpretive (attempting to develop hypotheses linking chains of understandings) and most importantly, well grounded in empirical evidence, rather than speculative (G. and L. Spindler 1987c:19–23). As a consequence, theory without sufficient grounding in observed reality or without sufficient ethnographic documentation is weak and speculative. If culture is *not* an static entity or an appendix attached to peoples' behaviors, but a force motivating behavior, and directing peoples to engage in actions, then this concept of culture has clear implications for dealing with rapid social change as it occurs in modern China. While the foundations of Chinese culture remain strong and do not change much (family values, Confucian philosophy and Chinese lifestyle) the values associated with political and economic activities are changing rapidly and are having an impact on the family across nationalities. Indeed, all nationalities or ethnic groups in China are being influenced by rapid economic change and the opening of cultural boundaries to foreign immigrants. There are also thousands of Chinese people travelling abroad who return and influence lifestyles in China. Many of the Chinese who live abroad continue to communicate with relatives inside China. To some extent, the retention of Chinese cultural values for Chinese people living outside China depends on this close communication with people in China. In China, the status of nationality officially given to fifty-five groups does carry a measure of racial or physical homogeneity within groups, and a maximum cultural homogeneity reflected in languages, traditions, geographical location and folklore. The boundaries surrounding each ethnic group are a function of the need to retain ethnic autonomy, cultural traditions, and the control over land and resources traditionally forming the patrimony of each ethnic group. A discussion of the nature of ethnicity can better help us to understand the relationship of ethnicity and culture, in so far as they formed part of this study and were targeted in the research design. In the case of the Miao, the racial factor was not important in contrast with the mainstream or the main Han group, because the physical differences between these two groups are not significant. That is certainly not the case of other ethnic groups, for example, the Mongols, or Korean, and other groups living in the Northwestern part of the country. What is genuinely relevant is the concept of ethnic identity and the sense of belonging to the Miao group for centuries.

Culture and Ethnicity

What is the relationship of culture and ethnicity? Is culture a broader concept that includes ethnic enclaves and class groups, while at the same time permitting the accommodation of other common characteristics shared across ethnic and class clusters? What is the function of ethnicity? For some scholars, ethnicity is primarily a politically cohesive group created for purposes of defense and survival (Horowitz 1985:7–10).

To deal with ethnic conflict and ethnic pluralism it is important to clarify the concept of ethnicity. The use of the term ethnicity has regained currency and significance in social science research in the context of the real or perceived threats that ethnic minorities in Europe and in America represent for the mainstream populations. The discovery of the ever increasing numbers of Turks, Moroccans, Italians, Spaniards and other immigrants in France, Belgium, Germany, Sweden and other countries in Europe has gradually resulted in a series of studies sponsored by various governments related to the possible means of controlling or assimilating selected immigrant groups. To be sure, it is not the Spaniards or Italians that worry those countries; immigrants from other European countries are welcome and valued because they help in occupations where there is a need for additional labor, without causing interethnic conflicts; these immigrants are white, share cultural and religious values of other Europeans, are viewed as law-abiding citizens, and often go back home after their contracts are finished. What worries European countries are immigrants of color, especially if they are affiliated with Moslem religions (meaning to the European 'fanatic Islam fundamentalism').

> Ethnicity is a complex, comprehensive concept, related to issues of ethnic classification or affiliation. It is contextual, appearing only in contacts between peoples in some type of opposition. It involves psychological, cultural, socio-economic and political factors. It emphasizes

contrast and expresses the differences between 'us' and 'them' in terms of culture, kinship, language, race, religion or societal organization.
(Alvarsson 1990:12)

Ethnicity, social mobility and colonialism in Latin America are discussed by Mörner (1990), and ethnic conflict in Belgium is discussed by Roosens (1989a, 1989b, and 1993). Both in the history of colonialism and of interethnic conflict within Europe, European values have provided the underlying motivation to achieve and control. Naturally, there are cultural values and patterns intricately wed to class values and racial prejudice. Some Africans in certain parts of Europe (for example, in Belgium) gave us the impression that their opportunities for upward social mobility are not as good in Europe as those offered to African Americans in the United States or Latin America. Parenthetically, class and culture concepts have drastically changed in the United States and Latin America in ways that the cohesiveness of North American culture and/or Latin American culture is recognized as being deeply diversified, cutting across class and racial strata. Music, history, economic and political institutions, etc., are highly diversified (though not totally free of race and gender biases).

Ethnic pluralism in Latin America is also historically dependent on the stratification patterns (or caste structure) brought to the Americas from Europe; it is linked to a rather sophisticated system to assess the breed or relative miscegenation of mixed-blood natives. The hierarchy of power was historically linked to the caste system, and the functional value of such systems was to maintain political and economic control in the hands of Europeans.

The struggle for power and for liberation on the part of oppressed ethnic groups often results in terrorism, as it occurs now in Bosnia, Croatia and Herzegovina. Hostility and conflict have been historically intertwined with ethnic cultures and political struggles. Ethnographic accounts of terrorism can provide important insights into the local cultures and the psychodynamics of power struggle and of abuse of force (Suárez-Orozco 1989, 1990). The analysis of terror has led to a better understanding of the process of self-identification of victims and their ethnic/cultural affiliation. Changes in popular culture and religious practices are associated with the empowerment of peoples previously terrorized. The present study on the Miao is an ethnographic case study of empowerment; but a study based on the painful psychological journey that each student took from a peasant village — characterized by poverty and ignorance — to the university life among the most selected young people of China, such as scholars and middle-class intellectuals. The issue of empowerment will be discussed in the final chapters. For now, however, it is important to note that ethnography is an appropriate instrument to focus on empowerment issues. Modern ethnographies of empowerment can fruitfully use a number of methodological tools — interviews, questionnaires, participant observations, journals, historical research, etc., to investigate issues of equity, access to schooling and public services, especially in the context of migration waves and psychological adjustment of ethnically different peoples.

Ethnographers have studied empowerment and disempowerment behaviors of immigrant ethnic groups and others, in relationship to the social reality of war, terrorism, prejudicial treatment, or racism. Recent studies of literacy for empowerment (Diaz, Moll and Mehan 1986; Delgado-Gaitan 1990) and the relationship between home and school values and a successful integration of these values needed by students to become empowered in school (Delgado-Gaitan and Trueba 1991; Trueba, Cheng and Ima 1993; Trueba, Rodríguez, Zou and Cintrón 1993) are examples of how ethnographic research is applied to empowerment processes. Indeed, the process of empowerment, as described by Freire (1973) must be grounded on a better understanding of the historical context of one's own existence, and the need to achieve instrumental competencies (literacy, for example) in order to participate in the democratic social institutions. The use of an ethnography of empowerment recognizes that in understanding the past, one is also defining the present and anticipating the future. Denying reflection about the past (the kind of reflection Freire calls *conscientization*), implies a tolerance of past abuses of power and a willingness to permit the repetition of the past. Indeed, Freire insists that people must become socialized into protesting abuses, they must 'yell in protest' against insolence, as long as they do not lose hope, because human existence does not make any sense without hope, '*a esperança é una necessidade ontológica*' (Freire 1993:10).

One of the reasons why modern ethnography represents hope and is seen as instrumental in social and educational interventions is that it makes sense of the past, provides a link between ethnohistorically grounded studies, and current long-term, comparative and interdisciplinary research. This way, modern ethnography allows us to understand the dynamics of social change and the role of culture in redirecting social change toward the fulfillment of equity and democratic principles. Learning about life, the mysteries of human behavior, and the motivations to act gives the ethnographer the proper perspective to make inferences about observed behavior, and to reinterpret the present in ways congruent with the past. What ultimately constitutes the natural linkage between ethnohistorical and contemporary long-term research is precisely the fundamental concept that culture is not static, it is not an entity attached to peoples, but is action and continuous interaction expressing and reinforcing values and perceptions.

Theoretical debates over the use of culture and ethnography must be contextualized by methodological, theoretical and other ideological currents that can make our discourse difficult and seemingly politically loaded. Ethnographers welcome with mixed feelings the popularity of qualitative research and the technological advances to gather and analyze data. They often express their feelings of anxiety about possible misunderstanding and oversimplification of the concept of culture and its role in ethnographic research. To discuss methodological tools in a vacuum, in the absence of appropriate theoretical frameworks that make research designs meaningful, looks rather dangerous.

Therefore, the discussion of the relationship between culture and ethnicity will be continued in the analysis and implications of this study.

Research Design

This study utilizes several methodological approaches to pursue diverse areas of inquiry: ethnohistorical inquiries have been made through the use of written historical and archival documents and personal interviews. The collection of biographical data on students and their families was obtained through personal interviews and the elicitation of written accounts by each student; subsequently, we used sociolinguistic methods to analyze the text generated by interview and biographical materials. The description of schools and other general data on Chinese culture and lifestyles is taken from personal participation in Chinese society by the researcher over the last forty years, from current reading of China's main newspapers and magazines, from conversations with important Chinese leaders via phone and face to face, and from a number of TV and video-recorded programs on recent cultural events in China. Inferences about intra-psychological processes in ethnic identification, achievement motivation and personal adaptive strategies to culture change are made on the basis of ethnographic data gathered from interviews and the analysis of historical data. The model followed here is used by a number of ethnographers G. and L. Spindler 1982; Trueba 1989; Trueba, Jacobs and Kirton 1990; Delgado-Gaitan and Trueba 1991; Trueba, Rodríguez, Zou and Cintrón 1993; and Trueba, Cheng and Ima 1993.

The organization of the study was planned at least a year in advance and the data was gathered after the summer of 1991. A trip to China under the auspices of the School of Education of the University of Wisconsin–Madison, with the research team organized by Henry T. Trueba (which included several professors from the Central University for Nationalities in Beijing, and the Guizhou Institute for Nationalities) was extremely useful in producing important data on Miao students. The trip which took place in the fall of 1992 was followed up with intensive data collection through correspondence with the help of our Chinese colleagues in Beijing and Guizhou. Our efforts have been directed to identify the existence of important Chinese sources on the eduction of minorities in China, as well as in the development of strategies for emancipation on the part of Miao people. Through our efforts, new colleagues from China have begun to share with us studies they had conducted earlier or to produce new studies addressing our concerns. Specific questions as to the role of Miao people in modern China, the role of education in the upward mobility of the Miao people, the conditions for the development of new educational leaders among Miao university students, etc., have been answered by our new friends and recognized scholars working in China.

Prior to the 1992 trip to gather data from the Miao students, we conducted a search of the literature in Chinese and in English and communicated with a number of professors in Beijing. The follow-up activities that led us to the identification of historical materials continued for two years. It was not until a few months ago that we obtained additional original material from several professors of the Guizhou Institute for Nationalities. Yali Zou has been able to translate and we have used much of these materials. The logistics of written and oral communication with professors in Beijing and Guizhou were cumbersome and time consuming. In Beijing alone we established contact and spent many hours with the Director of the Foreign Affairs Office, Prof. Li Yan Qing; Prof. She You Ling (extremely fluent in English and knowledgeable of the local politics and appropriate protocols); University President Ha Jing Xiong, who was extremely generous with his time and is an nationally-recognized expert on issues of nationalities (and who has written several books); Prof. Lin Yaohua and Prof. Chen Yongling, anthropologists and linguists trained at the University of Chicago and Stanford respectively, were extremely useful in providing us with the social and cultural context of the Miao in the larger national setting; Prof. Yan Yingjun, who gave us a historical account of the development of the various nationalities and their official recognition; Prof. Gujie Hua, also from the History Department in Beijing, whose specialty is minorities in China; and other specialists in history, such as Mr. Huang Xiuyi, helped us as well. The Director of the Institute for Nationalities a linguist, Prof. Dai Ginxia, gave us a very important introduction to the historical development of the Miao language. From the Department of Minority Language and Literature, Prof. Wu Dekun was the most helpful and dedicated. He is a Miao and one of the most erudite and fluent speakers of the Miao and Mandarin languages. His writings and his frequent visits were always inspiring and insightful. Perhaps no one else was as close to the Beijing Miao students as Prof. Wu; his mentorship and nurturing spirit came across in every word and action we observed. From the same department, Prof. Pan Yingjiu gave generously of his time and knowledge.

In Guiyang, during our visit to the Guizhou Institute for Nationalities, we were assisted by many professors and administrators, such as Prof. Li Jin-Ping, a lecturer in the Nationality Language Department, Prof. Wu Zhinguo, who was both a scholar and President of the Institute, Prof. Shi Juncen, Prof. Yan Zhenwei, but especially Prof. Pan Dingzhi whose original research became extremely important to make sense of the history and culture of the Miao in the Provinces of Yunnan, Hunan and Guizhou. We are deeply indebted to Prof. Pan and his associates.

In the Central University for Nationalities in Beijing we interviewed nine well-known scholars and professors of minority nationality and minority education and eighteen Miao students. We conducted eight interviews with faculty members for a total of eighteen hours. First we interviewed two internationally-recognized anthropologists. This interview lasted three hours. Then we interviewed three professors of minority languages and literacy for three hours. We interviewed the director of the Central Minority Research

Institute for two hours. We talked and had dinner together with the president two times with each time lasting more than two hours. We interviewed professor Wu three times, each time lasted two hours. We interviewed students three times — all together six-and-a-half hours. The first interview with eight students lasted three hours. The second with seven students lasted two-and-a-half hours. The third with one student lasted one hour. In addition to our interviews, we were able to observe their daily life (because we lived on campus) and the daily classes.

In the Guizhou Institute for Nationalities, we interviewed faculty and students both individually and in groups several times over a period of three days. First we talked to the president and three other professors for about two hours. Later, we interviewed eight scholars for more than four hours and groups of individual students and professors three times for several hours. The interviews with a group of eighteen students were intensive and lasted for over four hours. Subsequently students were asked by their professors to write their biographies. We selected seven student biographies from Beijing and seven from Guizhou for further transcription and text analysis. Furthermore, we communicated in writing with individual students and professors to obtain additional information and responses to some questions related to their values and achievement motivation. We sent students a questionnaire with topics ranging from their home village lifestyle, family income, parents' education and social status, to their educational experiences, their transition from elementary to junior high school, and from junior high to senior high school and college. This questionnaire is analyzed in Chapter 4. The compositions or biographies of students are analyzed in Chapter 5.

We are aware that this study is eclectic and combines different methodologies. However, the central methodological thrust that unifies the various approaches is the strong ethnographic foundation and philosophy behind all these approaches. This means specifically that we have attempted to be systematic, to gather data that allow us to improve further data gathering efforts, to examine interactional settings and data obtained in them (such as data from ethnographic interviews, life histories and participant observations) as contextualized by larger social and cultural structures linked through, and manifested in, concrete communicative exchanges. The use of narratives from students is essential to this study, and their analysis is seen in the light of historical, cultural and social contexts in which they function. At a higher level, all these interactional data are seen as linked to the broad macrosociological structures of Chinese society, with its old and recent historical dimensions that make understandable the liberation of minority persons such as the Miao.

To be still more specific, at the same time that we were gathering concrete data on the history of minorities, on the Miao people, their folklore and their lifestyles, and on the impact of modern technology on minorities, we were also reading the theoretical literature on cultural ecology, critical pedagogy, ethnography of communication, educational anthropology and the sociology of education. We found it essential to combine data gathering, data analysis and the reading of cross-cultural research on minorities from various disciplinary perspectives. Therefore, this study is primarily ethnographic and ethnohistorical in its method, and cross-cultural and interdisciplinary in its theoretical direction. While the data is essentially limited to the Miao and other Chinese minorities, its theoretical analysis has relevance for minorities from many other nations, and for issues that affect minorities all over the world, such as the formation of ethnic identity, the processes of empowerment, the role of knowledge acquisition in the processes of empowerment, and the like.

In the following chapter a brief history of the various minority groups in China and of the Miao in particular will serve as the context for the specific data collected among the Miao students of Beijing and Guizhou. The arduous task of finding, securing, studying and summarizing in English the content of original and rare materials, made the next chapter one of the most difficult ones.

References

ALVARSSON, J. (1990) 'Ethnicity: Some introductory remarks', in ALVARSSON, J. and HORNA, H. (Eds) *Ethnicity in Latin America*, Uppsala, Sweden: Center for Latin American Studies, Uppsala Universitet, pp. 7–14.

AU, K.H. (1980) 'Participation structures in a reading lesson with Hawaiian children: Analysis of a culturally appropriate instructional event', *Anthropology and Education Quarterly*, **11**(2), pp. 91–115.

AU, K.H. (1981) 'The comprehension-oriented reading lesson: Relationships to proximal indices of achievement', *Educational Perspectives*, **20**, pp. 13–15.

BAKHTIN, M.M. (1981) *The Dialogic Imagination: Four Essays by M.M. Bakhtin*, Michael Holquist (Ed), HOLQUIST, C. and M. (translators), Austin, TX: University of Texas Press.

BAKHTIN, M.M. (1986) *Speech Genres and Other Late Essays*, EMERSON, C. and HOLQUIST, M. (Eds), McGEE, V.W. (translator), Austin, TX: University of Texas Press.

BOOS-NUNNING, U. and HOHMANN, M. (1989) 'The educational situation of migrant workers' children in the Federal Republic of Germany', in ELDERING, L. and KLOPROGGE, J. (Eds) *Different Cultures Same School: Ethnic Minority Children in Europe*, Amsterdam, The Netherlands: Swets & Zeitlinger, pp. 39–59.

CHAVEZ, L.R. (1992) *Shadowed Lives: Undocumented Immigrants in American Society: Case Studies in Cultural Anthropology*, SPINDLER, G. and L. (Series Eds) New York, NY: Harcourt Brace Jovanovich College Publishers.

COLE, M. and D'ANDRADE, R. (1982) 'The influence of schooling on concept formation: Some preliminary conclusions', *The Quarterly Newsletter of the Laboratory of Comparative Human Cognition*, **4**(2), pp. 19–26.

DELGADO-GAITAN, C. (1990) *Literacy for Empowerment: The Role of Parents in Children's Education*, London, England: Falmer Press.

DELGADO-GAITAN, C. and TRUEBA, H. (1991) *Crossing Cultural Borders: Education for Immigrant Families in America*, London, England: Falmer Press.

DEVOS, G. (1973a) 'Japan's outcastes: The problem of the Burakumin', in WHITAKER, B. (Ed) *The Fourth World: Victims of Group Oppression*, New York, NY: Schocken Books, pp. 307–27.

DeVos, G. (Ed) (1973b) *Socialization for Achievement: Essays on the Cultural Psychology of the Japanese*, Berkeley, CA: University of California Press.
DeVos, G. (1983) 'Ethnic identity and minority status: Some psycho-cultural considerations', in Jacobson-Widding, A. (Ed) *Identity: Personal and Socio-cultural*, Uppsala, Sweden: Almquist & Wiksell Tryckeri AB, pp. 90–113.
DeVos, G. and Wagatsuma, H. (1966) *Japan's Invisible Race: Caste in Culture and Personality*, Berkeley, CA: University of California Press.
Diaz, S., Moll, L. and Mehan, H. (1986) 'Sociocultural resources in instruction: A context-specific approaches', in Bilingual Education Office (Ed), *Beyond Language: Social and Cultural Factors in Schooling Language Minority Students*, Los Angeles, CA: Evaluation, Dissemination, and Assessment Center, pp. 187–230.
Erickson, F. (1977) 'Some approaches to inquiry in school/community ethnography', *Anthropology and Education Quarterly*, **8**(3), pp. 58–69.
Erickson, F. (1982) 'Taught cognitive learning in its immediate environments: A neglected topic in the anthropology of education', *Anthropology and Education Quarterly*, **13**(2), pp. 149–80.
Erickson, F. (1984) 'School literacy, reasoning, and civility: An anthropologist's perspective', *Review of Educational Research*, **54**(4), pp. 525–44.
Erickson, F. (1986) 'Qualitative methods in research on teaching', in Wittrock, M.C. (Ed) *Handbook of Research on Teaching*, New York, NY: Macmillan Publishing Co., pp. 119–58.
Frake, C. (1964) 'Notes on queries in ethnography', *American Anthropologist*, **66**(3), pp. 132–45.
Freire, P. (1973) *Pedagogy of the Oppressed*, New York, NY: Seabury.
Freire, P. (1993) *Pedagogia da Esperança: Um reencontro com a pedagogia do oprimido*, São Paulo, Brazil: Editora Paz e Terra, S.A.
Goldman, S. and McDermott, R. (1987) 'The culture of competition in American schools', *Education and Cultural Process: Anthropological Approaches*, Second Edition. Prospect Heights, IL: Waveland Press, Inc., pp. 282–89.
Goodenough, W. (1976) 'Multiculturalism as the normal human experience', *Anthropology and Education Quarterly*, **7**(4), pp. 4–7.
Gumperz, J. (Ed) (1982) *Language and Social Identity*, Cambridge, MA: Cambridge University Press.
Gumperz, J. (1986) 'Interactional sociolinguistics in the study of schooling', in Cook-Gumperz, J. (Ed) *The Social Construction of Literacy*, Cambridge, MA: Cambridge University Press, pp. 45–68.
Gumperz, J. and Hymes, D. (1972) *Directions in Socio-linguistics: The Ethnography of Communication*, New York, NY: Holt, Rinehart, and Winston.
Gumperz, J. and Hymes, D. (Eds) (1964) 'The ethnography of communication', *American Anthropologists*, **66**, p. 6.
Horowitz, D.L. (1985) *Ethnic Groups in Conflict*, Berkeley, CA: University of California Press.
Hymes, D. (1964) 'Directions in (ethno-) linguistic theory', *American Anthropologist*, **66**(3), Special Issue: *Transcultural Studies, Part 2*, pp. 6–56.
LeCompte, M. and Goetz, J. (1984) 'Ethnographic data collection in evaluation research', in Fetterman, D. (Ed) *Ethnography in Educational Evaluation*, Beverly Hills, CA: Sage Publications, pp. 37–59.
McDermott, R. (1977) 'Social relations as contexts for learning in school', *Harvard Educational Review*, **47**(2), pp. 198–213.

McDermott, R. (1987) 'Achieving school failure: An anthropological approach to illiteracy and social stratification', in Spindler, G. (Ed) *Education and Cultural Process: Anthropological Approaches*, Second Edition. Prospects Heights, IL: Waveland Press, Inc., pp. 173–209.

Mörner, M. (1990) 'Etnicidad, movilidad social y mestizaje en la historia colonial hispanoamericana', in Alvarsson, J. and Horna, H. (Eds) *Ethnicity in Latin America*, Uppsala, Sweden: Center for Latin American Studies, Uppsala Universitet, pp. 29–43.

Roosens, E. (1989a) 'Cultural ecology and achievement motivation: Ethnic minority youngsters in the Belgian system', in Eldering, L. and Kloprogge, J. (Eds) *Different Cultures Same School: Ethnic Minority Children in Europe*, Amsterdam, The Netherlands: Swets & Zeitlinger, pp. 85–106.

Roosens, E. (1989b) *Creating Ethnicity: The Process of Ethnogenesis*, in Bernard, H.B. (Series Editor) *Frontiers of Anthropology, Volume 5*, Newbury Park, CA: Sage Publications.

Roosens, E. (Ed) (1993) *The Insertion of Allochthonous Youngsters in Belgian Society*, Special Issue of *Migration*, sponsored by the Verlagsabteilun des Berliner Instituts für Vergleichende Sozialforschung, erscheint vierteljährl. Berlin, Germany: Edition Parabolis.

Spindler, G. (Ed) (1955) *Anthropology and Education*, Stanford, CA: Stanford University Press.

Spindler, G. (1959) *Transmission of American culture*, The Third Burton Lecture. Cambridge, MA: Harvard University Press.

Spindler, G. (with Spindler, L.) (Eds) (1970) *Being an Anthropologist: Fieldwork in Eleven Cultures*, Holt, Rinehart and Winston republished by Waveland Press in 1987.

Spindler, G. (with Spindler, L.) (1971) *Dreamers Without Power: The Menomini Indians* New York, NY: Holt, Rinehart and Winston, republished by Waveland Press in 1984.

Spindler, G. (1977) 'Change and continuity in American core cultural values: An anthropological perspective', in DeRenzo, G.D. (Ed) *We the People: American Character and Social Change*, Westport, CT: Greenwood, pp. 20–40.

Spindler, G. (Ed) (1987) *Education and Cultural Process: Anthropological Approaches*, Second Edition, Prospect Heights, IL: Waveland Press, Inc.

Spindler, G. (Ed) (1988) *Doing the Ethnography of Schooling: Educational Anthropology in Action*, Prospect Heights, IL: Waveland Press, Inc.

Spindler, G. and Spindler, L. (1982) 'Roger Harker and Schoenhausen: From the familiar to the strange and back again', in Spindler, G. (Ed) *Doing the Ethnography of Schooling*, New York, NY: Holt, Rinehart & Winston, pp. 20–47.

Spindler, G. and Spindler, L. (1983) 'Anthropologists view of American culture', *Annual Review of Anthropology*, **12**, pp. 49–78.

Spindler, G. and Spindler, L. (Eds) (1987a) *The Interpretive Ethnography of Education: At Home and Abroad*, Hillsdale, NJ: Lawrence Erlbaum Assoc.

Spindler, G. and Spindler, L. (1987b) 'Cultural dialogue and schooling in Schoenhausen and Roseville: A comparative analysis', *Anthropology and Education Quarterly*, **18**(1), pp. 3–16.

Spindler, G. and Spindler, L. (1987c) 'Teaching and learning how to do the ethnography of education', in Spindler, G. and Spindler, L. (Eds) *Interpretive Ethnography of Education: At Home and Abroad*, Hillsdale, NJ; Lawrence Erlbaum Associates, Inc., pp. 17–33.

SPINDLER, G. and SPINDLER, L. with TRUEBA, H. and WILLIAMS, M. (1990) *The American Cultural Dialogue and its Transmission*, London, England: Falmer Press.

SUÁREZ-OROZCO, M.M. (1987) 'Towards a psychosocial understanding of Hispanic adaptation to American schooling', in TRUEBA, H. (Ed) *Success or Failure: Linguistic Minority Children at Home and in School*, New York, NY: Harper & Row, pp. 156–68.

SUÁREZ-OROZCO, M.M. (1989) *Central American Refugees and US High Schools: A Psychosocial Study of Motivation and Achievement*, Stanford, CA: Stanford University Press.

SUÁREZ-OROZCO, M.M. (1990) 'Speaking of the unspeakable: Toward a psychosocial understanding of responses to terror', *Ethos*, **18**(3), pp. 353–83.

SUÁREZ-OROZCO, M.M. (1991a) 'Dialogue and the transmission of culture: The Spindlers and the making of American anthropology', *Anthropology and Education Quarterly*, **22**(3), pp. 281–91.

SUÁREZ-OROZCO, M.M. (1991b) 'Migration, minority status, and education: European dilemmas and responses in the 1990s', *Anthropology and Education Quarterly*, **22**(2), pp. 99–120.

TOMLINSON, S. (1989) 'Ethnicity and educational achievement in Britain', in ELDERING, L. and KLOPROGGE J. (Eds) *Different Cultures Same School: Ethnic and Minority Children in Europe*, Amsterdam, The Netherlands: Swets & Zeitlinger, pp. 15–37.

TOMLINSON, S. (1991) 'Ethnicity and educational attainment in England — An overview', *Anthropology and Education Quarterly*, **22**(2), pp. 121–39.

TRUEBA, H.T. (1989) *Raising Silent Voices: Educating the Linguistic Minorities for the Twenty-first Century*, New York, NY: Harper & Row.

TRUEBA, H.T. (1991) 'Personal interview with George Spindler', unpublished manuscript, Madison, WI: School of Education, University of Wisconsin-Madison.

TRUEBA, H.T. (1992) 'The Spindlers as ethnographers: The impact of their lives and work on American anthropology', in BOYER, L.B. and BOYER, R.M. (Eds) *Psychoanalytic Study of Society*, **17**, pp. 73–94, Hillsdale, NJ: The Analytic Press.

TRUEBA, H.T., CHENG, L. and IMA, K. (1993) *Myth or Reality: Adaptive Strategies of Asian Americans in California*, London, England: Falmer Press.

TRUEBA, H.T., JACOBS, L. and KIRTON, E. (1990) *Cultural Conflict and Adaptation: The Case of the Hmong Children in American Society*, London, England: Falmer Press.

TRUEBA, H.T., RODRÍGUEZ, C., ZOU, Y. and CINTRÓN, J. (1993) *Healing Multicultural America: Mexican Immigrants Rise to Power in Rural California*, London, England: Falmer Press.

TRUEBA, H.T., SPINDLER, G. and SPINDLER L. (Eds) (1989) *What do Anthropologists Have to Say about Dropouts?*, London, England: Falmer Press.

VYGOTSKY, L.S. (1962) *Thought and Language*, Cambridge, MA: Massachusetts Institute of Technology Press.

VYGOTSKY, L.S. (1978) *Mind in Society: The Development of Higher Psychological Processes*, in COLE, M., JOHN-TEINER, V., SCRIBNER, S. and SOUBERMAN, E. (Eds) Cambridge, MA: Harvard University Press.

WERTSCH, J. (1981) *The Concept of Activity in Soviet Psychology*, New York, NY: M.E. Sharpe, Inc.

WERTSCH, J. (1985a) *Vygotsky and the Social Formation of Mind*, Cambridge, MA: Harvard University Press.

WERTSCH, J. (Ed) (1985b) *Culture Communication, and Cognition: Vygotskian Perspectives*, Cambridge, MA: Cambridge University Press.
WERTSCH, J. (1991) *Voices of the Mind: A Sociolcultural Approach to Mediated Action*, Cambridge, MA: Harvard University Press.
WITTROCK, M.C. (Ed) *Handbook of Research on Teaching*, New York, NY: Macmillan Publishing Co.
WOLCOTT, H. (1987) 'On ethnographic intent', in SPINDLER, G. and SPINDLER L. *The Interpretive Ethnography of Education: At Home and Abroad*, Hillsdale, NJ: Lawrence Erlbaum Associates, Inc., pp. 37–57.
WOLCOTT, H. (1988) '"Problem Finding" in qualitative research', in TRUEBA, H. and DELGADO-GAITAN, C. (Eds) *School and Society: Learning Content Through Culture*, New York, NY: Praeger Publishers, pp. 11–35.

Chapter 3

The Miao among Chinese Nationalities

This chapter is intended to provide the historical, sociocultural, demographic and economic context for the study of the Miao. China is one of the most complex and mysterious countries with cultural and demographic features never imagined by the Western mind — and seldom understood. To study *ethnic minorities* or *nationalities* in China is a still more difficult task. Our terminology is deficient. Eberhard (1982:3–4) finds the use of the term '*minorities*' somewhat problematic because it stands in contrast with the use of the same term for Western stratified societies. It is not necessarily a numerical minority. The term minorities as used in the context of China 'implies not simply difference but dominance and subordination' (Eberhard 1982:3). Obviously minorities see themselves as different from the majority — socioculturally, politically and economically. In the Chinese context racial differences do not play an important role in defining minorities, but rather in contrasting Western and Asian people. There are racial differences within the various Chinese groups. Northern Chinese (and other Asian groups in the region, such as the Koreans and Mongols) are taller and stronger than Southern Chinese. Our research in Beijing and Guizhou brings new dimensions to the understanding of ethnic diversity in China. A superficial comparison of the various physical characteristics of different Chinese minorities within the Beijing Central University for Nationalities is enough to persuade us that there are significant racial differences within China, but that the degree of difference is trivial in comparison with racial differences with some European groups.

In order to have some parameters to attempt to understand modern China, we must remember that, according to Poston and Yaukey (1992), the population of China from the time of Christ until the seventeenth century fluctuated from 50 to 110 million, and that in the 1770s, during the Qing dynasty, China's population was stabilized at over 100 million. They add:

> By 1840 the population had grown to 400 million, which was six to eight times greater than the traditional level of the country's population. In the Ching dynasty, people were finally able to live up to the perpetual Chinese ideal of 'numerous descendants'. But is indeed ironic

that it was the overpopulation achieved during the Ching [Qing] dynasty that resulted in its downfall in 1911, and in the downfall as well of the imperial dynasty system in China. All previous dynasties collapsed with the decline of population, but the Ching was overthrown because of an increase in population . . . By the birth of the People's Republic of China on October 1, 1949, the population exceeded 500 million.

(Poston and Yaukey 1992:1)

Many of the recent political and economic events in China during the last three decades have been relatively unpredicted and unpredictable. The intimate relationship between technological modernization for economic competition (which has brought a drastic change in communication technology and access to Western ideas and lifestyles) and political changes in the delicate balance between minority nationalities and mainstream China is evident. Even the most recent failure in attempts at curtailing the use of fax machines, to prevent Chinese students educated abroad from impacting the Chinese intelligentsia running higher education institutions in China are signs that there is no way back to the old China.

New China's Territorial Organization

The genius of Mao Zedong was to create a radical socioeconomic change in China without losing the large populations and territories of the ethnolinguistic minority nationalities living on 68 per cent of the Chinese land where some of the most valuable agricultural and mineral resources were located. The creation of Chinese provinces and autonomous regions with a negotiated semi-autonomy was central to Mao's campaign in the late 1930s. China's policy to deal with the 'problem' of nationalities was carefully defined in a document entitled *China's Common Program*, made public in 1949. This document defined the relationship of the geographical areas that had a concentration of minority nationalities to the Chinese Government of the New China as understood by Mao Zedong. In fact, article 9 of the Common Program declared that no part of China could secede. The right of secession that was part of the rhetoric up to the mid 1930s (and indeed was given serious consideration, following the Soviet pattern) changed in 1938 and was dropped. The reason was that the Chinese saw the efforts of other nations who tried to spilt China (Benson and Svanberg, 1988:56).

Why was it so difficult for Mao to create a coalition of provinces and autonomous regions supportive of his new policies that were meant to emancipate the large masses of Chinese peasants who had been mistreated for centuries? This is a very complex question linked to Chinese history and philosophy, the massive rebellions against feudal powers, and the religious traditions linked to political ideals. The existence of secret societies in China is linked with the religious traditions (Buddhism, Taoism, faith-healing, etc.) and with political ideas. When the Manchus came to power two secret societies actively supporting the expulsion of the conqueror and the restoration of the Ming dynasty were the White Lotus Sect (白蓮教) in the north and the Triads (三合會) in the south. These societies caused major rebellions and maintained connections with village leaders and lawless bandits in order to organize cadres of insurrection (Crespigny 1992:10). Crespigny describes some of the events of the mid-nineteenth century as follows:

> In 1851, the combination of economic distress and government weakness culminated in the Taiping rebellion. The rebellion was centered on the God-Worshipping Society led by the preacher Hong Xiuquan, a man of Hakka background who had been influenced by Protestant teaching in Guangzhou. The very phrase *taiping* ('great peace') was an ancient slogan of religious rebellion, and Hong Xiuquan interpreted his faith with Chinese rather than European concepts. His achievement, albeit short-lived, was to unify disparate groups of the discontented, bandits, pirates and smugglers, secret societies and landless men, under a single authority with a levelling creed which opposed the hierarchy of the traditional empire.
>
> (Crespigny 1992:10–11)

Within the following two decades, the Taiping rebellion spread rapidly throughout the poor and frustrated rural areas of China. Those peasants who refused to convert and join the movement were slaughtered. The violence marked the routes taken by the new converts step-by-step. The upper classes, conservative peasants and Westerners remained loyal to the dynasty against the claims of the rebels. This support did not stop the rebels who continued their destructive path to Nanjing in the north, the Hunan and Hubei provinces in the west, and to Hangzhou, Suzhou and Shanghai to the east:

> On every frontier there was constant warfare, bitterly contested ground, and a policy of attrition with a death toll in millions. Both Chinese and European travellers described regions of devastation, abandoned villages, overgrown roads and fields, and cities in ruins with no more than a dozen houses inhabited. For fifty years afterwards there was vacant land in Jiangzi, Anhui, and Zhejiang to attract immigrants from surrounding territories, and even in 1953 the latter three provinces still showed a net decline in their population. During the last half of the nineteenth century, similar human and natural disasters followed a comparable record of devastation and slaughter. There were major floods and in 1855 a change of course of the Yellow River from the south to the north of the Shandong peninsula, inundating thousands of square miles and drowning thousands of people with their farms,

while in every region of the empire there were droughts, insect plagues, and famine.

(Crespigny 1992:11)

While the Taiping rebellion was devastating part of the country, two additional rebellions also caused massive bloodshed: the Nian movement of the North China Plain and the holy war of the Muhammadans in Shanxi and Gansu. It was not until 1864 that the capital of the Taiping rebellion, Nanjing, was captured, while the other two rebellions continued for many years:

All these campaigns were accompanied by massacre on both sides, with cities, temples, and houses looted and razed to the ground, and in nineteenth century China, when we are told that ditches were choked with bodies and that rivers ran red with blood, it is very likely the descriptions were literally true.

(Crespigny 1992:12)

Finally in the last two decades of the nineteenth century the massive rebellions had subsided, and the central and provincial governments began to restore their strength and curtail disorder and abuse, but 'the anger and hatred of the people was directed against the men from the West, the soldiers, the traders, and the Christian missionaries' (Crespigny 1992:12). In the most populated regions, the Yangzi valley and the North China Plain, outsiders, especially foreigners — who had 'established their presence with legal privileges and treaty ports' (Crespigny 1992:12) — were viewed as responsible for all the misfortunes, and consequently motivated secret societies to target not only the Manchus, but Europeans.

For centuries China had been closed to outsiders. The sporadic contacts with the West during the Ming dynasty were limited to events such as the visits of the Jesuit missionaries, who displayed their skills and knowledge in clock-making and cannon-foundry as well as their vast knowledge of the sciences of the time, and the European traders in silk, tea and porcelain. However, towards the end of the eighteenth century the British discovered and exploited the opium trade and brought massive shipments of the drug from Calcutta to China. Opium use, forbidden in Britain and its territories, had become an obsession in China and became the most important concern of British traders. According to Crespigny, 'by the 1830s opium represented half the value of British imports into China, thirty or forty thousand chests a year — and China was importing silver to pay for it' (1992:13). The continuous problems between traders and Chinese officials responsible for port regulations and negotiations led to very tense situations, including an attempt on the part of the Chinese authorities to stop the opium trade. This led to the Opium War between the British and the Chinese in 1839. British naval power and the discipline of its troops found no match in the Chinese soldiers:

By the Treaty of Nanjing in 1842 and by the supplementary Treaty of the Bogue in the following year the Chinese agreed to payment of an indemnity, to cession of the island of Hong Kong, to the opening of five major 'treaty' ports to foreign trade and residence, and to the rights of British subjects to be tried by their own court and legal system. Almost incidentally, the Chinese also agreed that they would no longer attempt to prohibit the trade in opium.

(Crespigny 1992:14)

Series of unequal treaties resulting in indemnities in cash and transfers of territory and further privileges for foreigners resulted in the 'most-favored-nation' status for British, French, Americans, Russians, Germans, Italian and Japanese; a status first mentioned in the Treaty of the Bogue (Crespigny 1992:14).

There were a number of conflicts between the Chinese and Europeans, especially when the latter proselytized actively and demanded special treatment for their Chinese converts so they would be handled by Western laws. There were many profound misunderstandings. Both Chinese and Europeans saw each other as barbarians, a nuisance and potentially dangerous (Crespigny 1992:16). Crespigny describes the last two decades in terms of the political and economic changes that led to contemporary China.

Han Hegemony

The job facing Mao's Revolution in the first half of this century was formidable. The proposed constitution seemed to give the Han people certain privileges. Article 50 of the same document recognizes the unfair and chauvinistic attitudes of the Han people scattered all over China and the history of rebellions against the Han on the part of many nationalities, especially the ones occurring in Xinjiang and Inner Mongolia. Therefore, this article formulated an official policy of opposition to inequality and chauvinism. Perhaps the most significant parts of this document were articles 51 and 52. Article 51 established autonomous units of government in areas largely inhabited by national minorities. Article 52 guaranteed equal rights to all members of all nationalities, and freedom of religion, culture and traditions to each and all citizens of China (Benson and Svanberg 1988:56).

Although Article 53 declared that the Central Government had the obligation to provide support for the development of national minority areas, the actual aid also increased unwanted intervention from the Central Government. It was not until four years after the publication of the CCP that the Central Government began to implement Article 51 by means of a Program for Enforcement of National Regional Autonomy. Mao decided to implement this program by creating districts with substantial ethnic minorities under local ethnic leaders. Because of the ethnic conflicts among these minorities, Mao managed to structure the geographic boundaries of these districts to obtain a balance of power among them under close Han supervision (Benson and Svanberg 1988:57–8).

A central question is what was the nature of the power originally allocated to the autonomous areas (regions, prefectures and counties)? Was this power ever used by any of these areas? If not, why not? Benson and Svanberg address this issue very clearly in a historical perspective. In the first decades after the establishment of China's Common Program in 1949 there is doubt that autonomous areas were given a great deal of latitude. In theory, at the beginning the powers given to the autonomous governments were significant; they could establish new laws, local militias, use their home languages for official purposes and control their finances. However, a number of political factors prevented this autonomy. No autonomous region or district could be formed by a single ethnic minority group; the People's Liberation Army, controlled by the central government, retained most of the military power, and all ethnic rulers were placed or removed at the will of the central government (Benson and Svanberg 1988:58). The implications of Mao's policies for the minority nationalities in the New China were very significant and delicate:

> The formative period in the creation of the Chinese identity was that of the Han dynasty (206 BC–AD 221). To this day, the people of the Great Tradition call themselves Hanren, the 'Han people'. This term remains particularly useful to anyone interested in the ethnic and subethnic groups within China today, since it is the primary way of distinguishing the Chinese proper from the Tibetans, Mongols, Zhuang, and other minority nationalities who also live in China and are obviously Chinese in citizenship . . . The invention of Chinese characters long preceded the Han dynasty, as did their systematic organization into a writing system capable of expressing the full flow of human speech. The classical period of Chinese history, marked by the careers of philosophers like Confucius (551–479 BC), Laozi (sixth century BC), and Mozi (ca. 470–390 BC), also preceded the Han era. The Han era was, however, the watershed in the development of the unified China we know today. It is therefore fitting that the majority nationality within China, making up about 94 per cent of the 1 billion people of modern China, should call themselves Hanren . . . Confucius can be described as a key historical figure in Sinitic culture: to describe him as a Han would be more than a bit illogical, since he died 273 years before the founding of the Han dynasty.
>
> (Moser 1985:2–3)

Part of the ethnic diversity and political complexity of China originates from the clustering of individual groups who were never an integral part of mainstream Chinese society and culture, and who were not influenced by the Han people.

Ethnic Diversity and Political Complexity

According to Schwarz (1984) there were in Northern China many groups who remained isolated from Han cultural influence. Based on the research in Chinese and other languages that he conducted prior and during the 1970s, he contends that there are in that region of China three main linguistic/cultural groups: Turkic, Mongolian, and Manchu-Tungus; in addition, he lists a series of unrelated smaller groups, Hui (primarily in the Central and Western part of China, the Korean, Tajik and Russian (Schwarz 1984:v). While there is no total congruence between the names of these groups as he lists them, and the names as they are listed today by the current census in the Central University for Nationalities in Beijing, we could trace the main groups as follows:

Turkic: Uygur, Kazak, Kirgiz, Salar, Uzbek, Yugur, and Tatar
Mongolian: Mongol, Dongxiang, Tu Daur, and Bonan
Manchu-Tungus: Manchu, Sibe, Evenk, Oroqen, and Hezhen.

Among Others Schwarz lists the Hui, Korean, Tajik and Russian. These groups according to Schwarz (1984:v) account for 23.4 million. We will discuss some of these groups below.

Before we look at some of the most visible groups and their location in the various geographical regions of China today, it is important that by the mid 1970s the Cultural Revolution had lost its momentum and was clearly unsuccessful in comparisons with foreign technological achievements. The dissatisfaction with the Maoist regime was shown at the death of chairman Mao Zedong and the new pragmatism of Deng Xiaoping prevailed. It seems that Deng Xiaoping's influence increased to the point that by 1980 Mao's Cultural Revolution was considered dead, and his thinking was criticized. Indeed Hua Guofeng, who had succeeded Mao, was removed from power, and new freedom was granted to private individuals and enterprises. The result was a net loss of revenue for the central government and less funds for building the economic infrastructure of the country (Crespigny 1992:276–7). Additional pressures were placed by the rapid increase in population and a new generation of students seeking new freedom for their country with massive demonstrations, as those of May 1989 in Tiananmen Square that ended with the bloody tragic crushing of young Chinese by the government troops:

> [The 1978] Tiananmen Incident was a new and unwelcome development, the first time for many years that people had gathered of their own accord and shown their true feelings... Hua Guofeng was confirmed [after Mao's death] as Premier, with demonstrations organized in his favor. Despite such manoeuvres, however, the show of public support for Zhou Enlai's model of leadership had circumscribed Hua's role, and the immediate loss for Deng Xiaoping gave him strength in the longer term.
>
> (Crespigny 1992:278)

Power in Education

Mao Zedong died on September 9, 1976 from a stroke, confident that his successor was going to be Hua Guofeng, who advertised this endorsement in billboards 'With you in charge, I am at ease' (Crespigny 1992:279) and immediately moved to control the army, thus managing to retain the loyalty of the Minister of Defense, Ye Jianying, and the commander in charge of the 20,000 body guard force, Wang Dongxing. The opposition of Deng Xiaoping was latent, and the many economic and political difficulties facing Hua Guofeng and the Cultural Revolution ultimately gave Deng Xiaoping a clear advantage as a pragmatist and able administrator. The slogan of the Cultural Revolution 'politics in command' was replaced by Deng's 'economics in command'. Public addresses by officials from the Communist Party spoke publicly against Mao, alluding to 'Mao's errors, his arrogance and loss of contact with reality', but in the end they recognized the contributions of the 'Thought of Mao Zedong' to Marxist philosophy (Crespigny 1992:279).

In 1982 China had its first complete census in 30 years and it showed a population of 1,008,175,288 (a conservative figure according to Crespigny 1992:285). The policy of one child per family was adopted in 1982 and was accompanied by serious penalties for those breaking it, and rewards for those observing it. The population doubled between 1950 and 1980 the average age is about twenty-five. There is a strong emphasis on primary schools and literacy. A weak economy and an underdeveloped industry were critical factors leading to the economic pragmatism of the 1980s and 1990s. Food production had gone down in the late 1950s, was restored in the late 1960s, and increased in the 1970s; yet an agricultural economy was inadequate to meet the country's needs. Deng Xiaoping returned decision making power to farmers and invested his energy in promoting industrial and export relations with significant success (Crespigny 1992:287–90). The Chinese government learned to encourage an open economy with incentives and tangible rewards for risk-taking industries. Private enterprises increased, capital was accumulated and used profitably, and the country as a whole began to mount what is today the third most powerful economy in the world. The favorable trade balance between China and Western nations has been consistently increasing since 1981. The designation of four Special Economic Zones in 1979: Shenzhen (north of Hong Kong), Zhuhai (across the Pearl River estuary), Santou (Swatow, in northeastern Guangdong), and Xiamen (Amoung, in Fujian, across Taiwan), have proven extremely productive. These zones have a high quality, low-cost work-force and facilities, and consequently they are very attractive for foreign — Western and Japanese — industries that facilitate rapid technological transfers (Crespigny 1992:293–95). Subsequently, a number of ports and coastal cities have been declared special economic zones.

The tensions between Taiwan and mainland China have decreased significantly after the deaths of Mao Zedong and Chiang Kai-Shek. The negotiations between China and Britain to restore Hong Kong to China in 1997 were based on goodwill and confidence in future progress. Crespigny notes: 'Sadly, however, in June 1989, security was broken, confidence proved false, and goodwill was lost' (1992:299). The effort to bring economic reforms (modernization) has been perceived as 'democratization' by the Chinese political powers. Massive posters on the so-called Democracy Wall in Beijing (during 1978), pamphlets and journals communicating the same messages were arguing that political and economic freedom were inseparable, and that both were preconditions for modernization. The government silenced these liberal voices but tacitly admitted the competition with the West, seeking to beat the foreigners at their own game (Crespigny 1992:300). The following economic reform of China was unexpected, and it resulted in unusual demographic pressures on the Eastern coast. According to Munzhen Li (1992:83–112) the largest concentration of population (1926 people per square kilometer) is in Shanghai, followed by Tianjin (297 people) and Beijing (556 people).

Political Organization of Modern China

The historical, economic and natural factors supporting a strong density of population in eastern coastal areas are linked to the European trade and rebellions of the previous centuries. One of the most crucial issues in the political and economic organization of modern China is whether or not territorial structuring of provinces and autonomous regions retain a functional value, and to what extent the economic development of China requires a new conception of such structure.

Soon after the foundation of the New China in 1949, the Chinese Government realized that the unity of the country depended on the way minority issues were handled. An important reason for the significance of minorities is that they occupied borders with the former Soviet Union, Mongolia, Korea, Pakistan, India, Vietnam, Laos, Burma and other countries. In order to prevent secession in some of the vast regions in which minorities lived it made sense to negotiate some autonomy with these regions in return for national loyalty. The strategic importance of those areas for China was undeniable. The loss of any of those regions would have been most dangerous for the Chinese nation. In order to strengthen Chinese frontiers the Central Government sent the People's Liberation Army (PLA) to the borderlands, along with a large number of Han people (presumed to be loyal to the Central Government). The pretext was to lend support and assistance to minority regions and to improve their educational level. In fact, most of the time the Han sent to these regions were also appointed as authorities and were responsible for keeping the region under control.

There was, therefore, a strong influence on the part of the Han and a centralized political and military control; but there were also some important efforts at developing minority nationalities in order to incorporate them into the Chinese nation. This policy to strengthen national unity is described by Ma in the context of the enacting of Electoral Laws relative to minority participation as follows:

When the total population of a minority nationality living in a compact community or in scattered groups represents less than 10 per cent of the total population in a locality, the number of inhabitants represented by each deputy from the minority nationality may be less than half that represented by other deputies to the local People's Congress. Elections could be held separately or jointly to have minority nationality deputies elected, taking account of the population composition and the relationship between various nationalities in respective localities. Added to the Electoral Law was a new provision formulated by the 5th National People's Congress in 1979. It states that even a minority nationality with an exceptionally small population 'shall have at least one deputy' to the National People's Congress. Among the deputies to the People's Congress at all levels and the national People's Congress, the proportion of ethnic representatives generally exceeds that of the Han population of a specific locality, so that generally every minority nationality, including those with a population of under 1000, is represented at the national local People's Congresses.

(Ma 1989:23)

Minority representatives who become public officers in their autonomous areas are brought to Beijing at regular intervals to receive special training and must use their power in compliance with regulations from the Central Government or else they will be removed. Having drawn historical lessons from the historical revolts of minorities who were fighting excessive taxes and levies, the Central Government have given special concessions to all minority nationalities, such as smaller taxes, additional financial support, and even favorable criteria for college admission (lower grade point required). These policies have gained the Central Government good will and cooperation. There has been some public criticism on the part of the people who tend to see minorities as earning money and eating the food of the Communist Party, but not working for the party. The fear is that such assistance may strengthen the independence and power of the ethnic minorities. For this reason, the Central Government keeps very close control of the autonomous areas.

In brief, therefore, what is the political organization of China? What are the nature and functions of provinces and autonomous regions? What type of control is exercised by the Central Government? There are twenty-four provinces (including Taiwan and, as of 1988, Hainan) and five autonomous regions. The autonomous regions are Tibetan (NW), Xinjiang (NW), Ningxia (North Central), Inner Mongolian (North), and Guangxi Zhuang (SW) (Ma 1985).

1 The Inner Mongolia Autonomous Region was founded on May 1, 1947, and has it headquarters in Hohhot. The minority nationalities living there are: Mongolian, Hui, Korean, Daur, Oroqen, Xibe, Ewenki, and Manchu.

The Miao among Chinese Nationalities

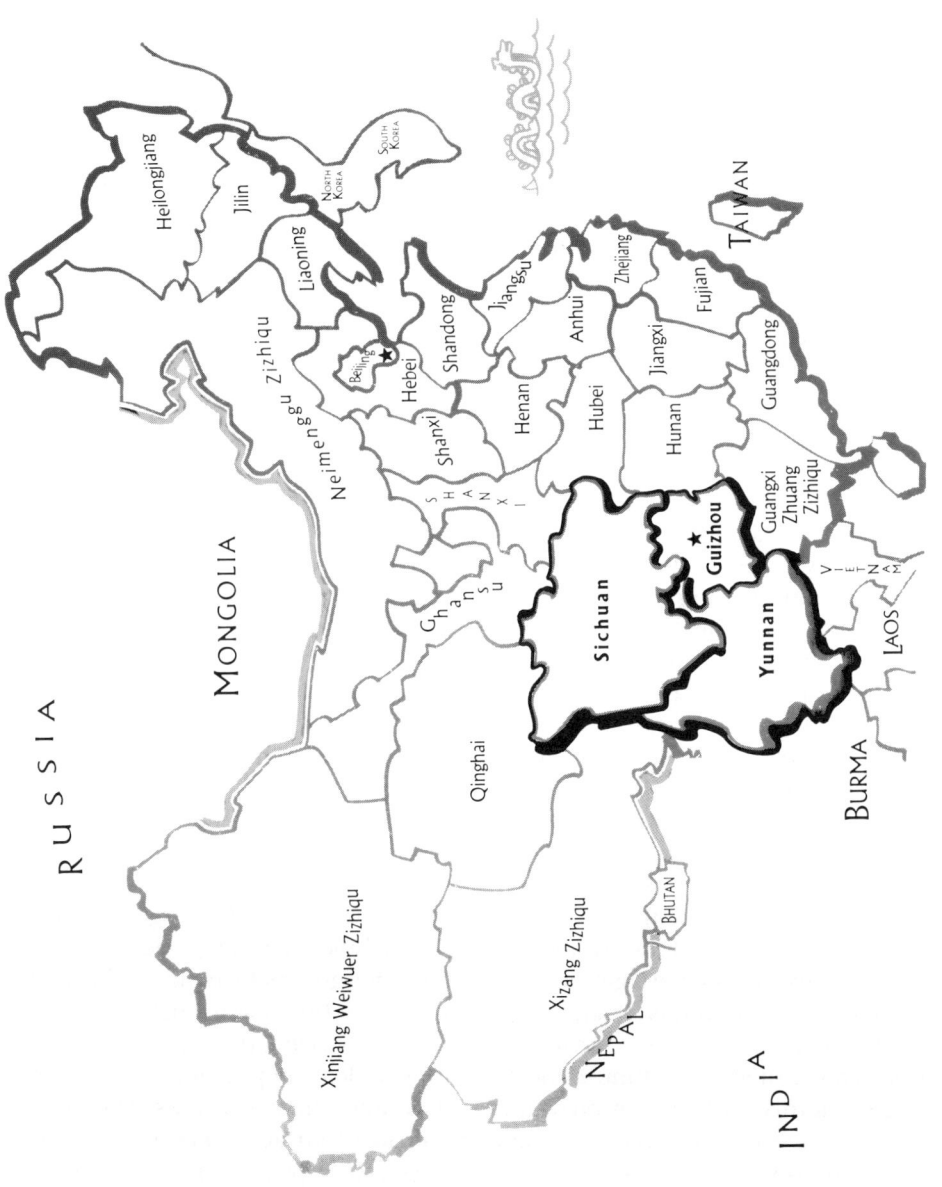

Map 1: Provinces and Autonomous Regions of China

2 The Xinjiang Uygur Autonomous Region was officially recognized by the Central Government on October 1, 1955. Its headquarters are in Urumqi, and the main minority nationalities living there are: Uygur, Kazak, Hui, Kirgiz, Uzbek, Mongolian, Daur, Xibe, Tajik, Tatar, Russian, and Manchu.
3 The Guangxi Zhuang Autonomous Region was officially listed by the Government on March 15, 1958. Its headquarters are in Nanning. The main ethnic minorities are: Zhuang, Yao, Miao, Dong, Mulanm, Maonan, Hui, Yi, Shui, Jing, and Gelo.
4 The Ningxia Hui Autonomous Region was accepted by the Central Government of Beijing on October 25, 1958, and its seat is in Yinchuan. The largest and most important groups in the region are: Hui, Dongxiang, Bonan, Salar, Tu, and Manchu.
5 The Tibet Autonomous Region became an official political entity on September 9, 1965, and its headquarters were established in Lhasa. The main groups are: Tibetan, Tu, Hui, and Mongolian

(Ma 1985:186–93)

China's major and primary government units are provinces and autonomous regions. The difference between autonomous regions and provinces is that the former are headed by local representatives of the ethnic groups in that region, presumably to give ethnic nationalities a larger degree of political autonomy and flexibility. Having ethnic representatives of the government is viewed by the Central Government as a means to empower minorities with some control of their own affairs and resources. In reality, however, the Central Government appoints these representatives and governors of autonomous regions. How did the Han people obtain political control in the first place? Obviously they had the largest population, and historically they enjoyed a cultural hegemony that managed to incorporate elements from many ethnic groups. A policy of political tolerance and a strong military control existed for centuries in China. Another element, according to Ma (1985), was the Han's advanced economy based on higher level of technology.

The popular notion spread in China is that China's basic governance policy of regional autonomy means that all ethnic minority concentrations have the same collective rights as the Han or other groups living in established provinces. Autonomous Regions have the same functional attributions of the provinces, but they have besides the privilege of being ruled by individuals representing their own ethnic minority groups (at least in principle). There are different terms for heads of provinces and of autonomous regions. The head of a province is called governor, and the head of an autonomous region is chairman. Both chairpersons and governors are appointed by the Central Government and rule their areas according to the policies of the Central Government. Consequently, they can be changed or removed at will by the Central Government. Here is where the questions of genuine political power, in contrast with symbolic gestures of power, rests. How powerful are the autonomous regions? Are they as powerful as the provinces? They are as powerful as the Central Government wants them to be. Ma suggests that both the autonomous regions and the provinces are first-level administrative divisions under the leadership of the Central Government, and that they constitute inalienable parts of the territory of China (Ma 1985:26–9). Thus, the main differences between the autonomous areas (that is, not only regions but prefectures and counties) and their counterparts in the provinces are as follows:

> The self-government organs of the autonomous areas are composed mainly of members of the nationalities exercising regional autonomy while the other nationalities inhabiting the areas concerned are also entitled to appropriate representation. As prescribed in the Constitution, the chairmanship and vice-chairmanship in an autonomous area are to be held by a citizen or citizens of the nationality or nationalities exercising regional autonomy in the area concerned. Moreover, the administrative head of an autonomous region, prefecture or county is to be a member of the nationality, or of one of the nationalities, exercising regional autonomy in the area concerned.
> (Ma 1985:28–9).

The use of the local languages has been given special attention by the Central Government, which has strongly supported the use of the spoken and written local language or languages by government employees in the regular functions. In the Xinjiang Uygur Autonomous Region the Uygur language is frequently used for official communication via documents and news broadcasts. The same occurs in Inner Mongolia where the Mongolian language is the official language along with Han, and in the Yanbian Korean Autonomous Prefecture where Korean is the main language (Ma 1985:29).

It is understood that the self-governing autonomous areas manage independently the administration of cultural, educational and scientific affairs, as well as matters related to public health. Furthermore, autonomous areas are given the freedom to enact additional laws if necessary beyond the national legal code. This is the case of the marriage laws which permit the marriage of persons under the nationally-stipulated ages of twenty years for women and twenty-two for men in some areas (Xinjiang, Ningxia, Liangshan and other places (Ma 1985:29). Taking the special situation of some autonomous areas into consideration, the Xinjiang Uygur Autonomous Regions has forbidden the nationally-accepted divorce of simply notifying the spouse verbally or in writing. The Tibetan Autonomous Region has approved a law to support divorce for the party requesting it, if his/her spouse has practiced polygamy. Another important area of local autonomy is the responsibility for handling local finances and formulating local economic development policies (Ma 1985:30–1).

Contemporary Ethnic Minority Groups or Nationalities

Ethnic minority populations account for 8 per cent or 91,200,314 of the 1,133,682,501 (the total population of the People's Republic of China as of 1990). Minority populations occupy 68 per cent of the Chinese territory, leaving only 32 per cent of the territory for the mainstream Han people (The 1990 National Census data, presented by Tian 1991:758). The Han nationality totals 1,042,482,187 people (92 per cent of the Chinese national population), and extends over the Eastern, Northcentral and portions of the South (in the border with Thailand and Vietnam, and in the Southeastern Province of Guangdong and Fujian). The distribution of ethnic groups (or nationalities) in China can be grouped in four regions. The Miao is one of the largest ethnic groups in China among fifty-five (the Han nationality is seen as the mainstream society) as we will see below. The reason why it is important to provide a historical, geographical, linguistic and demographic context for the study of the Miao is that China is an enormous country with an ecological and human diversity unmatched by any other country in the world. The sheer size of its ethnic populations and their territories is difficult to imagine. First, we will deal with the general distribution of ethnic groups and their populations; second, we will discuss the four ethnic groups, and in the following section, we present the Miao people, their population distribution, socio-political history, folklore, economic and religious organization and their cultural traditions.

The fifty-five ethnic minority groups (or nationalities) listed in Tables 1 and 2 encompass a very large portion of the population, and reflect an even larger share of control of the national territory. Table 1 is a list of nationalities in alphabetic order with their respective populations. The fifty-five nationalities are distributed throughout China and can be organized into geographical areas — which do not correspond exactly to the Autonomous Regions discussed above — (see Table 2): 1) Northeast China and Inner Mongolia, 2) Northwest China, 3) Central South and Southeast China 4) Southwest China. These areas represent the heaviest concentration of ethnic minority groups occupying 68 per cent of the total territory of the People's Republic of China.

These ten largest ethnic groups (or nationalities) presented in Table 3 are the Zhuang, Hui, Miao, Uygur, Yi, Tujia, Manchu, Tibetan, Bouyei, and Dong. Their populations, and regional locations are presented in Table 2. Of the entire fifty-five ethnic nationality groups (not including the Han, the fifty-sixth nationality), the top seven largest minority groups account for 40.6 million people, which is 43.5 per cent of the entire minority population, and the top ten account for two-thirds of that same population. The fifty-five Chinese ethnic groups listed in Table 1 represent a very substantial portion (8 per cent) of the total national population, 91,200,314 people, including 750,000 people belonging to unidentified ethnicities. The distribution of ethnic and mainstream groups is presented in Map 2. Even in the areas where the Han population is predominant, there are many other language groups. There is a great deal of

Table 1: The fifty-five ethnic minority groups of China

Achang	27,708	Maonan	71,968
Bai	1,594,827	Miao	7,398,035
Blang	82,280	Moinba	7475
Bonan	12,212	Mongolian	4,806,849
Bouyei	2,545,059	Mulam	159,328
Dai	1,025,128	Naxi	278,009
Daur	121,357	Nu	27,123
De'ang	15,462	Oroqen	6965
Dong	2,514,014	Pumi	29,657
Dongxiang	373,872	Qiang	198,252
Drung	5816	Russian	13,104
Ewenki	26,315	Salar	87,697
Gaoshan	2909	She	630,878
Gelo	437,997	Shui	645,993
Hani	1,253,952	Tajik	33,538
Hezhe	4245	Tatar	4873
Hui	8,692,978	Tibetan	4,593,330
Jing	18,915	Tu	191,624
Jingpo	119,209	Tujia	5,704,223
Jino	18,021	Uygur	7,214,431
Kazak	1,111,718	Uzbek	14,502
Kirgiz	141,549	Va	351,974
Korean	1,920,597	Xibe	172,847
Lahu	411,476	Yao	2,134,013
Lhoba	2312	Yi	6,572,173
Li	1,110,900	Yugur	12,297
Lisu	574,856	Zhuang	15,489,630
Manchu	9,821,180		

linguistic diversity within each of the fifty-six ethnic groups or nationalities. As discussed earlier, Eberhard (1982) has remarked that it is not totally correct to speak of minorities in China, because very often the nationalities or ethnic groups are the majority in the territories they occupy. In the West and South central, that is the case of the Tibetans (who number 4.5 million), the Yi (6.5 million) and the Miao (7.3 million); in the Northeast the case of Inner Mongolia (4.8 million) and the Manchu (9.8 million); and in the Northwest, the cases of the Hui (a Moslem population of over 8.6 million) and the Uygur (7.2 million); however, the clearest cases of ethnic concentrations occur in the Zhuang, the lowest part of Southcentral China (almost 15.5 million people), and the Tujia, the upper part of Southcentral China extended to Yangtze River (5.7 million). Chinese linguists consider that there are at least eighty major distinct languages which belong to five language families. The debate about languages and dialects, both within and across ethnic groups, continues today. As we will see later, the Miao have at least three distinct languages which are not mutually intelligible and which are distributed through the provinces of Sichuan, Yunnan and Hunan, among other areas.

China has been for centuries a multinational country with the largest population in the world. Since 1949 when the New China was established as a result of Mao Zedong's Communist Revolution that intended to emancipate

Table 2: Ethnic groups by region and population

Northeast China and Inner Mongolia	
Daur	121,357
Ewenki	26,315
Hezhe	4245
Korean	1,920,597
Manchu	9,821,180
Mongolian	4,806,849
Oroqen	6965

Northwest China	
Bonan	12,212
Dongxiang	373,872
Hui	8,692,978
Kazak	1,111,718
Kirgiz	141,549
Salar	87,697
Tajik	33,538
Tatar	4873
Tu	191,624
Uygur	7,214,431
Uzbek	14,502
Xibe	172,847
Yugur	12,297

Central South and Southeast China	
Gaoshan	2909
Jing	18,915
Li	1,110,900
Maonan	71,968
Mulam	159,328
She	630,878
Tujia	5,704,223
Yao	2,134,013
Zhuang	15,489,630

Southwest China	
Achang	27,708
Bai	1,594,827
Blang	82,280
Bouyei	2,545,059
Dai	1,025,128
De'ang	15,462
Dong	2,514,014
Drung	5816
Gelo	437,997
Hani	1,253,952
Jingpo	119,209
Jino	18,021
Lahu	411,476
Lhoba	2312
Lisu	574,856
Miao	7,398,035
Moinba	7475
Naxi	278,009
Nu	27,123
Pumi	29,657
Qiang	198,252
Russian	13,104
Shui	645,993
Tibetan	4,593,330
Va	351,974
Yi	6,572,173

Table 3: Largest ethnic groups in China

Ethnic Group	1990 Population	Region
Zhuang	15,489,630	S.Central
Manchu	9,821,180	N East
Hui	8,602,978	N West
Miao	7,398,035	S West
Uygur	7,214,431	N West
Yi	6,572,173	S West
Tujia	5,704,223	Central, S East
Tibetan	4,593,330	S West
Buouyei	2,545,059	S West
Dong	2,514,014	S West

Source: Census Bureau of China, 1990. Museum of Nationalities. Beijing: Central University for Nationalities.

The Miao among Chinese Nationalities

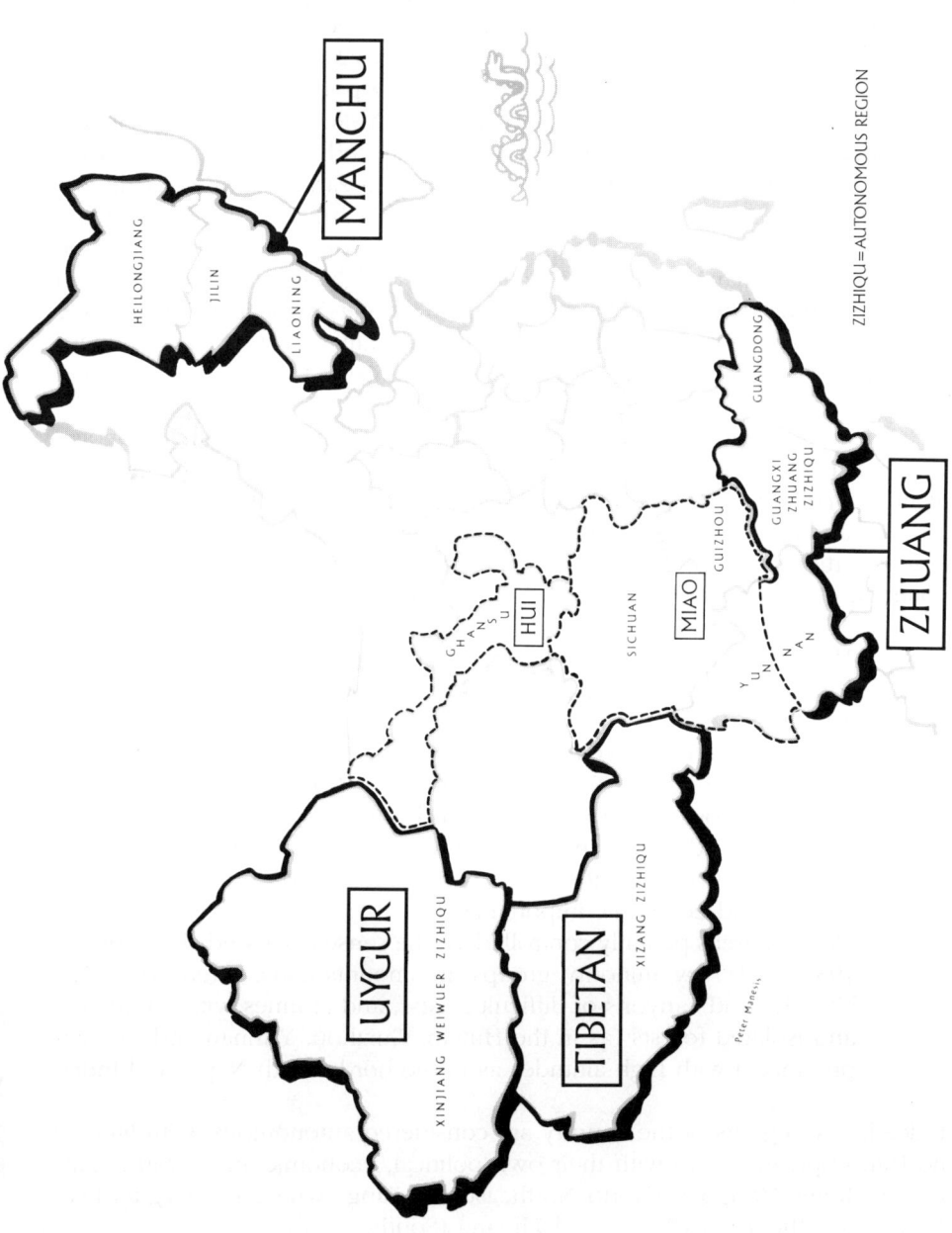

Map 2: Largest Ethnic Groups in China

oppressed peoples from all (including the Han), the ethnic groups, Chinese government officially recognized fifty-six nationality groups as equals — the fifty-sixth being the Han. Nevertheless, the Han group, the largest and most powerful nationality group is viewed as the main sector of society, or mainstream society. In ancient times, the Han Dynasty (206 BC–AD 221), members of the Huaxia (華夏) group, adopted, with the support of related groups, the name Han. First, the Han people lived along the Yellow River, but eventually they spread all over China and gained political and economic power over other groups (the reasons for this were alluded to earlier; for further discussion, see Moser 1985; Piao 1990; Crespigny 1992; and Poston and Michklin 1993). Today, the majority of the Han people live along the Yellow River, the Yangtze and Zhujiang River basins, and in the Songhuajiang-Liaohe Plains in Northeast China. They speak Mandarin, which belongs to the Tibetan language family. The Han, therefore, have played a dominant role in the modern political, social, economic life of China by maximizing the hegemony of Han cultural traditions, literacy and philosophy.

The remaining fifty-five ethnic groups mainly inhabit Inner Mongolia, Xinjiang, Tibet, Guangxi, Ningxia, Heilogjiang, Jilin, Liaoning, Gansu, Qinghai, Sichuan, Yunnan, Guizhou, Guangdong, Hunan, Hebei, Hubei, Fujian and Taiwan, and share control with the Han, as it was mentioned earlier, over the largest portion of Chinese territory (68 per cent). These regions present important common characteristics:

1. They have the richest and largest mineral resources in China, and consequently the greatest potential for industrial productivity (much of it untapped as yet).
2. They constitute border areas between China and other nations: Russia (Kazakhstan) on the Northwest and North; North Korea on the East; Vietnam, Laos (close to Thailand) and Burma in the Southcentral and Southeast; and Nepal, India and Pakistan (close to Afghanistan) in the Southwest. Consequently, these border areas have a unique political, military and economic importance.
3. Many of areas partially controlled (in the sense discussed above by Ma 1985:25–31) by minority groups are mountainous, often with high altitudes and canyons of difficult access, and at times with impressive and isolated forests (as in the Hunan, Guizhou, Yunnan and Sichuan provinces) with high altitudes as in the border with Nepal and India.

Indeed, vast regions of the country are considered autonomous, with little or no Han population and with their own political, economic and social organization: Inner Mongolia (North/Northeast), Xinjiang (where the Uygurs live, Northwest), the Tibet (West), and Zhuang (Southcentral).

Most minority groups have their own language except the Hui and Manchu who speak Han (Mandarin) as a lingua franca, but who are allowed to use

The Miao among Chinese Nationalities

other languages. Among the regional languages spoken by Chinese minorities, there are twenty-nine languages spoken by groups who live in Central, South and Southwest China which belong to the Tibetan linguistic family. Seven language groups, spoken by people who inhabit Northeast and Northwest China, belong to the Altaic language family. Three language groups, spoken by people in the South are of Asian origin, and two of Indo-European origin. The Gaoshan group (some 3000 people from Central South and Southeast and several thousand living in Taiwan) speak an language from Indonesia. There are many enigmas associated with the language distribution and the linguistic origin of those languages. Much of the language distribution, including the predominance of Mandarin, has to do with the economic and political power of the various groups.

The social, economic and political participation of Chinese ethnic groups in the modern development of China is far from being equal. The social and economic development of Han people is far more advanced than that of any other nationality. Some minority nationalities who live close to the Han communities adopted Han culture and its economic system, thus fostering industrial development, production systems, and technical skills, so they share similar social and economic conditions. But those nationalities who live in isolated and remote areas are still inaccessible and their lifestyle and standard of living are very modest; in fact, many of them live in terrible poverty. The Miao, Yao, Lisu, and Va, to give a few examples, still practice slash and burn agriculture and supplement their diets with some animal husbandry. Railroads and roads for trucks and cars either do not exist or are in very poor condition. Part of the problem is, therefore, the lack of a network of communications.

What follows is a more detailed discussion of the largest, historically most important, and representative ethnic nationalities: the Zhuang, Manchu, Hui, Miao and Uygur. These groups exemplify the diversity of ethnic minorities, whose adjustment to the Chinese single political and economic system represents an unprecedented diversity and tolerance among today's countries in the world. They have unique features tailored by cultural history, national economy and local ecology, and they reflect Chinese unity in diversity. It is important to describe their cultural characteristics, geographical distribution and socio-economic system in order to understand the modern political cohesiveness of China and the place of modern Miao in China (see map 2).

The Five Largest Minority Groups: Zhuang, Manchu, Hui, Miao and Uygur

In this section we will discuss the five largest ethnic minority groups in China. However, because we need to provide a more detailed context for the Miao, we have left them at the end in a different section. The Uygur population is smaller than that of the Miao.

Power in Education

The Zhuang Nationality

The Zhuang people, the largest ethnic group in China with a population of 15,489,630, live primarily in the Guangxi Zhuang Autonomous Region in the Southwest, and in the Yunnan, Guangdong, Guizhou and Hunan provinces. The Guangxi-Zhuang region is one of the most beautiful parts of China, a mountainous area where limestones and rocky peaks attract many tourists from all over the world. This region enjoys abundant water sources for irrigation, navigation and hydropower, and plenty of mineral resources such as iron, coal, wolfram, gold, copper, tin, manganese; aluminium, stibium, zinc and petroleum. The Zhuang people plant rice, yams, corn, sugar cane, bananas, longan, litchi, pineapple, shaddock and mango. Immediately after the founding of the People's Republic of China in 1949, the Zhuang area was established as one of the first Autonomous Regions (Ma 1989:371–2; see also Eberhard 1982; Schwarz 1984; and Moser 1985). Education has been developing rapidly since 1949 (Piao 1990). In 1950, when the language of instruction was only Han, there were only three colleges in Guangxi and no ethnic minority persons were able to attend. In 1989, the region counted nineteen universities and colleges, with thousands of minority students. By that year, more than 14,000 ethnic minority students had graduated from the Guangxi Institute for Nationalities alone.

The Manchu Nationality

The National Census of 1990 (Tian 1991:758) indicates that the Manchu people have a population of 9,821,180. Most of the Manchu live in the three provinces of Liaoning, Jilin and Heilongjiang in Northeast of China; the rest live in Hebei, Gansu, Shandong, Inner Mongolia, Xinjiang and Ningxia, with a few in Beijing, Chengdu, Xian, and Guangzhou, among other cities. The Manchu originally had their own language and writing system. Manchu people became very powerful in the middle of the seventeenth century and moved south of the Shanhaiguan Pass (山海關) where a large number of Han people lived. In order to interact with the Hans (who had a highly developed civilization) the Manchus learned Mandarin. At the same time, many Han people moved north of the Pass and shared their language and culture with the local Manchu populations.

According to several scholars (Schwarz 1984; Ma 1989; Pan 1993), the Sushen, a distinct linguistic minority who lived along the Heilong River and in the Changbai Mountains (長白山) in northeast China about 2000 years ago, is considered to be the ancestor of the Manchu. In brief, the splendor of the Manchu people extended not only to their religious rituals, but also to their science and literature. They had nationally respected mathematicians, geographers, historians, linguists and folklorists whose famous works were written during the seventeenth, eighteenth and nineteenth centuries (Ma 1989:47–9).

The Miao among Chinese Nationalities

The Hui Nationality

The Hui nationality is one of the largest ethnic minority groups in China with a population of 8,692,978 (Tian 1991:758). Most of Huis live primarily in the Ningxia Autonomous Region, as well as in the Gansu, Qinghai, Xinjiang, Henan, Hebei, Shandong and Yunnan provinces; but Huis can be found all over China. The full name of the Huis is Huihui. Historical records indicate that the Hui ethnic group was formed by various domestic and foreign nationalities which had the Islamic religion in common, and that this religion played an important role in the organizational, socio-economic and political history of the Huis. The earliest known Hui people are found in Anxi, also called Xinjiang, a region in the Northwest part of China since the Tang Dynasty (618–907). We know that the Hui culture began to be recognized in the thirteenth century during the ruling Yuan Dynasty (1271–1368). Military and political activities greatly influenced the founding of the Yuan Dynasty, in which the Hui occupied a high position, even higher than that of the Han people. However, the Hui remained still under the oppression of the Yuan rulers. It was not until the fourteenth century, during the Ming Dynasty (1368–1644), that the Hui began to emerge as a single nationality with a cohesive ethnic identity recognized by other nationalities. Modern Hui living in Beijing share religious traditions, diet, home lifestyle and a worldview with Moslems from other countries.

The Uygur Nationality

In the mid-eighth century the Uygurs came to rescue the Tang dynasty, and the Chinese capitals of Chang'an and Loyang (threatened by the Mongolians) in which there were Sogdian missionaries of the Manichean religion. When the Uygurs returned home they brought Sogdian missionaries and adopted both the Sogdian script and the Manichean religion (Schwarz 1984:3). The Uygur people spoke a Turkic language which was later used as a lingua franca in Northern China by other groups. The Sogdian missionaries were highly instrumental in the development of the writing system used by the Uygurs. The literary and cultural developments of the Uygur were characterized by the use of 'arabic' symbols (Schwarz 1984:vi).

In the thirteenth century the Uygur fell to the Mongols that conquered the states of Karakhanid and Turfan and other states that became part of the Mongol Empire governed by the Yuan (Schwarz 1984:4). The Uygur play many types of musical instruments (some with chords) and women have very elaborate embroidery (Schwarz 1984:10–14). Education has become very important since 1949, and public health has also greatly improved, primarily with non-Western medicine. In 1949, Communist armies entered Xinjiang peacefully and the Uygur accepted the control of the Communists after four years of relentless civil war in China. The 1982 Uygur population was 5.9 million, and in ten years the population increased to 7.2 million.

Power in Education

The Uygur ethnic group, with a population of about the same size as the Miao, 7,214,431 people, lives in the Northwest region of China, in the Xinjiang Province, and constitutes the Uygur Autonomous Region, which has a territory of 1,709,400 square kilometers, that is, approximately one-sixth of China's total area. Xinjiang is very rich in natural resources, in water, lands, forestry, and minerals such as gold, coal, and iron. The land is very fertile and produces, among other major crops, wheat, maize, rice and cotton, which is the major cash crop (Tian 1991:158–60). The name Uygur means unity, alliance and cooperation. Indeed, they share a common language with its own written form. The Uygur language belongs to the Altaic language family. They use the Altaic-Turkic alphabet (Gladney 1991:20) in their writing system.

The Miao Nationality

The Miao group is a nationality with a long history, large population and broad distribution. According to the 1990 National Census (Tian 1991:758), the Miao nationality has a population of 7,398,035, the largest after the Zhuang, the Manchu and the Hui. It is the fourth largest minority group in China. Since the People's Republic of China was founded, the Miao population has been increasing very rapidly. Based on the national census, in 1953 the Miao had a population of 2.51 million; in 1964 it had 2.78 million; in 1982 it had 5.03 million. The factors in the rapid expansion of the Miao population are first, natural increase, and the second — and most important — in the past under national oppression, some of the Miao people dared not claim that they were Miao. Since 1949, especially in the past ten years, as the policy towards the minorities has been implemented, minorities have received respect and care and they gradually revealed their real nationalities.

The Miao nationality in China is mainly distributed in the Southwest and South central areas. Guizhou is the main area for the Miao groups. The largest population of the Miao nationality live there — 3,686,900. In the southeast part of Guizhou there is a Miao nationality autonomous region which is the biggest compact community area, including 1,458,912 people. Hunan province has 1,557,073 Miao people, most of whom inhabit the west part of Hunan, the second biggest compact community. Yunnan province has 896,712 Miao people who mainly live in Wenshan (文山) Zhuang, Miao Autonomous Region and Pingbian (屏邊) Miao nationality autonomous region. Sichuan province has 535,923 Miao people mainly distributed in the southeast part of Sichuan province. Guangxi Zhuang Nationality Autonomous Region has 425,137 Miao people. Most Miao people live in the Miao nationality autonomous county in the northwest part of Guangxi. Hubei Province has 200,702 Miao population who mainly inhabit the Tujia Nationality and Miao Nationality Autonomous prefecture in the western part of Hubei province. Hainan province has 52,044 Miao people who mainly live in the counties of Tongshen (通什), Qiongzhong (瓊中), Baoting (保亭), Wanning (萬寧), and Lingshui (陵水). Most of the Miao live in mountainous areas where they cultivate a number of crops: rice, maize, potatoes, Chinese sorghum, beans, tobacco and ramie among many others. Their land is extremely beautiful and relatively isolated (Pan 1993; Tian 1991).

The name Maio appeared for the first time in bone inscriptions as early as the eleventh century BC, during the Shang Dynasty (sixteenth–eleventh century BC). Miao people call themselves Guo Xiong in the West part of the Hunan Province, but in the other areas they call themselves Meng, meaning the heart or pulp of a tree in the Miao language. It is said that the heart of a tree gave birth to the *mei bang mei liu* (the mother of butterfly), then *mei bang mei liu* gave birth to the earliest ancestor of the Miao named Jiang Yang. From that time on the Miao people used the name Meng to refer to their entire ethnic group or nationality (Tian 1991).

The Miao people have a very long history which can be traced to the last 5000 years. It is said that there was a powerful group headed by Chi You, the leader of the nine Li groups considered the earliest ancestors of the Miao who lived by the Yellow River. At the same time, there was another powerful group led by the Yellow Emperor. The two groups were rivals in various fights and competitions. Finally, the Miao group was defeated and was forced to cross the Yellow River, and went down along the middle and lower reaches of the Yangtze River. According to the folklore (Compiling Group of the Brief History of the Miao Nationality 1985:1) during the period of the emperors Yao, Shun, and Yu, the Miao people stood up again to fight against the three emperors, and once more they were defeated and had to move along. The history of the Miao is believed to have been a history of migrations and military struggles against the powerful Chinese emperors. Indeed, these migrations led them west to the Hunan province, or to the east and central parts of the Guizhou province. The people who lived in the western and central parts of Guizhou continued the migration patterns partially due to lifestyle and living conditions which became harder. Some of the Miao moved to the Guangxi, Yunnan and Sichuan provinces, and some continued from Yunnan to Laos, Thailand, Vietnam, Burma, and other areas of Indochina (Tian 1991:507–9).

There has been a great deal of research done on the Miao, according to Jun Wei Liu who examines the distribution of various ethnic minority groups in China as essentially adapting to the land available to them and its ecological conditions. Thus, for example, the Miao arrived in the Yunnan and Vietnam areas after other groups had already taken the flat valleys, and therefore the Miao had to take the mountains and adapt to the high altitudes; this is the reason why they were called the High Mountain Miao. Thus, each minority group adapted their lifestyle and cultivation patterns to the ecology in which they lived (Liu 1991:20). In fact, the Miao people originally did not live in the high altitudes, for they lived as aborigines of the Guizhou and Yunnan provinces. They migrated on a large scale. The Miao people that eventually migrated to Indochina, Thailand, and the Central Southern Island came from many places, but especially from Guizhou via Yunnan (Liu 1991:21).

There were two main Miao migration routes, one to the west and the

Power in Education

other to the east of Guizhou. The ones who migrated to the east were primarily White Miao, and some of them were also the so-called Flower Miao and Green Miao. They entered Yunnan from the south and southwestern corner of Guizhou through Xingyi, continuing through Danfeng and arriving finally at Mengzi. The details of the route are explained by Liu (1991:20–2), but eventually the Miao arrived at the northern part of Vietnam and the western part of Laos to settle down in Mengxinjing in Nancan.

The western Miao migration route (taken by mixed groups of White Miao, Green Miao and Flower Miao) left west Guizhou, and the region between Guizhou and Sichuan to head for Qujing in Hunan. Afterwards they continued west to Gaoming (Northern part of Kunming, in Yunnan), and to Fumin (富民), Niangbi (漾鼻), Yongping (永平), Menhua (蒙化), and finally crossed the Lanchang River (瀾滄江) to enter Burma via Shunning (順寧). The eastern migration was larger in population and many of the Miao settled in the mountain areas of Laos. Both eastern and western migrations are supposed to have taken place five to six hundred years ago, and were probably extended in greater or lesser numbers for the last two centuries. We know that the history of Laos describes a famous massacre of Miao immigrants by the Vietnamese, in 1479 during the so-called White Elephant Incident (Liu 1991:21), an incident that has not been forgotten by the Miao people.

According to the historical records, the Miao people went to Central Yunnan during the Ming Dynasty, in the first half to the fourteenth century, but the large scale migration of Miao people to Central South Island took place during the early Qing Dynasty, between 1644 and 1911. It is likely that one of the largest migrations in Laos, into the area of Shangliao (上寮), took place in the eighteenth century. It is also believed that the migration of the Miao in Vietnam occurred in three stages. First, probably in the mid-seventeenth century, some eighty households migrated to Tongwen (同文), in Hexuan (河宣), a Vietnamese province, and lived there for fourteen or fifteen generations. Second, perhaps sometime at the end of the eighteenth century, some 180 households, coming originally from Guizhou, migrated to Huangshupi (黃樹皮), Beihe and Ximajie (西麻界). There is some archaeological evidence of stones carried to Vietnam. Third, during the nineteenth century, over 10,000 Miao people migrated to other places, Laojie (老街), Hejiang (河江), Anpei (安沛), Laizhou (萊州) and Shanluo (山萝), and remained there for six or seven generations which brought them to the twentieth century. It seems that the Miao migration may have extended for some four or five hundred years (perhaps starting as early as the fourteenth century), but the most intense periods date from the seventeenth century to the present. There are historical records of Miao soldiers and their uprisings as a result of deaths due to shortages in rice and other food supplies in the fifteenth century. There are documents showing that the Miao people fought courageously against the Qing Dynasty whose corrupted officials had mistreated the Miao people consistently. One of the uprisings took place in 1735, another in 1795, and the Miao were again massacred in 1799. The history of oppression lasted for four or five centuries, from

The Miao among Chinese Nationalities

the Yuan Dynasty to the Qing Dynasty, and this history shaped the fighting and migrating spirit of the Miao (Liu 1991:22–3).

The Miao nationality suffered a lot and developed slowly. Since the San Miao were defeated, the Miao nationality has always been chased, enslaved and oppressed. Continuous wars and forced migration greatly damaged production and hindered the development of the socio-culture. In defeat, the Miao people were plunged into an abyss of misery and the culture was destroyed. When they moved, they always needed to throw their belongings away and build new homes in new places. The Miao people used to live in the flat land of plenty, then were forced to move into the mountains where they lost their flat land grain cultivation culture and were forced to adjust to mountain life and create a mountain culture. The long struggles against class oppression, national oppression and adverse natural situations strengthened the resolve of the Miao people and allowed them to bear hardships and persist in the face of struggle.

The Miao nationality economy has developed since 1949, especially since 1978 when China began to carry out economic reforms. The developments differ from area to area. Some areas have good natural conditions and therefore have been developed faster than the remote and mountain areas where most people still live under the poverty level.

In the northwest part of Guizhou and the northeast part of Yunnan, most people do not have enough food to eat. In the Hezhang county (赫章) in northwest Guizhou for example, there are 7158 households. Among them 1111 households live in *ChaChaFang* (叉叉房) which were made by a few tree trunks put together covered by grass, and tree branches. People live together with their livestock; five households live in caves; ninety-one households do not have any so-called houses in which to live; 2305 households do not have enough food to eat (Pan 1993). In 1986 the township (a structural unit formed by several villages) of Shimenkan (石門坎) in the county of Weining (威寧) in the Guizhou province (Miao country) had 984 households with 4823 persons. If we use as a basis for our calculations the currency exchange of 1993 ($1 US=5.77 Chinese dollars or Yuan), in 1985, 50 per cent of the households' annual income was less than 100 Chinese dollars (equal to $17 US); 10 per cent of the households' annual income was less than 30 Chinese dollars (equal to $5.20 US). The richest households' annual income is less than 300 Chinese dollars ($52 US); some households earn annually less than 10 Chinese dollars ($2 US). Most people in the township do not have enough food to eat and enough clothing to wear. Many children under seven or eight-years-old do not have any clothing to wear — even adults need to wear clothes by turn. Many people live in the so-called houses which are set up in tree branches without windows. They sleep on the wooden planks covered by grass (Yang 1989).

School education of the Miao nationality began in the early Ming dynasty (1368–1644). In order to 'Hanize' the Miao nationality so as to consolidate its control, the ruling class of the Ming dynasty set up schools in the areas where Miao people resided to spread Confucian education. During the reign of emperor

Power in Education

Hong Wu (1395), local officials in Guizhou province suggested to the emperor in a report that, 'since various kinds of Miao barbarians have no ideas of the royal ritual, it is advisable to set up Confucian education, enlightening them with the education of poetry and book learning'. The emperor Yongle (永樂) (1414) ordered the court to begin to 'send instructors there to teach the children of Miao people in order to enlighten them'. (Pan 1993).

At the turn of the Ming and Qing dynasty, there occurred several uprisings by the Miao nationality. In addition to armed suppression, the ruling class also emphasized the importance of Confucian education. With government funding, several free schools were set up in both Yunnan and Guizhou provinces. The modern Miao school education which began in the period of the Republic of China has a certain kind of development since the founding of the People's Republic of China. Generally speaking, primary education in urban areas, places with easy transportation and mixed communities of both the Miao and Han nationalities, is better developed. Children of school age go to school and can continue their study in a stable manner. Primary education in the cold mountain areas develops slowly, and 'the three rates' (the rate of attending school, the rate of continuing primary education and the rate of success) remain low. Because most of the Miao people live in the mountain areas which are poor, primary education is far more backward than in other areas.

The Miao people in Taijiang County at the foot of Leigong mountain account for 93 per cent of the total population. In 1982, the illiteracy rate went up as high as 53.3 per cent. Those who attended primary school account for 40.49 per cent of all the children of school age (7–11-years-old). In some countries, this percentage is only 20 per cent, and girl students amount to only 18.82 per cent with a low retention rate. In September 1978, the total number of students who attended the first grade of primary school were 4812. When they graduated in 1983 this number went down to 1407 with a low rate of retention of 29.23 per cent; the scores of these children were poor. In 1982, the graduates from sixty primary schools participated in a middle-school entrance examination. However, of these sixty schools fifty-one schools failed, with not a single one of their graduates passing the examination. This accounts for 85 per cent of all the schools which took part in the examination. Sidazhai Country of Ziyun County is a mountain area inhabited by the Miao people. In 1986 the rate of children attending school was 79 per cent, and the rate of retention was 10 per cent. The rate of girl students attending school was even lower, reflecting the high poverty rate in the high mountain area. Old customs of early marriage, of favoring the male over the female, as well as the ill-trained teachers and poor teaching facilities, all have greatly hindered the development of education.

Mashan (麻山) township of Wangmo County (望漠) is another example. It is located high in the mountains and is very poor. Before the founding of new China there was no state-run school. Now there is a complete primary school and seven village-run primary schools. The public primary school is the best of them all. However, it does not have a roof or walls. According to the statistics in 1985, the rate of the school-age children who attend school was 28 per cent, and the retention rate was 20 per cent. The rate of both male and female students who passed the state standard examination was 2 per cent.

To develop middle-school education is essential to raise the level of Miao culture and improve the quality of the Miao population. In order to enter universities, one must have a solid foundation laid in a middle school. In China, prestigious jobs such as technicians or scientists applying knowledge to farming, business persons, factory workers and managers, and teachers, need at least a junior high education. The Miao youth in county cities generally complete middle-school education, some of them enter colleges and universities. Some of the Miao youth in the country, especially in remote mountain areas far away from cities with no convenient transportation, complete their junior middle-school education, few complete senior middle-school education, even fewer enter colleges and universities. This is not because peasant children do not want to study, but because they are limited by poor financial conditions. If they go to district junior middle schools or county senior middle schools, they have to cover board and lodging and all tuition fees and other miscellaneous expenses by themselves. Regular middle schools have no financial aid. Since the problem of eating at home is not yet solved, it is too difficult to go to school. Those families who managed to solve the problem of eating rely on the resources from raising chickens and pigs or other side-line products to send their children to school. Even though they are very poor, parents try their best to let their children finish middle-school education and then continue for higher education. If their children fail to enter colleges and universities, they still will be able to find a job. Once they become successful, they bring glory to the family. Therefore, parents try to save money so that their children can receive an education. The children also understand their parents' expectations and live a plain life at school and study very hard.

After the founding of New China, the Chinese communist party and the people's government placed great emphasis on the development of higher education for the minority people by adopting a series of special supportive policies. First, in Beijing and other minority areas they set up institutes for nationalities: The Central Institute for Nationalities (in Beijing), The Guizhou Institute for Nationalities (in Guiyang), Southwest Institute for Nationalities (in Chengdu), The Central Institute for Nationalities (in Wuhan), Yunnan Institute for Nationalities (in Kunming), Guangxi Institute for Nationalities (in Nanning), Guangdong Institute for Nationalities (in Guangzhou), Xiangxi University (in Jishou, Hunan province), Hubei Institute for Nationalities (in Enshi), Qiandongnan Normal School (in Kaili, Guizhou province), Qiannan Normal School (in Jundu, Guizhou province), Qianxinan Normal School (in Xingyi, Guizhou), Wenshan Normal School (in Wenshan, Yunnan), as well as normal schools in other areas. All of these schools pay special attention to the admission of the Miao and other ethnic minority youth.

Second, historically, education for the Miao and other minorities was weak, and the number of middle school graduates was low and of poor quality. On the other hand, the government conducted a nationwide entrance examination which made it difficult for the minority youth to succeed. Because of this the government lowered the admission scores needed by ten to twenty points for members of minority groups depending on different areas. In some areas the admission score is reduced even more radically (Pan 1993).

The Miao language belongs to the Miao-Yao branch of the Chinese-Tibetan language family. It can be divided into three dialects, West Hunan dialect, East Guizhou dialect, and the dialect of Sichuan, Yunnan, and other parts of Guizhou, which is also called the Western dialect, used by the Miao people who live in Indochina. There are great differences among these three dialects, especially in pronunciation. For instance, eastern Guizhou dialect does not have duplicate consonants or voiced sounds, but the Western dialect has them. It is said in Miao folklore that in ancient times the Miao people had a written language, a script, which later, for various reasons related to their continuous migrations, disappeared. At the beginning of the twentieth century, an English missionary, Sir Poloart, who lived in the Shi Men Kan area (in the Western part of Guizhou) together with other scholars such as Yang Yage, Zhang Wu, and Lisitiwen, created an alphabetic writing system to record a form of the Miao language called Old Miao Script. Today, it is still used among the Miao of Guizhou and Yunnan. After the People's Republic of China was established, the Government organized a group of Miao scholars and linguists to reform the Old Miao Script on the basis of a national study, and to create a Latin alphabetic script; this initiative was welcome by the Miao people and has become increasingly more popular.

In the course of their development the Miao people have created many beautiful and colorful myths, poems and folk stories, and have expressed their artistic talents in music, dance and paintings. An example of their literature is the story called 'Yang Ya Shoots Suns and Moons' (楊亞射日月), which is said to have been written when the poet, Yang Ya, saw that the sky had too many suns and moons, and he thought human beings would be totally destroyed by them. According to the story, Yang Ya was so angry that he decided to shoot the extra suns and moons. He noticed that the only tree that had not died from the sunshine was one near the river. So, he cut the tree and turned it into the bow, using the branches to make arrows. Then he shot down seven suns and seven moons. Since then, the whole world became cool and crops began to grow, and people started to have a quiet life. Another folk story tells us that once upon a time there was a very serious flood in which all the people died except a brother and a sister. Therefore, in order to have descendents, they had to marry. Another story entitled 'Dog Got the Grain Seed' (狗取糧種) is known widely in Western Hunan. According to this story, people at the very beginning ate the leaves of trees and their wild fruits. Then they asked the dog to go to the sky to get the grain seeds which had five-inch stalks and five-foot grain ears. But because the dog was in a hurry and fell down, the dog forgot what the people told him. Finally, the dog brought back the grain seed with a five-inch grain ear and a five-foot stalk. So now a millet ear is five inches long, but the stalk is five feet long. Since it was the dog that brought human beings the grain seed, it is appropriate that the people worship dogs.

Poetry among the Miao is extremely popular. There are many poets who write about the quest of the Miao people for freedom in marriage. For example, 'Yang A Sha' (仰阿莎) is a story in which a beautiful girl was deceived by the matchmaker and was married to the sun. After she married the Sun, she was mistreated. In order to become free from the oppressive marriage, she eloped with the Moon. After that the Sun argued with Moon. The authority passed judgment on the case and decided that Yang A Sha and the Moon could be a couple. This reflects how the Miao people condemn the Sun's abuse of power and the Sun's mistreatment of the weak (Compiling Group of the Brief History of the Miao Nationality 1985:279–94).

The Miaos love singing and dancing. They have various musical instruments: *lusheng* (蘆笙 = pipes), flutes, copper drums, mouth organs, the *xiao* (簫 = a vertical bamboo flute) and the *suona* (嗩吶 = horn). The *lusheng* is their favorite instrument. They have also created many kinds of beautiful arts and crafts, such as, embroidery, weaving, batik, and paper-cutting which are well-known internationally. The Miao clothing is very colorful and beautiful; there are more than 300 styles of clothing among the various Miao groups.

> In northwest Guizhou and northeast Yunnan, Miao men usually wear linen jackets with colorful designs, and drape woollen blankets with geometric patterns over their shoulders. In other areas, men wear short jackets buttoned down the front or to the left, long trousers with wide belts and long black scarves. In winter, men usually wear extra cloth leggings known as *puttees*. Women's clothing varies even from village to village. In west Hunan and northeast Guizhou, women wear jackets buttoned on the right and trousers, with decorations embroidered on collared short jackets and full- or half-length pleated skirts. They also wear various kinds of silver jewelry on festive occasions.
> (Ma 1989:339–340)

According to the Miao women's clothing style, Miao people can be divided into many groups, such as White Miao, Red Miao, Flower Miao, Big Flower Miao, Small Flower Miao, Green Miao, and Black Miao. These groups are patrilineal clans, that is kinship groups formed by the male siblings who bring their spouses from other clans. The Miao, however, have a custom whereby a man can marry a 'cross-cousin', that is one's father's sister's daughter, or a woman can marry her father's sister's son, and either one can marry their mother's brother's child. Because clans are patrilinear, they are composed of males who have the same surname, their spouses and their unmarried children. People who have the same surname can not be married to each other. That is, one cannot marry one's father's brother's child (or 'parallel cousins'). The wedding ceremonies vary from area to area. In some regions the bridegroom brings the bride to his home the night of the wedding. In other regions both families choose the lucky day, then the family of the bride accompanies the bride to the bridegroom's home. For a more detailed discussion of the culture and history of the Miao see D. Pan (1993).

References

BENSON, L. and SVANBERG, I. (Ed) (1988), *The Kazaks of China: Essays on an Ethnic Minority*, Acta Universitatis Upsaliensis. Uppsala, Sweden: Almqvist & Wiksell International Stockholm.
COMPILING GROUP OF THE BRIEF HISTORY OF THE MIAO NATIONALITY (1985) *The Brief History of Miao Nationality*, Guiyang, China: Guizhou Nationality Press.
CRESPIGNY, R. de (1992) *China this Century*, New York, NY: Oxford University Press.
EBERHARD, W. (1982) *China's Minorities: Yesterday and Today*, The Wadsworth Civilization in Asia Series, THOMPSON, L.G. (Series Editor) Belmont, CA: Wadsworth Publishing Co.
GLADNEY, C.C. (1991) *Muslim Chinese: Ethnic Nationalism in the People's Republic*, Council on East Asian Studies, Harvard East Asian Monographs, Cambridge, MA: Harvard University Press.
LIU, J.W. (1991) 'The argument on the Miao minority's migration across country and the theory of national vertical distribution', In LI, T. PAN, D. and YANG, ZH. (Eds) *Miao Study, Volume II*, Guiyang, China: Guizhou Nationality Press, pp. 19–29.
MA, Y. (1989) *Chinese Nationalities*, Beijing, China: China Press.
MA, Y. (Ed) (1985) *Questions and Answers about China's National Minorities*, Beijing, China: New World Press.
MOSER, L.J. (1985) *The Chinese Mosaic: The Peoples and Provinces of China*, Westview Special Studies on East Asia, Boulder, CO: Westview Press.
PAN, D. (1993) *The History and Culture of the Miao Nationality*, unpublished manuscript, Guiyang, China, Guizhou Institute for Nationalities.
PIAO, S. (1990) *Educational Projections and Development of Minorities in China*, Beijing, China: Beijing Educational Press.
POSTON, D.L. JR. and YAUKEY, D. (Eds) (1992) *The Population of Modern China*, Series title: The Plenum Series on Demographic Methods and Population Analysis, New York, NY: Plenum Press.
SCHWARZ, H.G. (1984) *The Minorities of Northern China: A Survey*, Center for East Asian Studies, Bellingham, WA: Western Washington.
TIAN, X. (Ed) (1991) *The Nationalities in China*, Beijing, China: China Press.
YANG, Z. (1989) 'Yesterday, today and tomorrow of Weining Shimenkan: Search for exploring and developing way of Miao nationality areas from the lesson of a remote and backward Miao mountain village', in LI, T., PAN, D. and YANG, ZH. (Eds) *Miao Study*, Volume I, Guiyang, China: Guizhou Nationality Press, pp. 112–23.

Chapter 4

Miao Students Reflect on Their Lives: The Painful Journey From Home to School

Chapters 4, 5 and 6 are intimately related. Chapter 4 presents the students' own texts describing their arduous and painful journeys from home to the university, and the rationale for being committed to a university education. Chapter 5 describes the quality and variety of experiences that Miao students have in the university, and the relationship between these experiences and their own self-identity, as well as their motivation to achieve academically. These two chapters are the two sides of the same coin, that is the complementary experiences of students at the university in contrast with their home experiences. Chapter 6 provides an analytical statement of the key themes touched by students in their descriptions of their home and university lives. Indeed, Chapter 6 attempts to present a theory of self-identification and its significant impact on academic achievement; the argument in its simplest form is that being a Miao student means belonging to a Miao community and a Miao family, and that success at the university is the most logical means to show gratitude to one's own family and community.

The following pages will introduce the reader to fourteen Miao students, as they see themselves and share their most intimate and painful thoughts. Their words were often written as a means to share their anxiety and efforts in adapting to university life, and thus efforts to find peace within themselves. On other occasions, the predominant feelings are of gratitude to their humble parents. All fourteen students are proud of having reached the high status of university students, but all are close enough to their pasts to remember the tough days of hunger and the long journeys from home to school and back. In fact, many of these students still wait anxiously for the mail in the hope they will get a little money from home to help pay for food. Most of them receive a small stipend from the government that pays for tuition and fees, but not food. Their commitment to achieve academically is part of their life histories. After the reflections of students we present some specific comments organized by central themes emerging from the texts. The testimonies of the fourteen students interviewed for the study are presented in the same order as their responses to questionnaires that are discussed in the next chapter: the first seven students are from the Central University for Nationalities (CUN) in Beijing, and the other seven are from the Guizhou Institute for Nationalities (GIN). Additional information about both of these institutions, the students and their families is presented in Chapter 5.

Village Life among the Miao

The information on the village life is taken from personal interviews with Chinese professors and students, but especially from unpublished documents written by Professor Dingzhi Pan (from the Guizhou Institute for Nationalities) and Professor Dekun Wu (from the Central University for Nationalities in Beijing). The two written documents by these professors are placed in the references (Wu 1993; Pan 1993). While our information is somewhat fragmentary, it serves to provide a more concrete sociocultural context for the testimonies of the Miao university students. The information below will cover the organizational structure of Miao villages, the early experiences of children in the home, courtship, marriage and family life. Miao villages organize their lives around their agricultural activities which are planned according to the lunar calendar. Spring, summer and fall are busy seasons; winter is a time to relax. The most demanding time is during the months of April and May when the wheat is harvested and fields are plowed, and also when the rice seedlings are transplanted and the millet is weeded. February and March are used for plowing the fields and planting; June, July and early August are time for rice seedlings and to adjust water levels for the rice. Mid-August through September the harvest takes place, millets are dried in the sun and stored. In October wheat is planted. During November and December people leave their agricultural chores and deal with building or repairing their homes, arranging marriages, visiting relatives and friends, and preparing their instruments and tools for the following year.

Pan Dingzhi, a Miao and professor of Miao language and folklore at the Guizhou Institute for Nationalities (1993) describes the village life he has experienced using concrete examples, such as the Weining village located in the Yunnan Province, that has a single patrilineal clan with twenty households. Houses are built in different locations without forming streets or any other special configuration. Most households have two independent rooms, one for people and the other for animals, and a few of them have only one room in which animals are also allowed. The walls are made of clay and the roof is covered by long grass. The village of Weining is in a mountainous area. Consequently, in order to get water, villagers have to travel several miles and carry enough water for their animals and themselves. People eat two meals a day consisting of baked taro without vegetables. They feed their pigs, chicken, sheep and other animals, and sell them or trade them for salt and clothing. Living conditions are frequently very difficult. The villages in Southeast Guizhou are bigger, often composed of several patrilineal clans and hundreds of

Miao Students Reflect on their Lives

households. Homes are constructed on top of the mountain next to each other (often only three feet apart). Because the houses are made of wood, if one catches fire, it is likely that the entire village will burn.

The organization of the villages is very similar across regions. The people select a head who is responsible for presiding over the village affairs and offering sacrifices to the gods. On February 15th of the Chinese calendar, the head organizes all villagers to offer sacrifices in honor of the mountain god. If some people have had any disputes or disagreements with members of the village, they are invited to discuss their concerns. The contending parties must then obey the decision of the head, otherwise they can be fined; fines can take the form of wine, sheep or money. All villagers are invited to come and eat. After 1949, the role of the village head and village traditions were weakened, but they still exist. Now villages have a member of the Communist Party whose chair can serve for three years. Many small villages are formed by a single patrilineal clan with the same family surname, that is, one in which brothers, their wives and children form a political and economic unit. Sometimes different clans (including clans with the same surname) form a village. The village government organization is called *Gu She* (in Miao) or *Jiang Lue* (in Mandarin), and it is composed of a head who also has the functions of political leader, a judge called *Li Lao*, and a legislative and executive body that both advises the head and carries out his orders, called *Yi Lang* (in Mandarin). The *Gu She* or *Jiang Lue* has existed among the Miao since ancient times. The term literally means 'a drum place', or a place where the maple drums are played to honor the ancestors. Maple drums are believed to contain the souls of the ancestors, and when played during the sacrifices as offers to them, the ancestors 'talk' to the people. The *Yi Lang* (literally 'regulations discussion') is convoked by the head of the village to deal with petty crimes and to decide the punishment. A long stone without any inscription is placed on the ground; around it, the members of the *Yi Lang* (old and young, men and women) discuss a case; and whenever the head gives his verdict, he will hit the stone once; that means he put the final verdict in the stone, and therefore the stone must be buried. A serious offense may result in a fine; the culprit may have to give a cow which is killed, cut into pieces and given to the village families to take home. Serious offenses are, for example, the forceful occupation of someone else's land, the cutting of their trees, or stealing their property. The head of the village (*Li Lao*) must mediate disputes and make a judgment sometimes without the assistance of the *Yi Lang*.

Traditionally, Miao villages were considered to be fairly equalitarian. However, although not totally stratified, it is clear that government officials, scholars and students receive the highest status and receive public respect. Government officials have security of employment and are the highest paid. Next to them the village head has the highest status. Then the university students are viewed as the most respected, because they have knowledge and they will get government jobs and 'imperial grain' to eat. That is one of the reasons why families work so hard to get a child educated and hopefully become a government employee. The status of elementary and secondary education teachers is under that of village heads and university students, in spite of the fact that teachers have a salary and heads of village do not. Next in rank are witch doctors or sorcerers who conduct rituals and know how to cure people. The blacksmiths, tailors and other hand workers come after them in status. More recently, business persons have acquired high status because they have made a great deal of money, while in the past rich merchants were viewed with suspicion as being dishonest.

The education of the children is the sole responsibility of the parents (especially of the mother), not of members of the extended family. From birth to age four, the mothers are the exclusive caretakers, and teach their children how to talk, sing and function in life. Past the fourth year the mother's elder sister may help teach the girls to do household chores and feed the animals, and the father and his elder brother may teach the boys to go to the mountain and herd cattle. In the evening the elders tell stories to the children of both sexes. When children turn 7-years-old they must attend school. Girls have serious responsibilities in the home; they care for the younger siblings and from age nine on they learn how to embroider assisted by their mother. This is a particularly important occupation because clothing is often a status symbol and the most important possession of women; furthermore, girls' embroidering skills enhance their future as attractive potential wives. Singing is also emphasized in children's education. Boys and girls at age ten participate in the *You Fang*, a singing activity where children and adults sing love songs face-to-face as a way of courting.

Parents, however, concentrate their efforts on inculcating in children the moral principles and basic skills considered to be the foundations of a good life. There are a number of ceremonies and rituals that provide parents with an opportunity to socialize children into their cultural values of respect for the elders and the commitment to honor the family. The essence of family unity is hard work, fraternal unity, respect for adults, weaving skills for women and ploughing skills for men. When a family eats a meal, children should let adults eat first, and parents, do not let children waste any food. The birth of a new child is a happy occasion that brings relatives to feast together. The maternal grandmother gives a name to the child. The name giving ceremony takes place when the child is about a month old. Maternal grandparents are expected to bring wine for the family and clothing for the child. Miao people do not celebrate birthdays, and often children do not know their own birth date. When girls begin to menstruate they change clothing and hairstyles. In Guizhou, for example, girls wear pants and hats; when they become women they begin to wear skirts, they no longer wear hats, and they wear their hair as a knob on their heads to indicate that they are mature.

By the age of ten, boys must learn to dig the earth, fetch firewood, and help their parents during the planting and harvesting seasons. Elder sons are responsible for the education of their siblings, and when parents grow old they function as heads of the family. The youngest son does not have any special privileges. Parents divide their property equally among the sons; however, younger sons are expected to live in their parents' house and property until they die. At that point, they keep their parents' home and property. In general, men and boys are seen as superior to women and girls respectively. Boys are allowed to punish girls physically, as men do with women.

There are two different ways of selecting a spouse: free choice and by parental arrangement. The *You Fang* is important for boys to find a spouse. If an arranged marriage is not acceptable for a boy, he can bring home his own chosen spouse and face the anger of his parents and those of his arranged wife-to-be. Or the couple can just elope and come back to face the consequences. Boys in groups sometimes go from one village to another to look for girls. Often boys and girls express their love by exchanging gifts such as clothing or bracelets; these exchanges are seen as a potential engagement. That means that the boy and girl have chosen the *Yen Hun* (elopement) date for the informal wedding, or one in which the spouses chose each other. At midnight on the chosen day, the girl secretly packs her clothing and goes to a secret place to wait for the boy. Then the boy and two or three of his friends take the girl to the boy's home. The following day the boy will explain everything to his parents, and the parents usually support them in their decision and invite the elder members of the clan to come and drink wine. After two or three days, the boy's parents ask a matchmaker to go to the girl's house with a chicken, sugar and rice to ask for the girl's hand. Usually the girl's family agrees to the wedding by accepting the food and cooking it, and then inviting the boy's family to eat. For this kind of marriage the boy's family does not give money, nor does the girl's family give a dowry. This is the simplest ceremony.

Arranged marriages are more complicated. First the boy's parents must identify the appropriate girl, then invite the matchmaker to ask the girl's parents for her hand. When the matchmaker, usually a woman, goes to the girl's house for the first time, she merely presents the boy's parents' request, without making any gifts. No answer is expected at this time. A second visit by the matchmaker can result in a polite refusal or acceptance of the offer. If the offer is accepted, the matchmaker must take gifts (chicken, pork, wine, rice, etc.) and the acceptance of these gifts will constitute a formal engagement. Young people become engaged between the ages of 14 and 16 for males and 12–14 for females; they marry two or three years after their engagement. The matchmaker negotiates the wedding date, the dowry that the girl will bring (in clothing and other goods), and the amount of money expected to be paid by the boy's family. On the wedding day, the boy's family invites ten or twelve unmarried boys and girls (equal numbers) to carry the gifts of pork, wine, rice, etc., to the girl's house where the girl's family cooks a meal. After the meal the girl is taken by the young friends of the bridegroom to his home. The bride walks covered by a paper umbrella believed to protect her from evil spirits. When she arrives at the bridegroom's home she enters the middle room first and burns joss sticks to worship the ancestors, then she enters the bridal room. In

Power in Education

the evening they have a big feast which both families attend, and the bridegroom's family delivers the wedding money to the bride's parents. Then they drink wine and sing songs.

In determining the amount of money that the bridegroom's family agrees to give, three factors are considered: 1) the bride's physical beauty; 2) the girl's dowry in the form of clothing and jewelry; 3) local traditions. In the 1950s the average amount of money given by the bridegroom's family was 30 or 40 Chinese Yuan ($10 US dollars), in the 1970s 200–300 Yuan ($80–100), now it is 1000–3000 Yuan ($190–550 US dollars.). These amounts are extremely hard to obtain and this makes it difficult to arrange marriages. We have no information regarding the change in percentage of marriages that are arranged by parents or relatives, in comparison with marriages of choice by the two parties involved. There is no overt or formal sexual initiation for either boys or girls. Children may hear some jokes or something that makes them aware of sexuality. Parents feel embarrassed to discuss sex with their children. Sexual relations before marriage or outside of marriage are forbidden. The difficulties in addressing this issue reflect Chinese values. It is generally inappropriate to discuss such matters as sex in any form, but particularly sex related to family life.

Very few Miao youngsters manage to pursue their education above junior high school, and even fewer would ever go to the university. Thus, for most of them the crucial part of their life is marriage and the participation in the local clan as a new nuclear family. The Miao students who are fortunate to become eligible for college and who receive the necessary financial support from home, have to wait several years before they can select a spouse. The testimonies of university students who must postpone marriage (a difficult personal sacrifice) focus on the hardships of being away from home with meager financial resources and a great deal of pressure to achieve in competition with other students in college.

Testimonies from Central University for Nationalities (CUN) Students:

Text #1 by Wang Daqing (Male, born on August 9, 1971, in Guizhou)

My name is Wang Daqing. I am 23 years old. On August 9, 1971, I was born in a small village of Bijie county of Guizhou province. There are five children in my family. I am the second among them. When I began to learn things, I knew that the life was very hard in the village. All the people in the village, generation after generation, have made their living by growing crops on the poor and barren land. It is true that they were never able to eat enough and to wear fine clothing. Because of the poverty, many children in the village who were of the age for schooling could not go to school. They had to stay at home helping their parents, taking care of cows and horses. When I was ten years old, several officers [village leaders] in the village could no longer endure seeing that the young people in the village had to remain illiterate. Therefore they decided to establish a temporary primary school.

They turned a grain storage house in the village into a temporary classroom by putting two windows in the wall. In this way, together with twenty other children, I was able to study at the school. It is probably because our childhood wish was able to be realized that my fellow students and I were extremely excited and we studied very hard. In the winter, even though we were protected by worn-out and thin clothes, we never played the truant. When there was no firewood for heating the classroom, the instructor took us to the mountain in the back of the village to pick up the branches of the trees and build a fire to heat the classroom. In this study environment, the twenty other students and I studied very hard. No one dropped out from this hard environment. To tell you the truth, I had no idea that I would be like this today. Nor did I think that a poor peasant's son could be able to enter the highest national university for nationalities in Beijing.

Very quickly, I finished the third grade of the elementary school. In that year our class participated in the general examination [which is used in the county to evaluate the quality of instruction] held by the central school of the villages. All of us got excellent grades and I got first place. However, because our teacher had only an elementary school education, she was not competent to teach courses above the fourth grade. The students who wished to continue their study had to transfer to another school. Therefore I was transferred to a school in a Han nationality [the majority population] area which was five miles away from my home. Nevertheless, those of my fellow classmates with whom I had studied for three years had to say goodbye to school and stay home. Their parents were unable to pay the tuition fee even though it was only a few dollars. When I entered the school in the Han nationality area I was dressed in rags and very often I was looked down upon by people, and I was laughed at and neglected. However I did not care because in my mind there was only the encouragement given to me by my parents to study well. Perhaps it is because of the hardships in my life, although at that time I was only 13-years-old, that I was mature. Because of the differences in language I had to double my efforts to catch up with the other people in the school attended mostly by the Han nationality [who spoke Mandarin]. Therefore I worked even harder. Very often I would sit by the fireside with the weak light of a kerosene lamp and review my homework and do my assignments. As a familiar Chinese saying goes 'reward goes to those who work hard'.

After two years, I passed the examinations with excellent grades to enter a junior high school run by the government which was more than twenty miles away from my home. Ever since then my studies became even harder, and every week I had to make a trip more than twenty miles back home to carry provisions. Every Saturday after I took all my classes in the morning, I would run all the way home. By the time I reached home, it was already evening and the sun was already set. During the winter, because the daytime was short, I often had to walk in the darkness before I reached home. On Sundays, my mother would prepare for me more than twelve lbs. [1lb. = 0.9] jin of corn and twelve lbs. of potatoes. She would then see me off at the entrance of the village looking at my skinny figure carrying the bamboo basket and climbing over the mountain. Each time when we said good-bye my mother would cry and so would I. Sometimes my mother would insist on carrying the provisions and would walk with me for several miles over the mountain.

There were two ways to get from my home to the school. There was the walking route and there was a public bus. However, during my three years of junior high study, no matter how the wind blew or how hard it rained, I walked all the time along the rugged mountain path. It was not because I didn't want take the bus. It was because there was not one single penny in my pocket. Therefore all I could do was look at the passing bus and sigh. Because of these hardships and sad days, I made up my mind that I would enter vocational school so that I would be able to get rid of the poverty and share the worries of my family. In my own words at that time, 'I would make the journey that my feet made over the rugged mountain path worthwhile and I would reward my shoulder which was heavily hurt by the bamboo basket for those three years.' Most of all I would live up to the expectations of my parents who, in order to afford my study, worked very hard from dawn to dusk all year round bent over the yellow earth. Because of this I very often got up very early in the morning so the people could see me doing my morning studies all around the mountain path near the school. In the evening, I would review all my homework with the weak light of the setting sun. The three years of hard work enabled me to enter the only key high school [compared with the normal school, the key school recruits students from a broad pool of candidates, provides government financial support, quality teaching equipment and better teachers] in the district, although I was not able to enter the vocational school. I did not waste my time, and my family was proud of me because the school I entered was the one where many children of wealthy families could not enter even though they dreamed of doing so. This is because only those with real ability and learning and with high entrance examination grades could enter that school. However, after the moment of happiness and excitement, my family began to worry again because the school was located in the city, and there was a journey of about forty miles from my home to the school. To walk to school was no longer possible. What was even worse was that to carry provisions from home all by myself to school over such a long distance was by no means possible. The last worry was where would we get the money for my schooling? Later, my father said to me, 'Don't worry, my son, since you were admitted to the school, your daddy would feed the pigs to get money to pay for your schooling.'

I still remember the day when I left home. I still wore my peasant family clothes. I took with me only 50 Yuan (about 10 dollars), and went to the city. From then on there was an agreement that each month my family would send me about 20 Yuan (4 dollars) as my living expenses. However, very often this money did not reach me in time. When I was not able to support myself financially, I had to borrow money to travel back home to come up with some way out of my situation. Because I was short of money, I did not have enough clean clothes. I could wash all my clothes only when I returned home once a month. I still remember one time, at the end of the semester when final examinations were about to take place, but I still had not received the money from my home. At that time I did not have a single cent, but I could not give up my examinations to go home. So I had to borrow money from my classmates. One time I was not able to borrow any money from my classmates. So I took my meal box from the dining hall back to the dormitory, then I carried my books to the mountainside. When I was on the top of the mountain, I looked in the direction of my hometown and began to cry. Big tears came down my face. I shouted from the bottom of my heart: 'Mom and Dad, why didn't you send money to your son?' However, it was very clear to me that my family was not even able to buy coal to make the fire [fire needed to cook and keep warm]. Where would they get money for me? Nevertheless, even on the day of that hardship, I didn't give up my studies.

Very quickly another three years passed by. I graduated from senior high school. September 9, 1991, was an unforgettable day of my life. On that day an admission notice with yellow characters against a red background reached me in a small poor Miao minority village from Beijing, the capital. I had triumphed. The whole family shouted and jumped of joy. The whole village spread this good news. All of them were proud of the first university student that this poor village ever produced. Indeed, I was finally triumphant. I was successful. The past eleven years of hardship ended with a full stop. However, those past eleven years of hardship and sad experience will never be forgotten. I will remember this my whole life.

Now I study in the best university for nationalities — the Central University for Nationalities in Beijing. Although each semester my family can only give me about 100 Yuan (about 20 dollars), the school fellowship is sufficient for my meals. I will no longer suffer from starvation like the days in high school. Frankly speaking, all the money I used for my studies was obtained from loans. However, I feel more relaxed than before. This is because having entered the university, my future job will be guaranteed, and later I will be able to pay back in installments the money I borrowed.

This is my life which reflects the life of hardship of a poor peasant, son of the Miao people. Cases like mine are still prevalent among the Miao, as well as among other nationalities [in rural areas]. I am one of many who are living in a difficult situation. Therefore, I feel that I have a grave responsibility to do my best to help those people who are living in poor and backward conditions. At the University my major is minority languages. I am planning to be engaged in a job related to minorities to help those poor minorities get rid of poverty. Let them be rich as soon as possible.

Power in Education

> Text #2 by Long Jianhua (Male, Born on December 24, 1973, in Yunnan)

I was born to a peasant family in a remote mountain village in the northwest part of Yunnan province. There are seven people in my family, my parents, my four sisters and I. The fact that I could make progress to what I am now today, and that I am able to study very peacefully in the university has a lot to do with the hard work and support of my parents. What is worth mentioning is that I could not easily become successful without the help and support of friends and relatives. The village in which we live is a Miao village. I am proud of our community which offers a lot of mutual help and collective sharing of difficulties and hardships; this is one of the virtues of the excellent Miao nationality.

Each person has a path to follow; it may be smooth or rough. Of course, my path has not been smooth by any means; on the contrary, it has been full of hardships. Although my family was very poor when I started my elementary school, at that time relatively speaking, life was tolerable, because tuition fees and living expenses were very low. Before I realized it I finished my elementary school, and entered middle school. At that time I was very young [about 12-years-old], and to go to school I had to travel to a small town which is about fifteen miles away from my home. Of course, today with modern transportation a distance of fifteen miles is really nothing. But at that time, in an isolated mountain area it was a serious problem. It would take you at least five or six hours to cover that distance. You would have to climb over mountains and hills and walk with difficulty through a big forest. That was even harder for a little boy like me. Therefore, any time I returned to school from home, my mother would accompany me back. During my years of study in high school, my family was very poor, as I said, but my parents managed to save money and spent that money on me. They reluctantly bought clothes for themselves when their clothes were all worn-out. Every time that I returned home from school for the holidays, I saw my younger sisters dressed with old clothes with a lot of patches here and there. I felt very sad and I would hide to cry. For the first time I realized the hardships of human life, and how difficult it was for my parents to support me. I made up my mind to study hard and achieve well in order to return the love and kindness that my parents gave me.

I was admitted to senior high school after I graduated from junior high. At the same time my second younger sister also graduated from elementary school and entered a newly established junior high school. At that time my family was no longer able to finance the tuition fee for two children. My sister had no choice but to agree to quit school and return home to work on the land. At that moment I was really sad and felt terribly sorry for my sister. But what could I do? All I could do was to work very hard to be able to do things in the future for my parents, my sister and all my friends and relatives who had helped and supported me. Therefore, during senior high school, I always received excellent grades and was among the top students.

Now I have almost studied for ten years, and looking back down the road I took, I see it was full of splendor. Sometimes I fell down, but each time I got up again. I kept forging ahead and did not rest content with my achievements. I am the son of Miao minority people. In the final analysis, my path to adulthood is reflective of the development of the Miao people. There are thousands of other Miao people who are suffering in silence and struggling in silence just like me. I still remember Chairman Mao's remark: 'Each generation produces its own truly great men. However, it is in our age that we have enjoyed the real glory.' It is my belief that through these efforts and struggles they will have a bright future tomorrow.

Text #3 by Du Xiaobo (Female, born December 12, 1972, in Guizhou)

My name is Du Xiaobo. I am a Miao girl from the Guizhou province of China. In September 1991 I was admitted by the Central Institute for Nationalities in Beijing. My major is Miao language and literature.

In China, one of the characteristics of the Miao people is that they are spread all over the world, but wherever they go, they live together. Therefore the Miao people maintain their own language at different levels in different places. I spent my childhood in my grandmother's house. Like other kids in the same village, I studied from the first through the third grade in a private school run jointly by several villages. At that school our teacher used the Miao language for instruction, but he used a textbook in Chinese (Mandarin). We learned the knowledge from the Chinese textbooks and we could also read the Chinese characters. But we were not able to speak Mandarin very fluently. After the third year, I entered the primary school run by the county government [public school]. There were many students of Han nationality, and our instructors used Mandarin to teach. I mastered the Mandarin language very fast, because I was linguistically sensitive when I was small. After I graduated from elementary school, I entered the public middle school. My grades were always good. The Chinese Government adopted certain policies regarding minorities; one of them was to give minority students taking entrance examinations a special consideration [lower scores would not prevent them from entering], guaranteeing them college admission. That is how I managed to come to the Central Institute for Nationalities in Beijing.

During my years of high school I hardly spoke Miao because I was away from the environment and atmosphere in which I used my mother tongue. But after I entered the university, once again I chose my major in Miao language. I felt emotionally very much attached to my own nationality, and I also was determined to contribute my share to the development and progress of my own nationality.

China is a country which emphasizes equality and unity among nationalities. However, because of various historical reasons, the development of the nationalities is unequal. The development of each nationality is not isolated.

Power in Education

So, on the one hand, we should be aware of our own insufficiency; and on the other, we should learn from the other nationalities who have a rapid development. In the university, we not only learn Miao language, but also we learn classical Chinese, modern Chinese, philosophy and English. All students who are selected had excellent grades on the entrance examination, and therefore have a good command of Mandarin. Compared with the students of Han nationality, we know not only Mandarin, but also Miao. The courses which help us to receive and develop our cultural heritage and improve our proficiency in the Miao language are: The Division of Miao Dialects, Miao Language and Literature, The Grammar of Miao Language, The History of Miao Nationality. Except for the courses on Miao language and literature which are taught in Miao, all others are taught in Mandarin.

In China most Miao people live in the countryside in very isolated places that do not have transportation facilities. Therefore the economy and education are very backward there. So the Miao nationality development appears very slow as compared with that of other nationalities. I think that if the Miao nationality wants to develop itself, one of the most important things Miao people have to do is to develop their culture and education, to master knowledge, to broaden their vision, to understand the world, to improve the quality of their culture, and to change somewhat their old way of life, values and ideas. They should have more communication and ties with the other nationalities. At the beginning of elementary education, it is important that the instruction be bilingual and that we train more bilingual and bicultural Miao people. After my graduation, I would like to do some research on the Miao language, the history of the Miao nationality, and Miao folklore. Probably I will be working in a job related to minority languages. However, no matter what I do, I hope that I will be able to contribute my share to the development of my own nationality.

Text #4 by Tian Zhenmin (Male, born on July 7, 1972, in Guizhou)

I am from Guizhou province. My family lives in the small mountain town called Nayong located in Guizhou province. I came to Beijing to study the Miao language. There are eighteen people in my class, six of whom are girls. Most of my classmates can speak Miao language — with only a few exceptions. Most of the instructors are very well known and all of them are very concerned about us. They hope that some day in the future we will be able to contribute to our own nationality so that our living standards will catch up with the other nationalities. Therefore, we should work very hard along the lines and policies made by the government in order to develop the Miao nationality so that they can be liberated from their poverty and catch up to and surpass the other nationalities. We should work very hard because only in doing so will we be able to possess a position among the nationalities, and only in doing so will we be able to live up to the expectations of us, the Miao minority people.

There are four people in my family. My younger brother is a teacher of Mandarin. My mother and father are Miao. They speak Mandarin very well, but have never studied the Miao language. Therefore, they want me to study the Miao language in order to make some contributions to the Miao nationality. It takes thousands and thousands of years to change nature and mankind, therefore, treasure time very much. The working class people live in poverty and work day and night in order to survive. They work so hard that sometimes they forget even to eat. They are aware of the quick passage of time and realize that if they don't make good use of time, it will simply go by. In order to do things well we should treat in a positive manner the position our nationality occupies and we should value time. Today some young people still have some serious problems, one of which is the tendency to postpone until tomorrow what they should do today. When tomorrow comes they postpone it to yet another tomorrow. We all know that there are no end to tomorrows and we should make good use of today. Now that we are university students we should know that time never returns. We should treasure time. We should do well in whatever we do. We should work hard. Each step we take should leave behind full prints. We should lay a solid foundation for future careers and take responsibility for improving the Miao nationality.

In a word, time is man's life. Time means money. Although time can't be seen or touched we shouldn't let it go without making full use of it and we shouldn't waste any time.

Text #5 by Wang Zhongmin (Male, born June 10, 1973, in Yunnan)

I was born in June 1973 in a small town in Funing county, in the Wenshan autonomous region of Yunnan province. I was born into a peasant family. There are six people in my family, my parents, three sisters and me. My parents are typical peasants. From the time I was very young I was influenced by their kindhearted, simple and industrious spirits. I cultivated a good habit of bearing hardship and enduring hard work. I am the youngest one of four siblings in the family. Therefore, my parents are very fond of me and it is their wish to train me into someone who will be useful to our society. In our isolated mountain village, owing to various reasons, there are not many people who study. Even those who went to school gave up half-way. However, my parents were not afraid of all the difficulties they faced. No matter how hard their life would be, they would still try their best to send me to school. By the time I was 5-years-old, my parents sent me to a local school which was more than seven miles away from my home. The teaching conditions in the countryside, especially at that time, were rather poor. But worse was that my first language was the Miao language, because my first instructor was not from the Miao minority. In order to do well in my studies, I had to learn a new language. Fortunately, ever since I entered school, with the help of both my instructor and my parents, I very quickly learned Mandarin and made rapid progress in my studies. I went from being the last in the class to joining the top students of the class. In order to pursue further study, I carried a heavy bag and left my parents and my relatives to study in the central elementary school far from my home. From that time on I lived an independent life. Although I was very young, I tried my best not to disappoint my parents, instructors and relatives who were concerned about me.

In 1985, I passed the entrance examination held by the middle school for nationalities with excellent grades. That school was the only key middle school in our county. In this way I started my six-year study there. In the middle school I studied even harder than before so I could live up to the expectations of my parents, teachers and fellow villagers, and also have a bright future. In July 1991, I passed the national entrance examination for higher education and I entered the Central University for Nationalities in Beijing with good scores. In this way I realized my parents' wish for me to be a useful person in society and also I realized my dream of attending the university. These are some of my personal experiences and feelings from the primary school until now.

Today I am able to study in the quiet environment of the university. I owe all these achievements to the industrious training of my parents and teachers and, of course, to the concern shown by the Party and the Government. Frankly speaking, without the care of the Party and the Government, I have no idea where I would have been today. I spent my years of middle school in the school for nationalities. I would also spend my years of university life in the Institute for Nationalities. For many years, the Party and the Government have paid so much for me that I am unable to account clearly. Here I would first of all, like to thank the Party and the Government for their concern. Comrade Lei Feng remarked: 'A man's life is limited, but we should put it into the unlimited service of the people.' It is true that a man's life is limited, and man's ability is also limited just like mine. Our country is a developing country and our nationality is a relatively backward nationality. In order to change all this I am willing to put my limited life into the great cause of revitalizing our country and our nationality.

Text #6 by Yang Dexin (Male, born on August 10, 1972, in Guizhou)

My name is Yang Dexin. I am 20-years-old. I am from Shangshui village, Zhijin county of Guizhou province. My parents are peasants. From the time that I was very young I lived on a big mountain. When I entered elementary school, I had to walk about four or five miles across a small river to get from my home to school. In the summer there was heavy flooding of the river. Therefore, several times I had to take another route and the journey was made even longer. I still remember one time when I was crossing the river I was almost carried away by the water.

When I was the age for high school I had to go even farther to attend junior high school. Every morning after breakfast I had to spend all the time in school. By the time I returned home, it was already late afternoon. I attended senior high school in the county city. Although I didn't have to walk everyday, I was not able to avoid some hardship when I returned home. This is because in order to prepare half-semester provisions (food was not available or provided at the school), I had to carry these provisions to school all by myself, and I had to walk about fifteen miles before I took a bus. After getting off the bus I still had to walk a long way to get to the school. Only one who is educated and who has been civilized will be able to be free from ignorance, to be able to know himself, to know others, and to know the world. Ten or fifteen years in the future I believe that I will be able to contribute my share to the development of the economics and culture of the Miao nationality so that the Miao nationality will enjoy equal economic and cultural status in society.

Miao language and Miao literature are very helpful for me. Language can help people to communicate. As a university student of Miao nationality, I especially want to communicate with my fellow Miao people. To do so I have to be able to speak Miao language. The Miao language will be a great help in my future work. I grew up in the countryside. The first literature I learned was Miao literature. Fortunately I have a grandmother who told me many interesting stories in vivid Miao language and until now those stories influence me.

During my years of study, I felt the most difficulties I encountered were my years in senior high school. At the senior high school my study was very intensive. However I didn't have enough financial ability and I was unable to maintain good health. I was terribly poor in health. My happiest time is right now at the university. It is here I am able to study whatever I want to study and I will be able to give full play to my skills.

I would like to say a few words to my fellow Miao people in the United States. I hope you won't be unduly humble. You should have self-respect and dignity. You should be brave enough to identify yourselves in society and unite with the other nationalities to adjust to the new society. I hope you will someday come back to visit China and share your experiences with your fellow Miao people.

Text #7 by Xiong Qiang (Male, born September 1, 1972, in Yunnan)

I was born in a typical Miao village. When I reached the age to go to school I could not go like the other kids. It was not because my family could not pay tuition, but because my village was too isolated. Nobody taught there. This did not permit me to go to school until I was ten years old. At that time I loved books — I was crazy about books. All the time I finish my homework before the deadline. That did not last because the teacher was transferred to another place [without being replaced]. Therefore I had to move to my uncle's house and attend school elsewhere. At that time I came to value my schooling so much that I studied even harder than before. I was sent to fifth grade directly from third grade, and as a consequence I was not as well prepared as the other students. After a year of hard work I regained full confidence and I was admitted to the County Junior High School for Nationalities.

During my study in that school I never wasted a second. I wanted to change the situation at home. How could I forget my parents working hard in the fields, facing the earth, and bending their backs. For three years I studied in that school. I was the class leader and many times received awards for academic excellence and leadership.

During those three years I made significant progress but the results were not as good as I expected. Why? Because I wanted to attend a technical secondary school from which I could graduate in two years. I wanted this not to make my life more comfortable, but to help my parents who worked so hard to get money and support me. I was admitted to a junior high school, and after attending for three years I had no idea of what my future would be. At that time I was uncertain about being admitted and going to senior high school. If you go to senior high, you cannot find a job. You may continue your academic career by attending the university, but you don't know if you can be admitted to the university. After struggling with this dilemma, I made up my mind to spend a year at home studying and then apply again to the technical school.

After a year, bad news came. I faced another problem — the government does not allow a person admitted to senior high school, but who did not attend, to be admitted in the technical school. This news came to me as a thunderstorm that made me cry. I thought that a peasant's son had no alternative but to work in the fields. I finally decided to attend senior high school, encouraged by my parents. At that time the Government reformed the admission policy which separates applicants into social sciences and natural sciences. That benefitted me because I am good in literature but not in science. I, thus, had the chance to enter the Central University for Nationalities. I want to do some practical things to help the Miao in the future.

Testimonies from the Guizhou Institute for Nationalities (GIN) Students Addressed to the Hmong:

Text #8 by Tao Xiaoping (Male, born April 3, 1964, in Sichuan)

I am a youth of Miao nationality from Sichuan province. My name is Tao Xiaoping (my Miao name is Dub Tiaj). I am now studying at the Institute for Nationalities in Guizhou province. Today during my stay with the professor who is from your country, I wrote this letter and I asked this professor to take it to you. We are all fellow people. I would like to extend to you my best wishes for all my fellow Miao people in the United States. I hope that you live a good life and I wish you happiness in your family and hope all of your wishes are realized.

My family is in Yibin County of Sichuan province. There are many Miao people there. If you ever have the opportunity to come to China, please visit us as a guest of our village. We would surely warmly welcome you.

Best wishes,
Tao Xiaoping
One of the Miao people from Sichuan Province
October 31, 1992

Text #9 by Yang Li (Female, born on January 31, 1974, in Guizhou)

Hello to you all! My name is Yang Li. My family is in the well-known town of wax-dying, Anshun city of Guizhou province. I am now studying at the Guizhou Institute for Nationalities. We have a very good physical environment with green mountains and clean waters. All the people here are simple and kind.

There are various kinds of unique local customs and traditions here. There are buildings of different styles. There are beautiful songs for pipes and wind instruments. There are beautiful dances and the charming art of wax-dying (batiking). There are also many popular legends which have been passed down year by year, from generation to generation. The natural sights here are extremely beautiful. There is the grand Huang Guo Shu waterfall, the magnificent dragon paradise, and wonderful workmanship excelling in natural stone villages, as well as many other sightseeing places of national customs and traditions. I would like to introduce you to everything in great detail. That is why in addition to my study of the Miao language, I also study English very diligently. Hopefully one day in the future you can come here and I will be able to serve as your guide.

There are also rich natural resources and exquisite traditional arts and crafts here. Nevertheless, this place is isolated because transportation facilities are not very advanced. At one time it was poor and backward, but now there is more development. We need to be understood by the outside world, and also we want to understand the outside world, especially you, our fellow Miao people. I think I still need to learn many new things. Hopefully one day in the future I will be able to do something for the intercourse and interchange with the outside world. You are welcome to visit our city. We are looking forward to that day.

Yang Li
Guizhou Institute for Nationalities
October 31, 1992

Text #10 by Xiong Jinliang (Male, born on August 15, 1974, in Yunnan)

Hello to you! My name is Xiong Jinliang. My family is in Wenshan county of Yunnan province. I am a student at the Guizhou Institute for Nationalities. My major is Miao language. In addition, I also study English. In my country, China, there are basically three dialects of Miao. One is the dialect used in Sichuan, Guizhou and Yunnan provinces. The second is the dialect used in Eastern

Power in Education

Guizhou. The third dialect is used in Western Hunan. We are studying the dialects used in Sichuan, Guizhou, and Yunnan provinces and eastern Guizhou. I want to study Miao language so that in the future, when I return to my hometown, I will be able to pass on my knowledge to my fellow Miao people there. I also want to improve our national level of science and culture.

Here there are many unique petrified forests. We have a tourist area, Lu Nan stone forest. There are unique national customs and traditions, national art, buildings with national styles and national music instruments. The climate here is very suitable and good. It is good for growing various kinds of crops. However, our level of science and culture is still very low. To grow crops scientifically is still very rare. Nevertheless, our place has a lot of things to show for itself. We welcome you to visit our place. Thank you.

Xiong Jinliang
A student in the department of Minority Languages of Guizhou Institute for Nationalities.
October 31, 1992.

Text #11 by Wang Bingzhong (Male, born on April 20, 1973, in Guizhou)

My name is Wang Bingzhong. My family lives in the Longli county of Guizhou province. I am a student at the Guizhou Institute for Nationalities. As a member of the Miao nationality, I feel very sad about our Miao culture. I have heard that many American young people have lost their own national cultures. This is very frustrating.

The Miao nationality has a long history, from the myth in which Pan Gu created the universe and in which the Fu Yi sisters gave birth to humankind until now, the Miao nationality has left behind deep footprints. However, today the Miao culture has gradually disappeared and Miao youth has a strong sense of inferiority about their own culture. Many beautiful cultures of Miao nationality are now in imminent danger. All of this makes me feel that we should vigorously develop Miao culture. I also hope that my fellow Miao people in the United States will help encourage and develop our national culture and help it remain always young.

Wang Bingzhong
Guizhou Institute for Nationalities

Text #12 by Yang Yuxi (Male, born on October 20, 1973, in Guizhou)

My name is Yang Yuxi. I am very happy to have the chance to study at the university. My goal is to develop the national economy, especially the economy of minorities. I think I will be able to do this because there are rich mineral and water resources here in China. We have our unique and beautiful things, such as our national crafts. Our dance is also one of our rich resources. We need people of ability and knowledge to come here to help us develop these resources. That is why I am so confident about this.

Now our country is in a period of transformation and is opening up to the Western influences. Foreign businessmen should not worry about the business climate here. We welcome you to come here to invest.

Yang Yuxi
Guizhou Institute for Nationalities
October 31, 1992

Text #13 by Li Maohong (Male, born on April 15, 1972, in Yunnan)

Hello to you! I am the son of Miao nationality of Chahua village, Qiubei county, Wenshan autonomous region, Yunnan province, China. I am very much interested in the local customs and traditions of the Miao nationality. This is because from the time I was young I was brought up in this ancient cradle, and the place where I lived is as beautiful as a fairyland and full of rhythmical bird songs and guitar songs, like songs from streams and all these nourished the soul of nationality. It is this that motivated me to major in minority language. However, the development of local customs and traditions of this nationality is still not developed enough. Whoever is able to develop this culture to its full potential will become one of the richest people in the world.

Second, the place where Miao people live has rich natural resources which are waiting to be developed. Therefore I wish that you could come to China to celebrate our new year of the Miao nationality together, and hope that we can keep in touch. I would like to use this chance to ask about the American singer of the Miao nationality named Li Zheng Fang. Some time ago she wrote a letter to China to inquire about her family history. When I learned this, I had already misplaced her address. I would hope that you Miao fellow people could help me to track her down and give her my best regards. I wonder whether she could write to me when she learns about this letter.

I have to stop here, but I would keep corresponding with you. My best wishes to my fellow Miao people in the United States. I wish you good health and that all your wishes be realized.

Li Maohong
Class of 1991 Minority Department
Guizhou Institute for Nationalities

Text #14 by Tao Wencen (Male, born on May 5, 1974, in Yunnan)

Hello to you! You ((Hmong brothers in the United States) have been working hard. Although New Year has not come yet, I would on behalf of the Miao

Power in Education

people in China wish you a happy new year and wish you the greatest success in the new year! I am from Wenshan county, Wenshan autonomous region of Yunnan province, from the village of Huaqiao. I am 18-years-old. In September 1991, I came to study at the Guizhou Institute for Nationalities. I am a son of Miao nationality. I love my nationality very much, so after I came here, I chose to major in Miao language and literature. I would surely grasp all the knowledge in order to explore our culture, to carry out our traditional culture. In the end, I hope that you would come to visit us in Huaqiao village of Wenshan county. Thanks.

Tao Wencen
Class of 1991
Guizhou Institute for Nationalities
Huaqiao Village
Wenshan County, Wenshan Autonomous Region
Yunnan Province, China

Context for Students' Testimonies

All fourteen students originally came from rural areas in Guizhou, Yunnan and Sichuan provinces. Their parents are peasants and come from generations of peasants, although along with agricultural work some parents are teachers, government officials, and village heads. All families have a very low annual income. The students in this study belong to a generation that is in rapid transition from the New China established by Mao Zedong in 1949, and implemented in the following thirty years with a number of accommodations to a new economic philosophy of global competition and for equality and legitimacy for all ethnic groups or nationalities. Students are venturing into a world their parents never imagined; furthermore, students see themselves as central players in the creation of a new China with international significance and modern technology. In this context, any sacrifice is worthwhile if an academic degree and university training can empower students to become effective players in making China the most powerful and modern country of the world. There are important differences in the quality of self-expression and the articulation of the cultural values behind academic success. Undoubtedly, some of the students have discussed these matters many times and tend to give answers that reflect some uniformity resulting from rehearsal ('the party line').

The central themes discussed by students are: 1) hardship suffered by all family members (hunger, inadequate clothing); 2) a history of child labor and a life with adult-like responsibilities; 3) illiteracy and ignorance of villagers; 4) deprivation of food, rest and money to satisfy daily basic needs during life as students. The question is why anyone would want to leave his village and the comfort of family life to struggle far away in an isolated life as high school and college student? Why would a village boy want to leave his village life to work with people who speak a different language and ridicule him or see him as handicapped or stupid? Or why would his parents go along with that idea? The answer lies in the ultimate rewards expected to result from a university education: a permanent job with high pay (in comparison to any jobs one can find in a village) and the prestige associated with college education. Mr. Wang Daqing, for example, (see Text #1) does not mind those degradation incidents, because he is committed to succeed, encouraged by his parents, and motivated by the sacrifices they were making on his behalf. He recognized consciously that he had the judgment of an adult. To go to the Han school he had to walk twenty miles each way, often in the dark, and pack and carry to school about twenty-four lbs. of corn and potatoes several times a month.

The long-term goals of secure employment with the government and the immediate satisfaction of being admired and respected in their villages and receiving the special attention and affection of parents and siblings made life tolerable for students. There must have been very difficult, even desperate, moments for students. Mr. Wang Daqing, for example, not having money to buy food, and unable to borrow money from his peers, takes his meal box from the dining hall back to the dormitory, walks to the mountainside, and shouts in tears: 'Mom and Dad, why didn't you send money to your son?'

One of the contentions of this study is that postponed gratification and rewards or acceptance of satisfactions that are not tangible, such as the satisfaction of honoring one's parents or of preparing for the future, are not possible without a very long and intensive socialization that prepares young people for those sacrifices. What is the nature of this preparation? What is the role of Confucian philosophy, Chinese culture, Miao traditions and parental influence in preparing certain people to make painful sacrifices at a very young age? As we continued our research and followed up interviews with questionnaires (see Chapter 5) we began to answer some of these questions. One of the clues is in the above narrative of Mr. Wang Daqing:

> September 9, 1991 was an unforgettable day of my life. On that day an admission notice with yellow characters against a red background reached me in a small poor Miao minority village from Beijing, the capital. I triumphed. The whole family shouted and jumped of joy. The whole village spread this good news. All of them were proud of the first university student that this poor village ever produced. Indeed, I was finally triumphant.

At times with different words and emphases, certainly all students have expressed similar feelings that they are role models for success in academia. Honoring his parents was ultimately the best reward for his troubles. It seems that there is a hierarchy of values manifested in the way he structures his emotional experiences and views. At the top of the hierarchy is the value of being a responsible son, that is, filial piety and dedication to his family. This responsibility meant doing the very best he can in his academic life at any cost, even sacrificing every possible comfort and being deprived of food and sleep. Other values seem to be subordinated to that of responsibility; for example, the value of fortitude to tolerate anxiety and pain, to accept feelings of alienation and separation (as a poor Miao peasant boy away from home). Peasants, especially Miao peasants, are looked down upon by the Han people. The source of students' achievement motivation is drawn from their commitment to be good sons and daughters and thus honor their families. The feeling of belonging to their families, villages and communities, gives them the courage to put up with the laughing and disdain of other students.

Some students contrast their present comfortable situation with their tough lives as children forced to travel far from home, often climbing dangerous mountains and crossing forests. This recognition of hardships is at times expressed with an undertone of self-pity. They express the pain they felt seeing the misery of their families who were forced to sacrifice basic necessities in order to pay for their school and their food. The most logical decision students could make was to study hard so they could pay back their families. Thus, the main reason to achieve in school was to return to their parents the love and kindness received from them. At times students had to witness their own sisters quitting high school in order for their parents to afford to keep supporting their sons in college. The strong feeling of belonging to their families and the acceptance of a deep commitment to repay all the sacrifices that their academic careers had cost them is linked together with the obligation to love and honor their families via academic success; after all, thousands and thousands of other Miao people continued to suffer in silence and never had the chance to further their education and help their own people!

There are only two females, Du Xiaobo and Yang Li, in the sample chosen because there were very few women among the Miao university students. Du Xiaobo is a self-confident young woman who focused her efforts on studying the Miao language and literature in order to understand better her own cultural heritage. She is aware of the problems of language loss and language maintenance, and also of language change in cultural contact with dominant groups. She was well-groomed and displayed a composure that would give her a higher status. She attended a bilingual inter-village private elementary school for the first three grades and learned both Miao and Mandarin. She then moved to a public school run by the county government where she first came into contact with Han students. She is proud of her good grades and her skill in the Mandarin language. Her attachment to her ethnic group and to feminism seemed to be equally strong. Consequently she was vocal about her commitment to help the Miao people.

Both women are strong supporters of equity issues and China's multinational character, and both take subjects in school that enhance these perspectives: Miao literature, classical Chinese language, modern Chinese philosophy, English and social sciences. Other subjects also permit them to perform well in school and master the Mandarin language. In their view, there is a clear connection between the pursuit of an academic career with a high scholarly achievement and the fulfillment of ethnic and feminist goals. Intellectual leadership in education is a value subordinate to the service of the Miao people.

Ms. Yang Li, from the Guizhou Institute for Nationalities, is a very attractive and assertive young woman, who speaks English fluently and has a clear influence on her male peers. She tells her fellow Miao (Hmong) from America that Guizhou is a beautiful and healthy place and that the Miao people, although simple and kind, have a long history and an extraordinary folklore: songs, dances, wax dying, embroidery, etc., and world famous scenery, such as the Huang Guo Shu waterfalls. She sees the need for linking China with the outside world and hopes to visit America.

For these two women, academic success is not only a means to help the Miao and honor their parents, it is also a feminist victory in a country where women have traditionally held a very low status. Even younger male siblings are allowed to physically punish their sisters when they refuse to obey. Serving the Miao for them means to bring equity for women. Conducting research on Miao folklore is a means of grasping one's own roots and claiming a place in the hierarchy of Miao power and status. Controlling the Mandarin and Miao languages both orally and in writing is the means to obtain power in academia, a world run by males. Clearly, the Central University of Nationalities in Beijing and the Guizhou Institute for Nationalities are viewed by students as political institutions where knowledge and power go together, and the development of intellectual leadership is equivalent to reaching high political power.

There is a significant amount of repetitiveness in the testimonies of the students. The reason is that professors and students spoke a great deal with each other before writing their testimonies, and they also have been inculcated in certain answers that are politically safe. While we were in China, if one of the Miao professors or students departed from the previously approved schedule, security and intelligence officers who keep an eye on foreigners twenty-four hours a day would seem clearly upset, and often would prevent those professors and students from seeing us. When we changed our schedules and decided to visit some classrooms, the same problem appeared, and we were kindly reminded to submit our schedules to them in advance so that the appropriate authorities could prepare activities for us. There is, however, evidence of spontaneous and deeply felt sentiments in the numerous letters sent to us from China by students and their professors. In these letters there is a substantial repetition of themes and sentences. In the next chapter we will discuss in detail some of the more specific information about the university setting and the backgrounds of students. Suffice it to say at this point that practically all of the students repeated many times their gratitude to the government for giving them a chance for higher education, and their commitment to help their country by succeeding in school. The statements by Tian Zhenmin are perhaps the most emphatic. He implies that the underdevelopment of the Miao (so poor and isolated) requires national support and that university graduates are responsible for bringing solutions to the economic and technical problems of the rural Miao villages: 'We should work very hard along the lines and policies made by the government in order to develop the Miao nationality so that they can be liberated from their poverty.' This is a strong political statement that no one else articulated so clearly and forcefully. The unique nuance in this testimony is that Mr. Tian Zhenmin feels some responsibility to the Chinese government, and one that cannot wait until tomorrow. His logical conclusion is that Miao university students should lay a solid foundation for future careers and take responsibility for improving the Miao nationality. The question is whether Mr. Tian Zhenmin is making a political statement to the researchers knowing that it will be noticed by others (peers and professors), or is he stating a deeply felt conviction that he has internalized and acts upon daily? Perhaps in his mind and that of other students there is no way to differentiate between political statements and personal feelings related to China and the Miao nation. There is no freedom to disagree with political positions, and the risks and price for not accepting political truths inculcated in schools and universities are extremely high. Look, for example, at statements linking academic achievement to the sacrifices of the family and to government support, as in the testimony of Mr. Wang Zhongmin (text #5).

Many of the testimonies have nuances that remind us of the work of Paulo Freire (1973, 1993). They express a sense of urgency to emancipate the Miao people by educating them and helping them to get rid of their ignorance. Wang Zhongmin, who moved rapidly from the bottom to the top of his class, feels this way, but he equates modern technology with education. He represents a highly pragmatic person who understand politics and rhetoric. Whether he understands the relationship between literacy (both in its traditional sense of having skills to read and write, as well as in its broader sense of learning how to function in given historical and political settings) and equity is not clear from his testimony. But he definitely knows how to act with political wisdom in the university. He thanks the Communist Party and the Chinese Government for helping him become a productive citizen, and thus to enable him to discharge his most important responsibility of honoring his parents, his ethnic group and the entire nation. He goes on to publicly state: 'Here I would, first of all, like to thank the Party and the Government for their concern.' Similar statements are made by other students.

It is remarkable how important oral language (and to some extent written language) becomes in the political and intellectual development of young Miao university students. Communication with other fellow Miao students and other people is associated with political debates, public speeches, Communist Party celebrations, recognition ceremonies, political speeches associated with lobbying efforts to attract resources from the central government, and efforts to modernize and democratize China. Consequently, the appropriate use of language and the training to speak in public are viewed as most desirable and highly instrumental in obtaining political and academic goals. In other words, if Miao people just learned how to speak well and in public, much of their poverty would be eliminated because they would become efficient lobbyists with the central government presumed to have enormous resources. That feeling is expressed by all students, but most eloquently by Yang Dexin, originally from Guizhou but now a student in Beijing. Language skills are viewed as a weapon against poverty — the kind of poverty that at home caused him to be in bad health. In the minds of the Miao students, language is one of the key instruments of empowerment, both in the political Freirean sense of knowing 'the word and the world' in order to participate meaningfully in societal institutions, as well as in the Confucian way of acquiring virtue and wisdom. This relationship between language and empowerment is a driving force in the students' engagement to acquire a sophisticated knowledge of Mandarin, and in participating in political gatherings to represent the needs of the Miao. The importance of this relationship is particularly significant for students who felt totally isolated in their village life, such as Mr. Xiong Qiang (see Text #7). He just could not forget his parents scratching a miserable existence from the fields, their backs bent over until they could no longer move. Is it possible that one of the hidden reasons why Miao university students are committed to academic achievement is to avoid the hard labor in the fields and the isolated existence of their families? Indeed, academia has been the ticket to a better life out of the misery of agricultural fields for many immigrants in the United States. The strongest argument given by migrant workers to stay in the university was discovered by them while picking cotton in the south during the summer and feeling the pain of their bleeding finger tips and the unbearable weight of the noon sun over their heads and backs. Any sacrifice to obtain college graduation seemed so small!

We do not want to exclude other motives for academic success, such as a genuine love for intellectual work, for the world of ideas and the addiction to read and learn new things. Mr. Xiong is explicit about his need to read all the time since early childhood; he said he was crazy about reading and never wasted a second. Yet the image of his parents facing the earth bent over the fields was a vivid one that never abandoned him.

Other testimonies, especially those by the students from Guizhou, express their curiosity about other Miao people around the world, especially those in the United States. This may have been the result of much of our conversation during our visit to the Guizhou Institute for Nationalities. Imbedded in this curiosity is the hope that more fellow Miao living in the United States may want to acknowledge their Chinese roots (as in fact has happened — Hmong Americans have visited the Institute) and help bring the Miao into modern technology. University students are familiar with some American films and music. They think that the prosperity and powerful modern technology displayed in the American films could be obtained if Americans decided to invest in their province. Some of the students were talking about ambitious investment plans to renovate the infrastructure of China's transportation system, housing and city life. In this context, their description of personal vicissitudes and a personal introduction goes well with their expression of solidarity of all Miao around the world. The Miao students from Guizhou wanted to know as much as possible about the Hmong elsewhere, their lifestyles, their awareness of the Miao people in China, the treatment they received from the Americans, their jobs, the schooling of their children, the languages they spoke, and every detail about their lives. In an expression of traditional Chinese hospitality the Guizhou students invite Hmong Americans to visit China. The thought that some Hmong Americans would ever forget their cultural roots to the Miao people makes Mr. Li Maohong (#13) feel sad. Mr. Yang Yuxi (#12) goes a step further, he invites Hmong Americans to join him in his ambitious plans to develop an international economic base for the Miao. His goal is to make the Miao self-sufficient by using effectively its natural mineral and water resources, and establishing close economic relationships with Western businesses. So he invites Hmong and other Americans to invest in China.

In brief, common to all the above testimonies is the enthusiastic affiliation with their ethnic group, a profound sense of belonging, and the appreciation of Miao language and culture. Their obvious pride is also related to their surroundings and beautiful natural environment.

References

FREIRE, P. (1973) *Pedagogy of the Oppressed*, New York, NY: Seabury.
FREIRE, P. (1993) *Pedagogia da Esperança: Um Reencontro com a Pedagogia do Oprimido*, Sâo Paulo, Brazil: Editora Paz e Terra, SA.
PAN, D. (1993) 'The history and culture of the Miao nationality in China', unpublished manuscript, Guiyang, China, Guizhou Institute for Nationalities.
WU, D. (1993) 'Village life of the Miao people in China', unpublished manuscript, Beijing, China, Central University for Nationalities.

Plate 1: Miao students, professors and Yali Zou in the Guizhou Institute for Nationalities. November 1, 1992.

Plate 2: Henry Trueba with Chinese students at the Great Wall. October 24, 1992.

Plate 3: Pupils of an elementary school on a field trip to the Great Wall. October 24, 1992. Photograph by Henry Trueba.

Plate 4: A Miao girl selling Miao clothing in Guizhou Province. November 2, 1992.

Plate 5: Student dormitory of Guizhou Institute for Nationalities. November 1, 1992.

Plate 6: Henry Trueba with the professors of the history department of the Central University for Nationalities, Yan Yingjun, Gu Jiehua and Huang Xiuyi. October 20, 1992.

Plate 7: Yali Zou with two anthropologists, Lin Yaohua and Chen Yongling, in the Central University for Nationalities in Beijing. October 19, 1992.

Plate 8: Henry Trueba and Yali Zou with the President of the Guizhou Institute for Nationalities, Mr. Wu Zhiguo in front of the administration building of the Guizhou Institute for Nationalities. October 31, 1992.

Chapter 5

Miao Students' Experience at the University

Students have described in their own words the painful village and school experiences that prepared them to face the challenges of rigorous university life. We had also discussed earlier the rationale for the selection of Beijing and Guizhou and key sites to gather data for the identification of groups of students and professors who provided us with the necessary information on the social, cultural, political and economic history of the Miao in China. This chapter is focused primarily on the specific data on the Miao students' life in the university, obtained through interviews and questionnaires from fourteen students, seven from the Central University for Nationalities in Beijing, and seven from the Guizhou Institute for Nationalities, in Guiyang. These students were interviewed in groups and individually, and they were chosen to write a brief statement on their view of education, their ethnic background and their career aspirations.

Their statements are used here for an in-depth analysis of the central themes, values and positions that help us understand their achievement motivation, their adaptive strategies to university and city demands, and their role as educational leaders for their ethnic communities. Therefore, the chapter is divided into four major sections: 1) students' general characteristics and their home/family backgrounds; 2) categories for data collection, that is, central themes and statements of values; 3) text analysis; 4) basic evidence demanding theoretical explanations.

As we mentioned earlier in the context of the theoretical perspectives that frame this study, the early socialization process determines the role of ethnic identification in educational achievement. The fact that these Miao students left their small and poor villages to move on to education above the third grade, and gradually to junior and senior high school, until they became part of the Chinese elite that obtain a university education is not an accident; it has to do with these students' early years of training. The *Beijing Review* (Editorial Staff 1991) indicates that by the turn of the twentieth century mainland China had established only three universities: Tianjin University (1895); Shanghai Jiaotong University and Xian Jiaotong University (1896); and Beijing University (1898). Qinghua University was established in 1911. By the time of the founding of New China in 1949, there were 205 universities with 116,000 students and 16,000 faculty. Most of the universities were small. Today, China has 1075 institutions of higher education with 390,000 teachers (including over 100,000 professors and associate professors) with a total enrollment of 2.06 million students, of which only 113,000 are graduate students. The access to higher education in the last twenty-five years is marked by an increase in the student population from 856,000 (in 1978) to 2.06 million today. The number of institutions doubled and the increase in graduate students was also dramatic during the same period — from 11,000 to 113,000.

Unfortunately, we do not have detailed and reliable information about the rates of increase of the minority student population in higher education. From what the students and teachers we interviewed said, the number of Miao people ever making it to the university was negligible. Other students who belonged to upper economic ethnic groups, particularly those closer to the Eastern coast, had earlier access to university training. Consequently, indeed, in order to understand the adaptive strategies of Miao students to a new, democratic and technologically modern China, one needs to understand the process of early socialization in the rural villages of Guizhou and Yunnan, their profound commitment and deeply felt loyalty to their ethnic group and families, their appreciation of the sacrifices made by their parents to provide them with an education, the liberating role of literacy and the acquisition of knowledge, and the overall redefinition of the self resulting from higher education. The themes that will appear and reappear in their conversations and writings are the sacrifices made by the family members and the students in order that they succeed at a major university.

It will be important to identify the general categories of behaviors present in studies of ethnic identity and academic achievement. The actual texts from each of the students in the two groups (seven students from Beijing, and seven from Guizhou) will be presented, and finally the major configurations resulting in types of behavior identified will be displayed. The more detailed analysis of the data configurations, in contrast with other studies, is presented in the next chapter.

Selected Students' Characteristics

While the interaction with all of the students (many of whom did not submit written materials) provided the researchers with some insights about the rationale for pursuing a university career, those students who took the time to write their feelings and describe their home cultural environment, provided us with the most useful material. These fourteen students had a mean age of twenty, and were predominantly male (twelve out of fourteen). They all came from the provinces of Guizhou, Yunnan and Sichuan. Their general characteristics are found in Table 4.

Of the seven students from the Central University for Nationalities in

Table 4: Miao Students in Study

Text	Name	Birthdate	Age[1]	Sex	Province	County	Family Village	Rank/# Siblings	Parents' Education in Years ♂ ♀	Parents' Occupations ♂ ♀	Annual Family Income[2]
A. Beijing Central University for Nationalities											
1	Wang Daqing	08.09.71	21	M	Guizhou	Bijie	Yuqun	2/5	7 0	Peasants	90
2	Long Jianhua	12.24.73	18	M	Yunnan	Lufeng	Tianjingshan	1/5	3 3	Peasants	70
3	Du Xiaobo	12.12.72	18	F	Guizhou	Xiuwen	—	6/6	— —	Peasants	30
4	Tian Zhenmin	07.07.72	20	M	Guizhou	Nayong	Tianba	1/2	7 —	Teacher Peasant	700
5	Wang Zhongmin	06.10.73	19	M	Yunnan	Funing	Xiaoking	4/4	5 —	Peasants	30
6	Yang Dexin	08.10.72	20	M	Guizhou	Zhijin	Shangshui	1/4	3 —	Peasants	70
7	Xiong Qiang	09.01.72	20	M	Yunnan	Weixin	—	4/5	8 —	Peasants	80
B. Guizhou Institute for Nationalities											
8	Tao Xiaoping	04.03.64	28	M	Sichuan	Yibin	Caoying	1/5	7 7	Peasants	1200
9	Yang Li	01.31.74	18	F	Guizhou	Anshun	—	1/2	16 6	Government Official Factory Worker	950
10	Xiong Jinliang	08.15.74	18	M	Yunnan	Wenshan	Wulichong	1/6	— —	Peasants	600
11	Wang Bingzhong	04.20.73	19	M	Guizhou	Longli	Bimengchangba	4/4	— —	Peasants	70
12	Yang Yuxi	10.04.72	20	M	Guizhou	Longli	Basheng	5/7	7 —	Factory Worker Peasant	320
13	Li Maohong	04.15.72	20	M	Yunnan	Qiubei	Chahua	4/4	9 —	Peasants	700
14	Tao Wencen	05.05.74	18	M	Yunnan	Wenshan	Huaqiao	5/6	12 6	Village Leader[3] Peasant	900

[1] Age at time of interview in October, 1992
[2] Annual Family Income in US dollars
[3] Congress Representative

Beijing, four were from Guizhou and three from Yunnan. From those attending the Guizhou Institute for Nationalities, one was from Sichuan, three from Guizhou and three from Yunnan. However, their backgrounds and social, economic and educational levels were about the same. All came from small villages, from peasant families with very few economic resources, and all had to search for special support from the Government to finance their undergraduate and graduate work. All students were at least bilingual in Miao and Mandarin, and some knew a little bit of English or other languages.

The average annual income of the students' families is $415. However, one of the families, the Tao Wencen family whose head is the village leader, alone earns $900, the third highest income among the families. Without counting this family, the average income goes down to $285 per year. In their conversations and in their responses the students alluded continuously to their concern over having enough food to eat. The family income is correlated with the parents occupations. Most of them are peasants, with the exception of Tian Zhenmin's father who is a teacher; however he earns less than other peasant families (for example, Mr. Tao Xiaoping's family who earns $1200) and less than the government officials and the village leader. The average size of the household is 7.7 persons per household (including parents and extended family members living at home). The family of Xiong Qiang has an annual per capita income of $8 per family member; the family of Wang Zhongmin $4.28 per year, and the family of Du Xiaobo a per capita income of $3.75.

These students come from eleven different villages, twelve different counties, and from three different provinces: Guizhou (7), Yunnan (6), and Sichuan (1). Their personal backgrounds and social classes are also different in important ways. As we will see below in their statements about their families and villages, one can tell the types of expectations they have from home and the sacrifices they are forced to make to complete their degrees.

In general, from our conversations with them, they all seemed very happy and enthusiastic about being students in the university and deeply committed to their intellectual work. Also, all of them were committed members of the Miao group of students across the campus (regardless of their fields of study). Many of the social and recreational activities (playing, eating, trips to town, picnics, economic ventures, etc.) were carried out in the company of their Miao peers. Also many of their academic activities (most of the classes and field-based activities) permitted them to keep a close working relationship with other Miao students.

Their lives as students were subject to very modest financial support and very rigid schedules. Every morning, loud music broadcast across campus via loudspeakers would wake them up exactly at 6:00 a.m. and all students were expected to go outside for calisthenics or other exercise (about half an hour). By seven o'clock all the students had washed up and were on their way to the kitchen or cafeteria to pick up their ration of food and drinks. Between 7:30 and 8:00 students began to go to their classrooms. There were between six and eight students per room in the dormitories, and they used several layers of bunk beds, with little space for work or storage. Some students had only a few pieces of clothing. In fact, during the cold season (and at times when no heating was provided in the dormitories) they had to wear a double layer of clothing. There were classes in the afternoon until about 4:00 p.m., and then students broke for recreational sports, at times very competitive, including basketball and soccer. There is a substantial amount of biking during the day, and continuous walking all day, from class to class, and from the campus to outside stores. The evening was always characterized by a mandatory study period (of quiet and dedicated work) which took place in many locations on campus. This schedule was the same for Monday through Saturday. On Sunday additional time was given for recreation and occasionally a dancing party (with a moderate Western flavor in the music, dancing styles and movies).

Sexual codes are extremely rigid. During class and social or recreational activities, there can be some communication between members of the opposite sex, but this is infrequent. There was no access to rooms or dormitories for persons of the opposite sex. Indeed, surveillance of all students, faculty and visitors is enforced twenty-four hours a day. The gates of the campus are closed at night, and both police and intelligence personnel keep an eye on the dormitories and entire campus.

There were important differences between the students at Beijing and those in Guizhou. In Beijing the students seemed a bit overwhelmed by their surroundings, and a bit more conscious of their low status and humble origins. There were more clearly defined social strata in Beijing, because the university has many more students from ethnic groups from the northern and eastern parts of China, groups that often display their ethnic clothes and jewelry, and who seemed to belong to upper classes. In Guizhou, however, most of the students seemed to belong to the low-income groups and lived in the surrounding areas, or in provinces such as Yunnan that are very poor. The Miao people living in Yunnan and Guizhou are considered among the poorest of China, with an annual family income of less than 30 US dollars.

Students from Guizhou, in contrast with our expectations, seemed to be more aggressive, determined, confident and free to express their values in group interviews. But when we looked at their written compositions, their statements did not have the forceful and powerful statements that often characterized the statements of the Beijing students. In both institutions, we found that students formed strong groups around specific faculty members. In Beijing, Professor Wu seemed to be the mentor and counselor for many of the students; in Guizhou, Professor Pan had the role of mentor. Another contrast between the two institutions was the status and overall intellectual climate. The Central University for Nationalities (CUN) in Beijing has high prestige, excellent facilities, and is placed in the center of China's economic, political and technological power.

The Central University for Nationalities (CUN) was established on June 11, 1951. It covers an area of 486 acres, including 197,000 sq. meters of buildings. There are more than 2300 faculty members and a total enrollment of more than

Power in Education

7000 students from all fifty-six ethnic groups. There are more than one million books in the library, 120,000 of which are written in over twenty minority ethnic languages, such as Mongolian, Tibetan, Uygur, Kazak, Korean, Zhuang, Buyi, Yi, Manchu, Jingpo, Kirgiz, Xibe, Naxi and Dai. More than 50,000 books are in foreign languages. CUN started by holding a training class for cadres of the army and government as well as a class in Tibetan language. In 1952 CUN accepted some departments and majors from other universities, such as the Sociology Department of the former Yanjing University (later this was called the Ethnology Department), the Sociology Department of Qinghua University, and the professional training school of minority languages of the Oriental Languages Department of Beijing University (including Tibetan language, Uygur language, Miao-Yi language). Those majors were transferred to CUN and formed the main departments and majors in the early days of CUN. At present CUN is made up of twenty-two departments: Economics; Law; Philosophy; History; Minority Ethnic Languages and Literature Departments I, II and III; Chinese and Literature; Ethnology; Computer Science; Art; Music and Dance; Biological Chemistry; Physics; Mathematics; Night University and Correspondence School; Ethnic Therapy Teaching Office; two centers: Audiovisual Education Center and Information Center. These Departments are subdivided into sixty-four fields, including Ethnology; History; Linguistics; Chinese and literature; Mathematics; Physics; Biology; Chemistry; Economics; Philosophy; Law; Journalism; and Music; but the institution is known for its specialists: Ethnology, Minority Languages and literature particularly Korean Language and Literature; Tibetology; Teaching Chinese as a Second Language; Art and Dance.

The schooling extends over four years for undergraduates. The students are selected from among high school graduates through National Examinations distributed and scored by a central government office working with students' home towns. The period of study for the Cadre-training Department is one or two years and it aims at training ethnic cadres in-service as well as Han cadres dealing with ethnic groups for an extended period of time. CUN strives to carry out the government's policy of education for the future, meaning for modernization and economic development. The primary principle of running CUN is to strengthen all aspects of human development through teaching, and to improve instructional quality in order to prepare qualified personnel for the construction of a socialist order. Both teaching and social benefit have brought about good results. As we mentioned above, in the last two decades the number of graduate students has increased dramatically. For example, from the class of 1984 graduating with a college degree in the History Department, 6.25 per cent were admitted to graduate school; in 1985, 15 per cent and in 1986 27.1 per cent were admitted. The qualifications required for admission into graduate work are extremely competitive. Only the very top ranking students can be allowed in the universities (see Luo, 1991).

The Guizhou Institute for Nationalities (GIN) was founded in 1951, and is located in the south of Guiyang City, an area well known for its natural beauty. GIN has over 2500 students, with 90 per cent belonging to eighteen different ethnic groups, especially Miao, Bouyei, Dong, and Gelo. GIN has 840 faculty distributed among the departments of Chinese, Law, Sociology, Administrative Management, History, Mathematics, Physics, Art, Ethnic Languages, Foreign Languages, and Economics. Guiyang City and its surroundings are clearly rural and not as developed as Beijing. The city, in spite of its modest size (less than 100,000) is becoming very polluted with fumes from local factories and industries. Within a few hours by car there are the world renown beauties such as Huang Guo Shu Water Falls and Long Gong (Dragon Palace), the largest caves in the world.

The setting and students for the research were chosen with the purpose of pursuing more in-depth exploration of achievement motivation, the constellation of family values, and comparative analysis of the behavior of the Miao students with other students who share the Miao culture but do not exhibit the same degree of academic achievement motivation, for example, some of the Hmong students in the United States, and many other Miao in China who never find the opportunity to pursue a high school, bachelor's or graduate degree. Our contention is that intellectual leadership of young Miao people is intimately connected with their educational aspirations and commitment to fundamental values such as responsibility, honor and respect for the family and community elders, and the work ethic associated with the economic and emotional support received from their families.

A questionnaire including forty-two questions and an essay was sent to each of the fourteen students in late Spring 1993. The first section on general information (questions 1–13) is summarized in Table 4 above. The second section on communication with family and community (questions 14–19) deals with the rationale for making inferences regarding the emotional bond between students, their families and their communities. The questions about frequency of visits and correspondence between students and their family (14–17) can be summarized as follows: most students visited their family twice a year. Parents never visited students on campus. Students wrote to their parents once a month, and parents and siblings wrote to students once a month (often to send money). A few students wrote to their brothers and/or sisters once a week. The more specific questions on the close emotional relationship between families and students (#18–26) are summarized in the next section.

Bond with Family and Community

There is continuous communication between students and their families, especially through letter writing (because of the high costs of travel). To the question: 'Do you feel that you are emotionally very close to your family? (do you often send gifts to your family?)' they answered as follows:

1. Wang Daqing said that he is very close to his family and often sends them pictures. He said: 'I have an obligation to my family and my

Figure 1: Questionnaire

I. *General Information*
1. Name
2. Sex
3. Birthdate
4. Place of Birth
5. Family village, county and province
6. Parents' education
7. Parents' occupations
8. General family economic situation
9. Annual family income
10. Members of family in household
11. Number and sex of siblings
12. Place of student among them
13. Education of siblings

II. *Communication with Family and Community*
14. How often do you visit your family?
15. How often do your relatives visit you?
16. How often do you write to your parents and siblings? (per week, month, year).
17. How often do your relatives write to you? (per week, month, year).
18. Do you feel very close emotionally to your family? Do you send gifts?
19. Do you feel that you have an obligation to your family?

III. *Experience in the University*
20. What are the most satisfying moments in your university life?
21. What are the most difficult moments in your university life?
22. With whom do you share your happy moments?
23. With whom do you share your difficult moments?
24. With whom do you talk most frequently?
25. Are all your friends Miao?
26. In what kind of activities do you participate the most at the university?

IV. *Marriage*
27. Will your parents arrange your marriage?
28. Will you obey your parents' will in marriage matters?
29. What criteria will you use to choose your future spouse?
30. Do you plan to marry a Miao person?
31. When do you plan to get married?
32. Where do you expect to build your future family life?

V. *Values and Social Status*
33. Have you changed your values since you left your home?
34. Is your lifestyle different from that of village people, or from that of city people?
35. Do you feel that you have adjusted well to the university environment?
36. What kind of adjustments have you made?
37. Do you think your social status has changed since you entered the university? How do you know?
38. Have you acquired a higher social status? How do you know?
39. Do you think university education helped you to acquire a higher social status? Please, explain.
40. How do people in your hometown perceive your social status?
41. What are your fellow students' attitudes towards you?
42. Do you think your instructors treat you as fairly as students from other ethnic backgrounds?

VI. *Future Plans*: State three of your top goals that you want to accomplish within the next five or ten years. Please, be as specific as you can.

Miao Students' Experience at the University

parents. In my family I am the second oldest child, and a man, so I have an obligation.'

2 Long Jianhua said: 'I feel very close to my family. Our feelings are sincere and simple, but because our economic condition is poor, my parents don't permit me to send any gifts to them. As long as I keep writing to them they will be very happy. Even before I get a job, I have a sense of obligation to them. I often write to share my thoughts with them, in order to have them trust me and relieve them from mental anxiety. I hope in the future I will be able to take care of them and return their kindness, and I hope their last years will be very happy.'

3 Du Xiaobo (female) wrote: 'I am very, very, very close to my family. And yes, I have an obligation to my parents and family. My parents gave me life, my family is the source of my strength... Therefore, I should take responsibility for my family. I have a special obligation to support my parents in the future. I also have an obligation to the other members of my family.'

4 Tian Zhenmin wrote the following: 'I don't think I should neglect the relationship with my family just because I am studying far away from it. On the contrary, anytime I go home I take some gifts typical of Beijing. From the first day I was born, my parents always took good care of me, loved me, were concerned about me, gave me complete financial support. In spite of the fact that my parents are old and have white hair, they still continue to support me financially in college.'

5 Wang Zhongmin wrote this statement: 'Yes, I am very close to my family, because my parents and sisters loved me so much; I always think about them and miss them. I have the total responsibility of my family, because I am the only male child.'

6 Yang Dexin said: 'Feelings... I always hide them deep in the bottom of my heart. In spite of the fact that my family is very poor, they still support me as a university student, because they want me to bring honor to our home. My family gives me the motivation to work hard.'

7 Xiong Qiang felt that he was not very close to his family: 'In some respects, they do not understand me. However, according to the Chinese law parents have the obligation to support their children, and children have the obligation to support their parents.'

8 Tao Xiaoping said: 'Yes, I am very close to my family. I miss them a lot. Every holiday I write a letter to my family. Family is a very important part of my life. I have the obligation to help them, to be concerned about them. My parents gave me life and nourished me to adulthood. Without my parents I would not exist. I am the hope of my parents. Of course, I have an obligation to take care of my parents.'

9 Yang Li (female) said: 'I am very close to my family. During the holidays I miss them particularly. Sometimes I send them small gifts, a card, etc., and when I go home I bring them some gifts. I think I

have an obligation to my family, because my parents gave me life, and my brothers gave me wonderful times. My family is a very important part of my life.'

10   Xiong Jinliang stated: 'I am close to my family; every holiday I send them some gifts to celebrate with them. I think I have an obligation to my parents and family. Because my parents gave me life and supported me, I should take care of them.'

11   Wang Bingzhong wrote: 'Yes, I am very close to my family, but I never sent any gifts, because I see them often, and don't have any money. Also, I do not like to exchange gifts, unless one separates from family members. My older brother married and left; my older sister left too. So my parents gave all their love to me, therefore I have the greatest obligation to them.'

12   Yang Yuxi also felt very close to his family. He said: 'I often visit my parents and buy gifts for them. I have an obligation to support my family. After graduation I will pay part of the tuition of my nephews and nieces, and will pay for my parents' expenses.'

13   Li Maohong strongly stated: 'Yes, I am very close to my family; whenever I need something, they immediately mail it to me. I caused my parents so many difficulties going to school. I feel that this obligation is so high that I should not only do something for my people and society, but I should help my parents lead a happy life.'

14   Tao Wencen said: 'I am very close to my family. Every holiday I mail cards and birthday gifts. I have an obligation to support my family, especially my parents, since they supported me to go to school.'

The bond between students and their families varies a great deal, and their expression of affection depends on how close to each other they live and on the frequency which they see each other. Most students express in vivid terms their love for their family members, their continuous communication with them and, in some cases, the exchange of gifts that takes place. Different students play different roles in their families depending on their particular place among siblings. No other feeling was expressed more emphatically than that of piety and love for parents and family. The connection between some of the students and their families has decreased in significance because of the lack of communication; parents often do not know how to read and students can hardly travel to visit with them. The normal reactions of most students is to make the commitment to help their families and to retain a close relationship with them.

The third section of the questionnaire focused on information regarding the best and worst experiences students had at the university. Questions were asked to assess the sacrifices made by students in order to achieve well in school and thus repay their debt of gratitude to their families and communities. The assumption is that even the most difficult situations in the university would have to be faced with the concern for the family and community in mind. A fundamental principle in Chinese ethics is to care for one's parents. Therefore, part of the traditional moral code of 'virtuous' behavior that can be traced to the Han Dynasty and that forms the centerpiece of the Confucian philosophy is that children should always respect parents and family by obeying them, by caring for them as they grow old, and following their example and advice. Consequently, Chinese youngsters grow up internalizing this moral code. If they do not follow this code, they will be criticized by members of the community and society at large. Miao students have been socialized in these values; they want to show the world (their peers, community members and society in general) that they are moral. They also are grateful to their parents, and this gratitude translates into a commitment to help their parents (noblesse oblige).

Best Experiences at the University

(Each number 1–14, corresponds to the same person as in the previous section).

1　Receiving a letter from home, and obtaining high grades.
2　Being with friends and receiving letters from home.
3　Learning new knowledge.
4　Being with friends.
5　Receiving letters from home.
6　Enjoying the Miao holidays.
7　Receiving letters from home and obtaining high grades.
8　Being recognized publicly as an excellent student leader.
9　Feeling competent in my studies.
10　Receiving money from home.
11　Knowing that someone cares about me and understands my thoughts and feelings.
12　Making money and buying something I need badly.
13　Events that occurred December 25, 1991 [Not disclosed by the student].
14　Breaking a university sports record and being recognized as an excellent sportsman.

Most responses emphasized human contact: the satisfaction of sharing success or failures with others, especially with peers and members of the family (just knowing that someone else cares). Also students mentioned the reward of learning and being recognized for the efforts made in the process of learning. Others focused on competitive sports, money and social festivities. Letters from home are important because they become the only way to communicate with loved ones, and consequently they take on a great deal of significance in the life of students. The anxiety associated with not knowing if parents are still alive and healthy, if other persons in the family are well, if siblings have what they need, is at times unbearable to students. In America it is common to pick up the phone and call one's parents, sisters and brothers. Neither Chinese students nor their families have access to phones. For the parents, sending a letter is the symbol of warm affection and care for children who are away and are presumed to be often suffering hunger and loneliness. A letter brings news that students need to retain some internal peace of mind, because letters announce crucial events, states of health and provide encouragement to motivate them to study hard. Often letters determine the students' decisions for the future, as well as news relevant to daily survival (money for food, for example). Peer groups tend to become surrogate families when students are deprived of communication with their relatives. They are also support groups and a stimulating social unit to acquire new knowledge. The satisfaction of acquiring new knowledge has a social dimension of making one's peers proud and happy. Part of the mechanism that binds student peer groups together is the celebration of the holidays, the reaffirmation of their own culture, and the relaxation of daily student duties. Sometimes, students gather spontaneously to dance and sing their traditional songs, or to celebrate folk activities. However, prolonged separation from family is always extremely painful for all students, as is the case, for example, of Chinese students working in the United States who have access to their relatives both by phone and letter.

Worst Experience at the University

1. Not receiving money from home.
2. Not receiving money from home and not having money for food.
3. Being treated like an enemy by my classmates.
4. Not being accepted as a member of the Communist Party.
5. Not receiving a letter from home in a long time.
6. Running out of money for food each month.
7. Running out of money for food each month.
8. Worrying about food and studies.
9. Having difficulty in my studies.
10. Running out of money for food each month.
11. Having emotional problems.
12. Not having enough time to participate in extracurricular activities.
13. Events of April 15, 1993.
14. Running out of money for food each month.

Although education in China is free, and students do not pay tuition/fees and room and board, they must buy their own food and books. In the case of students whose parents have very modest incomes, the university provides them with a small stipend for basic food needs. That means that these students from low income families are always hungry. All but one or two of the students in this project received the small stipend. The stipend is the same for boys and girls, small and large students, physically active and relatively sedentary ones.

The result is that some students are much hungrier than others, and men more often than women.

Sharing the Best and Worst Experiences

To the question, 'With whom do you share the best and the worst experiences?' the fourteen students responded:

1 With nobody.
2 With best friend, teachers, classmates and parents.
3 Good times with best friend, bad times with nobody.
4 With best friends and with people who know me.
5 With best friend.
6 With girlfriend and friends.
7 Good times with teachers, parents and friends, and bad times with nobody.
8 With fellow Miao students.
9 With best friends.
10 With classmates.
11 Good times with best friend, and bad times with nobody.
12 Good times with my roommates, and bad times with nobody.
13 With classmates.
14 With teachers and classmates.

Why did no one mention their family, in spite of the fact that they feel very close to it? In American culture this may seem contradictory; the assumption is that you share both the sorrows and the happy moments of life with those closest to you. In Chinese society, you do not. Communications in China are not easy. Students may not hear from their relatives for a long time, if at all, and their need to share intimate moments must be met immediately. Therefore, if an event is going to be shared immediately, it should be shared with those around them, such as peers and teachers, who can respond and make their response known. There is also another factor — social distance. Because of the social distance between members of the same family or between man and wife, there is less sharing of all daily events. In other words, there is a selectivity of domains to be shared with different categories of people. One shares with peers and teachers what one cannot share with parents and siblings who may not grasp the significance of an event, or understand the underpinnings or nuances of particular issues. Finally, the sharing of important events affecting one's emotional balance is done when persons meet face-to-face and have time to talk; unfortunately for students, that rarely happens with their family members. Besides, in Chinese culture, one must be modest and should not brag. Consequently one would not write home to tell Mom that one has obtained the highest grade in class or honors. One would write saying that

Power in Education

things are going well thanks to the support of parents. Regarding the hardships and sad events at the university, it is extremely difficult to bring that up in communication with one's family. Sharing unhappy events is not a thing Chinese students want to do; and there are good reasons for it. Parents, after all, suffer so many deprivations in order to help their children that it does not make sense to worry them any further. Finally, there are gradual but radical changes in the students' personalities, lifestyles and values. Much of what they do becomes almost irrelevant or incomprehensible to parents and siblings. When the students write they attempt to keep the discourse at the level of their family, mostly in very general but affectionate terms.

Since one of the most rapidly changing cultural patterns is the selection of a spouse, we asked students: Will your parents arrange your marriage? The following answers are very telling regarding how different university students are if compared with the bulk of the population. All except three stated that their parents will not arrange their marriage. The other three indicated that perhaps their parents would suggest someone without attempting to force their own choice. In Chapter 4 we discussed village life, wedding patterns and the various social and cultural arrangements associated with a wedding. We asked students to describe their ideal spouse. To the question, 'What kind of person would you like to marry?', students responded in very eloquent terms reflecting clearly their changes in value orientations. Only student #3 (Du Xiaobo) and #9 (Yang Li) were female students. One of the students, (#8) is 29-years-old and already married, but the other thirteen students responded that they would like to marry someone who is:

1. Beautiful, caring, tall and slim, and younger.
2. Sincere, loyal, ambitious, willing to share happiness and sadness.
3. [A husband] Tall, of stable income and occupation, talented, with a pioneer spirit, with similar interests, and someone working in the city where I live.
4. Quiet, beautiful, easy to get along with, ambitious, innovative, handworker, and with a wide range of interests.
5. A girl who is beautiful, well educated and who supports and understands my work.
6. Not necessarily a beautiful girl, but lovely and understanding.
7. Without experience but with ideas and imagination.
8. I won't say anything because I'm already married. My wife is quiet, beautiful and a hard worker.
9. [A husband] Ambitious, talented, quiet and emotionally balanced.
10. Educated, caring, sincere, good-hearted and with a mild temper.
11. Just a girl with a job and a good heart.
12. A Miao girl, loyal, knowledgeable, educated, beautiful, with a good temper, and as tall as I am.
13. A good-hearted girl.
14. Educated, handworker, good-hearted, willing to be a good mother.

We can assume that all the students intend to marry a Miao person. That is a non-negotiable part of their tradition. The communication with members of other groups increases after college graduation, but there are a number of social barriers that most frequently persuade Miao students to seek Miao potential spouses. The choice of marriage partner is already an indication that these students have been exposed to modern trends of increased freedom for the youth and young adults. We were very interested in checking the extent to which students realized that they were changing radically since they left home. According to native Chinese people and scholars (Wu 1993; Pan 1993), young peasants would normally hesitate to articulate their expectations from future spouses in the way done by these students. Students emphasized education and knowledge as important attributes. Most people, including students, would be culturally inclined to emphasize beauty, but not education. Many peasants still rely on pre-arranged marriages; most students reject that form of marriage and are determined to make their own decision. Indeed, these higher expectations reveal a fundamental change in values on the part of students. Obviously their expectations are higher than those of their parents and villagers. Traditionally, peasant villagers would look for an honest woman, or an honest man, a hardworking, strong and healthy person. Of course, peasants do seek beautiful people, but they realize that there is a difference between finding a beautiful wife and being able to afford to pay the necessary dowry (see discussion in Chapter 4 regarding costs involved in weddings). Obviously, beauty is conceived as an attribute that is more affordable by the middle and upper classes. Even naturally beautiful peasant women do not have the clothes or the education needed to display that beauty in ways similar to those of urban people. Students are becoming part of the urban young educated people who have higher standards in seeking a spouse, regardless of their ethnic affiliation. Their answers to our question show that the Miao students have already been socialized into the middle- and upper-class values of educated urban Chinese.

Change in Values

To the question: 'Have you changed your values since you left home?' their answers were as follows:

1. Yes.
2. A great deal. I demand much more of myself, and I have a serious commitment to the educational development of my people.
3. No. I have not changed my values. I may have a deeper understanding of my own worth. Now I know I can realize my dreams if I work hard.
4. I never change my goals. I always wanted to enter the political arena and to make a lot of money in order to live a better life and help my family.

Power in Education

5 No.
6 My values changed a lot. In the past I thought that making money was shameful. Now I know that although money is not everything, without money you cannot do anything.
7 Before I just wanted to have a peaceful and quiet life. Now I want to study abroad.
8 I am more determined than ever to work for my people.
9 Yes. Before I was ignorant. Now I have become productive.
10 Yes.
11 I rediscovered that personal relationships are worthwhile and not only a means for getting money.
12 I have not changed my values. I value friendship and disdain the benefits of money.
13 No. I have not changed.
14 Before I came to the University I was uneducated, ignorant. Now I have found a high quality intellectual life in teachers and students, and have learned a great deal.

Not all students think that they changed their values, or they chose to respond 'no' because the question was either ambiguous or they interpreted change as no longer being attached to the Miao culture and lifestyle. Naturally, as the students spent more years away from the village and in educational institutions they must have undergone certain cultural changes. A change in values does not necessarily mean rejection of home culture and family values; more often, it means the acquisition of a deeper understanding of cultural differences along with adaptive strategies to function in culturally different settings. The question was meant to be ambiguous because the subject was delicate. We obtained, however, meaningful and significant information.

This was a very complicated question that could be interpreted in different ways. For example, it could ask: 'Did you abandon your cultural values?', or it could mean: 'Have you adjusted well to the life of a student and accepted the academic achievement values of the university?' The answers seem to imply some confusion about the meaning of the question and the meaning of 'values'. If they understood values as Miao culture and lifestyle, then accepting other lifestyles may be seen as abandoning one's cultural traditions and values, that is, renouncing one's own roots and family ties. Therefore, an appropriate answer to that question is 'no'. This interpretation makes it unacceptable to even consider the possibility of doing things according to different criteria, or things totally unknown to Miao villagers, or things deemed acceptable by the Miao villagers. The response by some was 'no'. In Chinese society, the higher you go up the social ladder, the more obligations you have to those people who helped you climb. You go to the university and achieve high status, but you cannot forget your family or your culture. Friends and peers always tell students: 'Do not forget us.' A very popular play in China tells about a man called Chen Zhimei who went through the Imperial Court civic examination, succeeded in his studies and became the 'Number 1 Scholar'. After that he divorced his wife, and the entire community became angry and called him ungrateful. Then the town Judge, called Bao Gong, sentenced him to death; capital punishment was by guillotine. This immoral man had violated the most important social code of behavior, that of loyalty to the family. This story warns those who reach high positions: 'Do not be a Chen Zhimei when you become successful.' Loyalty is greatly enforced by social sanctions. This represents one force, the force that makes students remain internally committed to be loyal and to keep village values. On the other hand, there are constant pressures to change. The backward traditions and way of life must change to allow them to live modern lifestyles compatible with university life. Their time must be spent in reading, writing, and participating in school activities. Subsistence activities in peasant life take most of the day. In the students' life, subsistence activities must give room to intellectual endeavors. That is a drastic lifestyle change.

Students seem to accept Western (modern) notions related to the international economy and the new values associated with capitalist economies. Money, specifically the use of money as a means to obtain personal goods and satisfaction, formerly rejected by many Chinese (especially peasants), is now a reality of life and a central concern in urban centers. In general, the acquisition of sophisticated knowledge about the national economy and about academic subjects, has a genuine impact on students' views on life, and their appreciation of Chinese refined arts, architecture, historical accomplishments, etc. We therefore feel that part of the changes alluded to by students are related to new physical and mental maturational stages, age, experience and the increase in knowledge, sophistication and status each student felt as he or she became part of a small elite of university students. In order to pursue the issue of status, we decided to ask directly about it.

Social Status Change

To the question, 'Did your social status change at home, in your village and community?', they answered in the following way:

1. Yes. The people in my village now think that I can do something for them because I became educated.
2. In my village, the people that used to look down on me now come to my home to court me. Family and friends think I will become a government leader and admire me a lot. My family's honor is greater.
3. Now I am trusted by others. In the eyes of the villagers I am now Number 1 Scholar, with rich knowledge and good judgment.
4. Villagers think I am not equal to them, but higher than them.
5. People in my village respect and admire me.

Power in Education

6   From a poor peasant son I became a student in a prestigious university, because out of 10,000 finishing high school, only twenty go to the university.
7   People in my village have high expectations of me. I do not know about other people's judgment. I work hard and I should receive some recognition, but some people admire me blindly.
8   I do not care about my status, whether it is low or high. There is a change in how people judge me because of the new environment in which I study. People praise me, admire me, and that motivates me to work hard, but I do not see that as a higher status. Old people in my village think I have a bright future, and they respect me, love me, admire me; but at the same time I respect and admire them. Whenever they praise me I always respond with a grateful smile and with modesty.
9   At home I am still a child. For the people of my village, I am now an educated university student who is not expected to do manual labor.
10 I became an intellectual and matured. I acquired a higher status through my own effort and with the support of my people. My people want me to have knowledge and have higher status, but not to forget them.
11 As soon as I became a university student, many people in my village praised me and know my name. Once I have a university degree, of course I will have a good job. There are very few university students in my village; they always praise me and that makes me feel embarrassed.
12 From a high school student without any reputation I became a star, the hope of my village. Everybody around me respects me. They think I rank higher than the village leader, because I am the only university student in the village. In China it is not easy to enter the university, unless you have money to pay tuition.
13 People respect me.
14 I am not sure that university education would bring higher status; status depends on your ability to use your knowledge and put it to practice. My people want me to come back after graduation.

From the perspective of the villagers (Pan 1993; Wu 1993), students hold a very high status. Schooling, education, acquiring knowledge, in the philosophy of Confucius provides a person with a higher status and a superior place in society. Even the most remote villagers do appreciate, admire and respect these young people who study and become university graduates. There is also an expectation on the part of the villagers that these students will become rich and will help the village. Therefore, it is politically appropriate to treat these students and their parents with deference.

During the informal group interviews we realized that Miao students, especially those in Beijing, acted shy and nervous in front of their professors, while students from other ethnic groups seemed to be more at home and self-confident. We felt that perhaps Miao students felt they were treated as an underclass. We therefore decided to ask them about the treatment they received from the faculty.

Instructors' Treatment

To the question, 'Do you think your instructors treat you as fairly as they treat students from other ethnic backgrounds?', they responded this way:

1   Some instructors look down on me because I am a Miao student.
2   Some do, others do not.
3   Some instructors treat the Miao differently. They do not understand the Miao, they think the Miao nation is backward.
4   Once I entered the university, the boundary between ethnic groups is very clear.
5   They always treat me differently.
6   They treat me equally.
7   I do not know, and I do not want to know.
8   Basically they treat me equally.
9   Equally.
10 Equally.
11 Equally.
12 Equally, but instructors sometimes treat me better than students from other groups.
13 The majority of instructors treat all students equally, but a few do not.
14 Equally.

Not everybody feels treated as an underclass. Half of the student do. Obviously, instructors who have a ranking order of minority students in their minds do not classify all Miao in the same rank. Personal merit and other personal qualities must play a role. There are about 7,000 students at the Central University for Nationalities in Beijing and about 2,500 in Guizhou. Can we assume that the external appearance of these students signals their ethnicity? Or that all the faculty knows the ethnicity of their students? If the answer is 'no' to these questions, then Miao students are looked down on for other reasons than their ethnicity. If the answer to the above questions is 'yes', then faculty members have certain ranks for certain ethnic backgrounds, but not all students internalize their treatment and the feeling of mistreatment the same way. University professors have access to all kinds of information; they know their students' personal backgrounds in detail. Elementary and secondary teachers, as well as professors, will write comments about each student. This is used as a reference to make decisions about student admissions and support. In sum, why are some Miao students feeling put down and others not? It may have to do with their fluency in Mandarin, their accents, their academic records, their relative success in the university, and their overall personal qualifications.

The last part of the questionnaire was formed by an open question about their personal goals, ambitions and planning for the next five or ten years. This question was intended to explore the long-term vision and goals of leaders committed to their political ideology and traditional Chinese values. Their responses are summarized in the following section:

Future Goals

We asked students: 'Please state three goals which you want to accomplish in the next five to ten years (be specific).' They gave us the following answers:

1 Find a good job. Use the knowledge I acquired at the University to serve people. To continue my studies. Find a beautiful wife and establish a happy family.
2 Return to the university to do graduate work. Help my village economy organizing chicken and pigs farms. Use part of my salary to support five poor university students.
3 Publish books, conduct research, and establish a happy family.
4 Become an administrator, find a lovely girl, and within seven or eight years save enough money to marry her.
5 Find a good job, improve my family economic situation, and help the Miao economy.
6 Study further to obtain a graduate degree (saving money first, if necessary); then, make good money and establish my own company.
7 Make enough money, then travel around the world, and establish a family.
8 Help the Miao people become literate; collect and edit Miao folklore and publish a book; write a book on the history of my Miao village.
9 After graduation, pass the state English proficiency test. Collect and edit Miao folklore and publish a book, and translate it for different people. Study and do research on the Miao language, and promote interchange among Miao people who speak different dialects.
10 To become a village leader and use my intelligence to develop it, and to increase my knowledge.
11 Translate Miao folk songs into Mandarin and publish them. Write one or two novels describing Miao life style and traditions. Establish a happy family.
12 The five years following my graduation I will not seek a job. I will organize a big research firm in charge of conducting surveys. After five years, I will organize county cooperatives and business firms. In ten years I will use the capital produced by these firms to establish a Miao city with tourist facilities. Where there is a will there is a way.

13 Write a novel about the Miao and work hard to realize my dreams.
14 Find my own worth and try to be successful, but without becoming arrogant. Live happily. Use my knowledge to develop the Miao groups to repay what they did for me.

All of the students have confidence in their future and display a great deal of ambition, not only personal ambition for academic achievement, but ambition to change the world around them, for example, the student who in five years plans to run a research firm and in ten years a cooperative of research firms. Most students expect to have an assigned job after graduation. The government guarantees all college graduates a position after graduation, except those students who, not having qualified to enter regular free public colleges, pay their own tuition and get a slightly different college education (one emphasizing technical and vocational skills). These students generally come from upper income families and do not seek government employment. Their payment for education is a recent phenomenon and is viewed positively by the public and the government. The Miao students are generating new ideas about what they want to accomplish on their own, independent from the Government. All students seek a certain degree of happiness one way or another, and material means that will allow them to help their community. They all seem more aware of the need to turn around the economy of the country. Their statement of goals represents important changes in their lives: a demand for the freedom to select their own spouses and to demand education, knowledge and a commitment to the newly acquired urban values. They have indeed developed in ways that show they think globally and they view the role of Miao intellectual leaders as important in the modernization of China.

Without college education the chances of obtaining a good job are very slim, and indeed college education means a secure job and a fairly good one, in contrast with other people who do not have a college education. The academic and capitalistic ambitions of these students stand in contrast to their many personal statements during the interviews and their slogans related to their unselfish dedication to their people and the educational cause of the Miao. They know that school teachers and university professors do not get rich.

References

EDITORIAL STAFF (1991) *Beijing Review*, December 2–8, **34**(48), p. 26.
LUO, B. (Ed) (1991) *The Central Institute for Nationalities*, Beijing, China: Knowledge Press.
PAN, D. (1993) 'The history and culture of the Miao nationality in China', unpublished manuscript, Guiyang, Guizhou, China: Guizhou Institute for Nationalities.
WU, D. (1993) 'Village life of the Miao people in China', unpublished manuscript, Beijing, China: Central University for Nationalities.

Chapter 6

Social Identification and Achievement Motivation among the Miao University Students

The interpretation of Miao students' university experiences and reflections on their academic lives, with focus on the transition from their home village to the university, has significant implications for a number of theoretical issues at different levels of specificity.

The Process of Social Identification for Achievement

At the macro-psychological and macro-sociological levels, that is, at the levels of the larger social, political and economic structures that form the infrastructure of a country and its value system as a whole, its ethos and self-image, this study deals with:

1. the process of social identification as Chinese and Miao in the national and international contexts. The dilemma between being a member of a less prestigious nationality, the Miao, and a member of an elite group in China, i.e., university students and academicians;

2. the process of empowerment of minority and immigrant groups which has national and international importance, as well as comparable issues of power relationships, drastic rapid sociocultural changes, cultural conflict, inter-ethnic, relationships, hyper- and hypo-marriages and overall social upward mobility;

3. the role of education in the process of modernization of rural communities, and specifically the role of members of the village who become intellectual leaders; the local expectations of rural villagers, the authority and power they invest in the educated sons and daughters who manage to attend a university and become cultural brokers for them with the larger society;

Social Identification and Achievement among students

4 the role of education in the democratization of the political systems as a result of changes in the national economy and the increased frequency of communication with economic centers.

At the micro-psychological and micro-sociological levels, the findings reported here have implications for:

1 the important mediating role that ethnic languages and cultures have for the academic achievement of students. The fact that ethnic students enhance the knowledge of their home language and culture, not only permits them to keep their ongoing communication with the members of their family and community, but also allows them to retain a strong self-concept and affiliation to the larger ethnic group, and thus to draw on this affiliation for an increased motivation to achieve academically.

2 a deeper understanding of the process of empowerment in the face of unexpected cultural and linguistic demands from a new learning environment. The ability of members of ethnic and minority groups to acquire a second language and culture, as well as social skills to participate in new cultural institutions, can be related to the strong emotional support found in one's own social identity and the sense of belonging in a family and community.

3 a better understanding of achievement motivation across cultures. In the case of the Miao, their willingness to suffer pain and deprivation, to delay gratification and rewards, and to pursue a long and arduous course of intellectual development becomes an opportunity to repay family and village members their own sacrifices with the prestige and honor they generate as university students and members of a new elite.

Indeed, the specific stories on the painful journey of many Miao students from the poverty and lack of formal education of the village home life to the prestigious position as university students, has important consequences for a better understanding of the 30 million Chinese persons living outside of mainland China and Taiwan, as well as for the millions of Indochinese people, many of whom have migrated to the United States. Beyond Chinese and Indochinese populations, there is a world-wide effort to study and better explain the differential adjustment and performance of various immigrant populations seeking opportunities for life improvement in Western societies. In some instances, the maintenance of the home language and culture and of the family cultural and social networks has made it possible for immigrants to succeed in the host country. Is this the case of the Hmong? How do we explain the world-wide spread of Hmong people who, belonging to one of the central branches of the Chinese Miao, have managed to maintain their Miao dialect and many of the

Miao cultural traditions throughout a tumultuous history of military and economic problems extending for about a century from Yunnan, Guizhou and Sichuan to Vietnam, Laos, and Thailand, and from Thailand to Australia, Canada, France, the United States, and many other Western societies?

The data used here are limited, but they raise important questions beyond China and Chinese minorities. Part of the strategy to gain some insights into the lives of the Miao people is to attempt to link macro-sociological or psychological analytical levels, with the micro-sociological and psychological levels of their day-to-day interaction. The initial chapters in the study attempted to provide the larger sociological and psychological contexts, and the last two chapters, the sociological and psychological contexts immediately surrounding the university students. The implications of a better understanding of cultural and linguistic links maintained across thousands of miles and through several hundred years are powerful in helping our understanding of both racial/ethnic prejudice in Europe, America, and other western societies, as well as in China and other Asian societies.

Furthermore, we can learn a great deal from the Chinese Miao that will help us understand the Hmong in the United States; the resiliency of certain cultural practices and traditions, and the problems of Hmong empowerment are similar to the resiliency of Miao students in China and their rapid empowerment as intellectual leaders. Can American pluralism be compared with Chinese pluralism? What are the differences in status and political representation of the Miao, as compared with the status and political representation of some ethnic groups in Europe or in America? These comparisons are well worth consideration and discussion later on. Rapid social change among the Miao in China is taking place through many channels and avenues, but especially through education.

The data presented here suggest that the process of empowerment for the Miao represents an increased participation in the national and international social, political and economic arenas, and that it takes place without destroying the social (ethnic) identity of the Miao people. Indeed, just the opposite, the process of empowerment depends on the maintenance of a strong ethnic identification and affiliation with the Miao culture, language and traditions. Modernization does not have to become a conflicting process that creates cultural marginalization. Under what conditions were the Miao capable of becoming an integral part of Chinese society while retaining their cultural traditions? The changes in education and technology are welcomed by the Miao because they bring about a higher status, and that status is used to enhance their unity, political strength and the traditional family values of loyalty and sacrifice for the sake of the common good.

Knowledge of the past, a deeper understanding of the cultural traditions, the Miao languages, and national context, are an opportunity welcomed by Miao university students who are determined to succeed without rejecting their cultural values. They are becoming better writers and speakers of the Miao language while at the same time they become fluent speakers and writers of standard Mandarin. They feel Chinese, i.e. members of a wonderful multicultural society which has been diversified for many centuries, and they understand better their role as cultural brokers between mainstream Chinese and their own people.

China's nationalities (minority groups) represent not only a very large population (close to 100 million people), but a population that is rapidly increasing its economic and cultural visibility, as well as its political power in the entire country. The largest Moslem nationality, the Hui who are close to ten million people, are now present in the main Chinese metropolis and largest business and industrial centers. In contrast, the Miao, close to eight million people, remain relatively invisible in China, and have not yet become a conspicuous economic and political force; a sleeping giant that controls the Southwest part of China is rapidly, but quietly, learning about its roots, history, and the wider society. The Miao are moving gradually to a position of power from the bottom of the social and economic ladder. The annual family income of the Miao families living in the provinces of Yunnan, Sichuan and especially Guizhou, is considerable lower than that of the other nationalities and of the mainstream or Han people. The significance of the data gathered in this study is that even among the Miao, the development of an intellectual elite is opening doors for their political and economic empowerment in the rest of the country.

At the center of this study is the basic hypothesis that education, the acquisition of knowledge, status and academic skills, is the main door to the empowerment of nationalities. Equally important is the hypothesis that education is pursued by Miao minorities as a mechanism to become empowered. Thus, at the heart of the educational process is the continued motivation to help one's own people, to reciprocate, to pay back debts of sacrifice and support. Education, in the final analysis, is seen by Miao students as the culmination of their parents' and community's dreams, as the realization of their own dreams and the public recognition for the sacrifices made. The paradox, however, is that the educated young Miao students become marginal, and the more distant they are (socially, economically and culturally) from their villages of origin and their families, the more they strive to keep their emotional ties with their culture and their people — as if the source of motivation to survive in a hostile and difficult world, the world of academia, is to remain linked with one's own people, loyal to their cause, a good son or daughter of the wonderful parents who made it possible for these students to become somebody.

In this respect, the psychodynamic mechanisms for achievement and the steps to achieve are guided by psychological processes similar to those of other minorities in America, Europe and other Asian countries (Japan and Korea, for example). This chapter is intended to place in the appropriate perspective some of these psychological mechanisms observed in the Miao students in comparison with other minority students seeking empowerment in other settings around the world. It should be noticed that the education of Miao students at the university was a rare phenomenon until a few years ago. Indeed, the few Miao scholars that became professors in various universities were 'passing' for mainstream students, had become effectively bicultural, and represented a very small minority within the universities. In contrast, the large number of university students from the Miao and other groups is viewed by the Chinese as the pride of their communist system, and the proof that Confucian philosophy and communist philosophies do produce a reality of fair opportunities for all, of justice and fairness in academia, of genuine commitment to learning even for the poorest students coming from the most remote villages.

The personal relationship of Miao students with their parents and siblings and other members of their village is characterized by a very strong bond that has some important features. The statement made by Wang Daqing, 'I have an obligation to my family and my parents. In my family I am the second oldest child, and a man, so I have an obligation' is similar to statements made by the other students. For example, Long Jianhua states, 'I feel very close to my family . . . I often write to share my thoughts with them, in order to have them trust me, and relieve them from mental anxiety.' Du Xiaobo puts it in the strongest terms: 'I am very, very, very close to my family . . . My parents gave me life, my family is the source of my strength . . . Therefore, I should take responsibility for my family.' Tao Xiaoping feels very free to express his feelings for his parents: 'I miss them a lot. Every holiday I write a letter to my family.' Other students feel close but express their love by working only in their studies.

These feelings are sometimes hard to express, especially when physical, emotional and academic survival are the main preoccupation of students, yet, as Yang Dexin put it, 'Feelings . . . I always hide them deep in the bottom of my heart.' Chinese seldom speak about their feelings in a direct and overt fashion. There is a cultural value in keeping to oneself, in being reserved. Chinese strive to feel inside without expressing these feelings or even appearing to have them. Poems and other literature stresses this value. The paradox of feeling closer to their parents and needing them emotionally, precisely when one is changing so rapidly and becoming so different, results in pain and frustration. After recognizing the close bond with his parents, Xiong Qiang says about his parents: 'They do not understand me.' There is a generation gap also. Traditional moral concepts in China demand that the younger generation honor the ancestors, the family and all the members of the clan.

The bonding goes beyond parents and siblings. Students express their commitment to help their other relatives as an expression of their affection for the family. Yang Yuxi says: 'I have an obligation to support my family. After graduation I will pay part of the tuition of my nephews and nieces, and will pay for my parents' expenses.' Indeed other students expand their commitment to the Miao people and the entire society, as long as parents are top priority. Li Maohong said: 'I feel that this obligation is so high that I should not only do something for my people and society, but I should help my parents lead a happy life.'

The forging of a strong will to achieve academically started from the early years of sacrifice leaving their village school and becoming minority children in Han language schools. The memories of these sacrifices presented in Chapter 5 do not end when students enter the university; they continue during college when their food money has been either paid by the student family or obtained in other ways. When asked what the worst experiences are, students will allude to their lack of money for food. Their dependence on their poor parents to help subsidize the cost of food is more painful the more students enjoy a higher level of living on campus. This sense of imposing on poor parents translates into guilt and profound commitment to bring some relief to parents after graduation.

The most difficult experience for Wang Daqing, Long Jianhua, Yang Dexin, Xiong Qiang, Tao Xiaoping, Xiong Jinliang, and Tao Wencen (half of the students surveyed) is running out of money for food each month. Other difficult experiences are being treated 'like an enemy' by classmates, not being accepted as members of the communist party, not hearing from home, and having difficulties with academic subject matter. In contrast, the most satisfying experiences are hearing from home, getting good grades, being with friends (Miao fellows), feeling competent in one's own studies, and being recognized for academic achievement. The bonding with the family and the expression of love through academic achievement are a form of reciprocity. Parents' support of children's studies is reciprocated with children's school achievement, and the benefits coming from success in education.

We have argued that academic socialization for success is based on the love of the family and reciprocal relationship of affection; parents' support at great sacrifice is the highest expression of love for their children; children's highest expression of love is academic achievement. This bonding is continued throughout the years at a distance, with relatively few visits of students to their home (once a year), and only a few letters from home (although some students write often to their parents or siblings). Are students free to share their good or bad experiences with their parents and siblings? Most of them do not; they would rather share these happy or sad moments with fellow students, classmates, teachers, and best friends, or with nobody. There is a profound and rapid change taking place during the lives of these students whose entire youth and adulthood is spent away from home with some visits to their village. Are students aware of these changes? How are these changes manifested? One of the most obvious changes is a departure from the traditional way to seek a spouse. In contrast with the old village traditions of having marriages arranged by the parents — the parents select spouses and negotiate marriage arrangements in every detail — all students plan to make their own choices and have a pretty good idea of the kind of spouse they want. However, the very choice of a spouse still represents a compromise with the old values. Yes, male students want to make their own choices, they seek a 'beautiful, caring, loyal, quiet and younger wife,' but at the same time they want a 'tall woman, with a pioneer spirit, ambitious, innovative, well educated and somebody who understands my work.' The two female students want to select their husbands, and seek a 'tall person, of stable income, who has similar interests and lives in the same city', and one who is 'emotionally balanced, talented, and ambitious'.

There is a combination of old and new values working in their minds. Students, however, are well aware that their lives are changing a great deal in important ways, but that they keep some of the old values. Long Jianhua says: 'I have changed a great deal. I demand much more of myself, and I have a serious commitment to the educational development of my people.' Yang Dexin said, 'My values changed a lot. In the past I thought that making money was shameful. Now I know that although money is not everything, without money you cannot do anything.' Xiong Qiang said, 'Before I just wanted to have a peaceful and quiet life. Now I want to study abroad.' And Wang Bingzhong made the most surprising statement: 'I rediscovered that personal relationships are worthwhile and not only a means for getting money.' Other students responded firmly that they have not changed their values, that their commitment to their Miao communities is as strong as ever. In fact, as aware of some of them are of their new social status, they essentially confess that this status enjoyed when they visit their villages only serves to increase their commitment to their traditional values and to serve their people. Wang Daqing said: 'The people in my village now think that I can do something for them because I became educated.' Long Jianhua said, 'In my village, the people that used to look down on me now come to my home to court me. Family and friends think I will become a government leader and admire me a lot. My family's honor is greater.' Other students feel they have earned the trust, admiration and respect of their fellow villagers, and modestly they point out that 'out of 10,000 finishing high school, only twenty go to the university', but deep down they feel the way Tao Xiaoping does: 'I don't care about my status, whether it is low or high', or as Yang Li put it: 'At home I am still a child.'

These statements express the complexity of the change occurring not only in the social life of the village, but in the mind of each student. While each retained his/her original sense of belonging to the village and attachment to traditional cultural values, each also recognized that he/she was becoming two different persons, one at home and another in the university. But even at home there were some contradictions. A student was at home a child, consequently, a person who obeyed his/her parents and followed orders from older siblings; yet, this child was also a leader and the center of admiration and respect, indeed the pride of the entire community, and the hope of the villagers for a better economic and social life. Returning to the university, however, was both difficult and a relief; at the university, Miao students often remained the underdogs, the low-status people, suffering poverty and always striving to compete with the richer and more sophisticated peers in an environment that was still somewhat unfamiliar and academically demanding. Yet, much of the university life is attractive, stimulating and enjoyable, because it brings Miao students the freedom and the opportunity to fully develop their human potential in a way never suspected by their village peers and community persons. Now Miao students think globally and read about international matters; they want to travel abroad and visit other countries; they want to display their knowledge and skills in several languages, and they feel they can reach higher levels of intellectual development. They never dreamed to aspire to such high levels in their entire lives before. Of course, these thoughts are both exciting and frightening. The dreams of reaching higher levels of academic excellence are understandable. But why fear? Fears are also very rational and perfectly understandable. The fear of losing their ethnic membership and their sense of belonging in their village and community is equivalent to the fear of death, because their *raison d'etre* is to bring honor and other rewards to the Miao people, to repay their parents and other members of the community. The more they stay in the university the more different they become, and the more their thinking changes. Yet, the role models they see in other professors give them confidence that one can remain emotionally attached to one's own village, yet quasi-permanently separated from it. However, the deeper emotional conflicts and contrasts students face as they go back home once a year are a vivid reminder of the possibility that socio-cultural change through education may be a one-way journey to mainstream Chinese society.

Before we pursue this analysis further and establish some cross-cultural comparisons with other groups discussed in similar studies, it is important to examine in a more detailed fashion the feelings of ambiguity faced by these students in the process of redefining their social identity during their lives at the university. Indeed, part of the ambivalence associated with their new social or ethnic selves is the recognition of the personal changes in values and behavior they see in themselves and their peers, as well as the awareness of the social distance between the university and their home village. They ask themselves? Will I ever fit back in my village? Could I ever give up this new lifestyle? Could I face the insecurity that this new and exciting life has brought about? Will I be able to deliver, to discharge my responsibilities, to produce, to fulfill the expectations of my people? These are examples of the profound thinking that takes place among the university Miao students, and these considerations form the context of their new social and ethnic identification.

Towards a Theory of Social Identification

One of the psychological approaches in the study of Asian and other minorities in the United States (DeVos 1992; and DeVos and Suarez-Orozco 1990) suggests that there are two main components in the analysis of achievement motivation and actual differential achievement: 1) one that focuses on the structure of the personality, that is the characteristics of individuals as they are exposed to socialization experiences in their specific interactional and socio-cultural environments — that is, the factors relevant to the intra-personality and cultural milieu immediately surrounding the person; and 2) the broader ecological factors that are formed by sociological structures, social, political and cultural systems determining peoples' rights and obligations, status and upward mobility. The proper level of analysis for these factors is the highest and broadest. Naturally both types of factors must be examined diachronically, over a period of time where variations can be analyzed. Unfortunately, the diachronical approach is not always possible, except in a well conceived plan of long-term research. Neither one can be neglected. While the former allows for individual variation within the same families and communities, the latter creates constraints and directions affecting the entire social group within which the individual functions, and the conditions for upward mobility at the broader levels (regional, national, international). This study is limited in its specific scope of the formation of social identity among the Miao students selected for this project. In another sense, the study capitalizes on the knowledge Yali gathered as a Chinese woman over the last forty years, both as a university student and professor as well as a citizen interested in the politics of ethnicity in China. The limitations of this analysis as well as its strengths will be apparent. 'I feel confident that my interpretation of what the Miao students described and expressed is accurate, because I had the opportunity of inquiring and probing with questions that required an indepth knowledge of the Chinese society and culture. The design of the questions themselves and the analysis of the various responses and other essays by students is based on my knowledge of Chinese society and culture in its broad macro-sociological structures, that is, on the larger human ecology of multicultural China,' (Yali Zou says).

We feel that the essays and various questionnaire responses, as well as our observations and written communication with students, are in complete agreement on every dimension of the process of social and ethnic identification. The crucial questions we are asking are:

1 Where do Miao students find sources of self-esteem?
2 Where do they find role models to handle the conflicts associated with changes in self-identity and the upward social roles they have to play?
3 How do they manifest their ambivalence about traditional behaviors and their newly adopted lifestyle?
4 How do they retain a strong self-concept as members of the Miao people, yet are prepared to display behaviors that characterize persons of higher status in Chinese society?

Perhaps an attempt to answer these questions first will give the reader a better understanding of the contrast between Chinese and American students, as well as a sense of the different processes of social and ethnic identification that Chinese (and Miao students in particular) go through. Finally, the following discussion will also address the issue of the sources of self-worth which allow students to change to adapt to university life, yet remain deeply committed to their family values.

Chinese students, in general, but especially students from ethnic or minority groups (nationalities) derive their personal self-worth and their social identity from key values collectively achieved. Consequently, the sources for personal self-worth are places outside and inside the individual. Those outside the individual are placed primarily in the family, peer group, village, and ethnic community. These collectively achieved values represent high standards of joint success and social distinction; thus, success is measured in terms of approximation to specific goals, that is, behaviors and activities that portray commitment to these goals. One of these central, collective values is honor. But honor is viewed in the context of a social attribution of virtues resulting from many individuals working together. For example, family honor consists of socially recognized achievements, especially in terms of knowledge and virtue, by the members of that family. Parents, for example, are the object of the attribution (the recipients of honor) if their children do well in school.

The need for analysis of the personal statements by each of the fourteen students included in this project (see comments in Chapter 5), helps in understanding the dynamics of ethnic identification for the Miao students. The longer they have been away from their villages and the more knowledge and status they have acquired, the more difficult it is for them to feel both as a Miao villager and a prestigious university student. Their early socialization maintains its impact through the continuous dependence on home, and the collective village recognition they receive (as local heroes) any time they go back to visit their families. It is impossible to imagine that these students could ever forget who they are, and abandon their personal commitment to achieve in order to pay back their debts of gratitude to their families, fellow community members, and the Miao people in general. Thus, the text to be presented here, will guide the reader to understand the reasons why Miao students sacrifice so much in order to obtain an academic career.

Of particular importance in this analysis is not only the identification of the hierarchy of values leading to students' commitment to succeed in school today as university students, but the chain of events that led to their present status as university students, and the chains of events that provided them in the home with the support system that allowed them to become members of a very select group in China, that of university-educated elites. The values that play a key role in student's lives are indeed the same values of Chinese families: respect for the family, commitment to honor the family and community, respect for learning and for teachers, mentors and scholars; a strong sense of belonging to a family, a community, and a village and province. This sense of belonging is essentially a deep knowledge of the history, language and culture of the peoples who share the same cultural values, lifestyle and traditions. If one asks a relatively simple question to a Miao student at the university, such as 'Why do you work so hard to achieve academically?', the answer is one that reveals a sense of obligation to the family and the community. The student feels that he or she has received so much, that he or she cannot disappoint parents, relatives, community and friends; that would destroy the honor of the family. The sacrifices of parents to support their children at the university on their modest income is a burden that brings tears to many students even as they speak about their family. To help one's own parents is an obligation for all children, including those who did not receive an education from their parents; for a child whose parents had to suffer hunger, cold and many deprivations related to poverty, the obligation to honor parents and pay them back for their sufferings is truly overwhelming.

Therefore, our basic assumption behind the interpretation of the data we collected is that the key motivating factor of academic achievement among the young Miao intellectual leaders at the Beijing Central University for Nationalities and at the Guizhou Institute for Nationalities is family and community; that is, their sense of obligation and responsibility to both family and community gives energy and inspiration to these young men and women to work hard in school in order to repay the obligations of love and sacrifice. The assessment of the frequency and quality of communication between students and their families — parents, siblings and other relatives living in the households — as well as other members of the community, helps us to understand the validity of our assumption that academic achievement is motivated by a debt of love and gratitude with those members of the group (family, community) to which the student belongs.

The Inner Miao Self

One of the fundamental premises of this analysis is that statements about the self and the world around us reflect our inner self-identity and cultural values, our affiliation and our perceptions of the world. The study of the self through text analysis is a search for human consciousness, but distinct from the study of psychological structures or types of personalities. While the analysis of social structural or environmental factors (as, for example, those that are provided for the Chinese nationalities and the Miao in Chapters 3 and 4) can help us to understand the adaptation of Miao students to university life and their internalization of their roles as intellectual leaders, it is essential to examine their personal experiences as expressed by them and their statements on their social roles. Personal experiences provide us with insights into the psychodynamics of motivation to achieve, to tolerate pain, to endure deprivation, to make sacrifices, and ultimately to succeed in the attainment of personal goals.

The differential response of ethnic or minority groups to status inequality and the differential cohesion or alienation resulting from attempts to respond to low status are both linked to a number of psychological mechanisms discussed earlier. These mechanisms that are designed by humans to protect themselves from pain and retain a measure of self-control are contingent upon the early socialization period, the relative strength of the support given by the family, community and peer groups, and the relative integrity of the personality of the individual. According to DeVos:

> Examining patterns of minority adaptation both in the US and Japan
> I have come to decry sociological theories considering delinquency or

deviancy solely in terms of the situational social factors such as those operative in American city ghettoes. These theories do not explain why different minority groups viewed longitudinally over several generations develop different patterns of adaptation in response to discrimination and economic hardship. On the other hand, anthropologists attempting to examine persistent culture patterns are too prone to dismiss psychological universals and advocate non-judgmental cultural considerations which rule out any possible judgment as to the relative adequacy or inadequacy of their attempts at adaptation... Social behavior found prevalent in some groups are often symptomatic of underlying psychological rigidities induced in childhood that make it difficult to adapt to change. There *are* psychological consequences that become evident in the behavior of members of some groups related to the deprivation and neglect as well as abuse experienced during their socialization.

(DeVos 1993a:9)

The rigidification of behavior, in DeVos' view, may be related to early socialization of children who seek coping mechanisms to protect themselves from adults and peers. De Vos identified three maneuvers or mechanisms: 1) introception; 2) exclusion or boundary protection; 3) expulsion:

Frozen into a rigid pattern during this early phase one finds them apparent in various forms of psychosis. Rigidification in their intermediate stages leads to character problems, or neurotic incapacities. They may appear as character problems influencing identity, such as 'identity diffusion'. They may appear in a neurosis as excessive repression, or in obsessive compulsive ideational patterns... Throughout their development these three processes remain in some form of continuous interactive balance, although one or another of these mechanisms may receive more use defensively, and hence, become characteristically more dominant. Such relative dominance in more or less rigidified interactive patterns become recognizable as fixed 'personality' patterns.

(DeVos 1993a:30)

The first type of defense mechanism is identified by DeVos as 'empathy' or the human capacity to resonate, which regulates the intake of early experiences, that is 'taking in or introception of experiences in Durkheim's idiom is basic to the continuing of a "collective consciousness" common to a society' (DeVos 1993a:31). This process of internalization starts early in life and leads to identification and a distinct concept of the self. Internalization may be a function of 'selective permeability', or of the culturally and socially mediated choice of relevance criteria for pursuing objects of knowledge, norms of behavior, cultural values and social identification.

These principles are relevant to the selection of analytical concepts and categories of human behaviors, values and attitudes present in the statements

Power in Education

Table 5: *Categories of Basic Interpersonal Concerns from Text*

	Positive	Negative
EXPRESSIVE	1. Pleasure: physical, sensual, emotional, ecstasy	Suffering: Pain, depression, anxiety, ambivalence
	2. Nurturance: advice, economic support, help	Abandonment: deprivation, refusal to help, withholding support, neglect
	3. Affiliation: Belonging to a group, close relationships	Isolation, marginalization, separation, discontent, incompatibility
	4. Appreciation: Recognition of status, deference	Humiliation, degradation, rejection, disdain
	5. Harmony, peace, happiness, satisfaction with life	Discord, conflict, disagreement, hatred, factionalism
INSTRUMENTAL	1. Dominance, control, disobedience, authoritarianism, autonomy	Subordination, obedience, dependence, lack of assertiveness
	2. Competition, entrepreneurship, aggression	Cooperation, accommodation
	3. Responsibility, observance of laws and behavioral norms	Irresponsibility, neglect, delinquency, crime
	4. Competence	Lack of competence
	5. Achievement (attribution)	Failure (attribution)

Source: Partially constructed from DeVos, 1993b

made by students. Analytical categories as applied to statements are either expressive or instrumental. Following DeVos' typology (1993b) *expressive* statements are those that merely convey a feeling, an attitude, a value position, a state of affairs; *instrumental* statements are those that convey a sense of means to ends relationship. Among the expressive statements are those manifesting pleasure or suffering, nurturance or deprivation, affiliation or isolation, appreciation or humiliation, harmony or discord. Among the instrumental statements are those statements that convey dominance or subordination, competition or cooperation, responsibility or delinquency, competence or incompetence, achievement or alienation. These expressive and instrumental categories of statements are subdivided into positive or negative and into active or passive. (See Table 5 inventorying the various categories).

Table 5 is based on the more comprehensive set of categories developed by George DeVos in his *Scoring Manual, Basic Interpersonal Concerns* (DeVos 1993b). The table simplifies a very sophisticated taxonomy of expressive and instrumental categories. In attempting to use such a complex taxonomy, we found that some of the Miao students' statements referred to behaviors that could function both as expressive and instrumental, and that with some frequency, students provided hints of subordinate relationships between expressions of achievement, search for competence, pleasure, nurturance, appreciation, or harmony, to higher level values associated with the basic value of responsibility to the family, to parents, to their community. Even statements alluding to the need for control (at least, control of their lives and their academic activities) and tolerance of suffering, abandonment, isolation, marginalization, conflict, and even failure, were always subordinate to the main value constellation of love to the family, especially parents, peers, Miao society, and devotion to the beliefs and practices keeping together the Miao people.

The use of these categories is primarily for the purpose of identifying crucial characteristics in the personality of the individuals under study, and then to explore the possible factors explaining those characteristics. The major hypotheses presented to explain those characteristics will form a part of the early socialization process. The nature of the socialization process is expected to shed some light on the basic research questions raised earlier:

a Why do Miao educated persons pursue their academic career with such intensity, and with such enormous personal and group sacrifices?
b What is the nature of their role as educational leaders?
c What is the nature of their ethnic identity and what is its role in academic achievement?

We thought that in order to examine in detail these issues we could use the testimony of Professor Wu, one of the recognized Miao leaders in the Central University for Nationalities of Beijing, and a dedicated mentor whose students provided me with eloquent testimonies of their values. There is a clear correspondence between the perceptions and values of students and Professor Wu, but it seems that Professor Wu is speaking out of long personal experience, and on behalf of many other intellectuals from Miao ancestry.

We asked Professor Wu to write a letter to the Hmong (Miao) people in the United States, and to share with them his life experiences and values, in the hope of establishing communication with them. The more mature and extremely eloquent statement of Professor Wu illustrates the psychological process of integration of academic values with Miao cultural values, and thus helps the argument that empowerment does not necessarily have to bring cultural conflict, self-rejection and marginalization of low-status groups. Here is the text of Wu Dekun's statement:

My Life History

A Letter to Fellow Miao People in the United States
Wu Dekun

My dear fellow Miao people in the United States:
You are in the United States, while we are in the Peoples' Republic of China. We are separated from each other by the deep ocean and high mountains and we are in different parts of the world. Our common forefathers can be traced back to ancient times. That was the time of the powerful tribal unit headed by Chi You, the leader of the nine Li tribes. At that time, they lived by the Yellow River. That society existed more than five thousand years ago. In the meantime, there was another tribal unit headed by a Yellow emperor who was very powerful as well. These two powerful tribal units competed with and

fought against each other. Eventually in the battle of Zuo Lu, the Miao tribe was defeated (Zuo Lu county today is in the Hebei province).

After having been defeated, the Miao people, old and young, men and women, withdrew. Successfully crossing the Yellow River southbound, they went down along the middle and lower reaches of the Yangzi River. By Dong Ting Lake and Pan Yang Lake they settled down to live. By the age of the Emperors Yao, Shun, and Yu, the Miao people, once again, formed a powerful tribal unit which was known as the 'Three Miao'. The Three Miao controlled a large population which was able to compete with the tribal unit headed by Emperors Yao, Shun, and Yu, and there were a lot of fights and battles between them. In the end, the Miao were again defeated. Therefore they had to begin a large-scale migration. Some of them entered the West part of the Hunan province. Some entered the east, west and middle parts of the Guizhou province. Those who found themselves in Western Hunan and Eastern Guizhou, where there are green mountains and beautiful rivers and a friendly environment were relatively better off and so their settlements were relatively permanent. In Eastern Guizhou, there are certain counties, e.g. Leishan county, where the Miao were about 85 per cent of the total population in the county. In some Miao villages there were as many as one thousand households. The Miao who lived in Western Hunan province also formed a large community.

Generally speaking, those Miao who live in the central and western parts of the Guizhou province had to look for a better life by moving around. Due to the natural environment which is what we call a 'high and cold mountain area', some of them entered Guangxi province, Yunnan province and Sichuan province, then from Yunnan they entered Laos, Thailand, Vietnam, Burma and that area traditionally known as Indochina. For various other reasons, some Miao people also emmigrated to the United States, France and the other countries. Consequently, the Miao people have become an international group. China, however, remained the headquarters of the Miao people where there continues to be a large population of Miao people. According to the statistics of 1982, there were more than five million Miao people in China. Up to 1990, there was a increase in the Miao population. It has now, in 1991, reached numbers as high as 7,398,035 people with about 3.68 million Miao people residing in the Guizhou province — about 50 per cent of all the Miao people in China. One of the characteristics of the distribution of the Miao people is that they are in large areas with small living settlements in which the village is the basic unit.

The language used by the Miao people can be divided into three dialects: 1) the Eastern Guizhou dialect; 2) the Western Hunan and Sichuan dialect; 3) the Guizhou and Yunnan dialect. Those Miao people who live in Laos, Vietnam, the United States, France and the other countries called themselves 'Mo' (or 'Hmong'). In a word, those Miao people who speak the dialect of Sichuan, Guizhou and Yunnan also call themselves 'Mo'. Those who use the same language can readily communicate with each other. However, the people who use other dialects have some difficulty in communicating.

My dear fellow Miao people, now you are living in the United States, a country with a high level of life, culture and scientific technology. I sincerely hope that you keep your own national [ethnic] language and maintain your national [ethnic] culture. In the meantime, I also hope that you, especially the young and the middle-aged people work hard to study English well and to study other disciplines, to be strong and people with high aspirations — specialists in different fields — so that you can contribute your share to mankind. In so doing you also will be able to contribute to your fellow Miao people, to help change the backward situation of your ancestral homeland. I hope you will not forget your ancestral background in China where there are thousands of thousands of your fellow Miao people just like me who place great hopes on you. The Miao minority people in China today are still poor and backward. It is my hope that you will be very successful in your studies and that you will use advanced science and technology to help your fellow Miao people in China to change their backward situation. Of course, Miao people in China, themselves, will work very hard to be self-reliant and to try to change their homeland . . . and reconstruct their hometown, and realize their great goal under the leadership of the Chinese Communist Party.

We all know that in today's society, the development in the fields of economics, science and technology are very important and the competition is very keen . . . That if you do not make any progress or you simply stay in the same place, you are already behind. It is my sincere hope that you will become numerous huge dragons who can summon the winds and rains [control the forces of nature].

In conclusion, I want to say that when you have time and it is convenient, you are welcome to come back to visit your fellow Miao people in China. You will surely receive a warm welcome and we will strengthen the ties between us.

Best Regards,
Wu Dekun, Miao Associate Researcher
Central University for Nationalities, Beijing, China

A Miao Cosmology: Comments on Professor Wu Dekun's Statement

An interesting and eloquent history of China includes as a central piece the struggles between the Han dynasty and the powerful Miao fighters who have resisted for the last 5000 years the oppression of the dominant groups. Defeat after defeat caused large scale migrations of Miao through the Yunnan, Hunan and Guizhou provinces and beyond into Indochina. The strong appeal not to forget their fellow Miao in mainland China goes along with the recognition of the power that Miao people in exile throughout the world have achieved, especially the Miao (Mo or Hmong) in the United States, France and other Western countries. Implied in this statement is a profound commitment to the Miao nationality or the recognition of Miao ethnicity and uniqueness. Mr. Wu did not speak of his personal life, although in passing he often said that his students' life histories were pretty much like his own.

Professor Wu Dekun, who teaches at the Central University for Nationalities in Beijing, often sat with his students during the group interviews and encouraged them to share their experiences with the researchers. Several times, as the students were describing the hardships and poverty they suffered as young children, and the sacrifices their parents made to send them to school, Professor Wu was unable to contain his emotion and the tears would roll down his face. Later on, after the above letter was sent to me, we received additional biographic materials he composed to show how he had gone through many experiences in life similar to those of his students.

Prof. Wu is a genuine scholar who can distinguish nuances in the Miao language that require a great deal of knowledge and phonetic training. For example, he explained to us how a single sound in eight different tones could have eight different meanings in Miao. His essay is a summary of the ethnohistory of the Miao people, but it is addressed to his fellow Miao living in America, and has the intent of opening communication with them. Recognizing the lack of technology and the poverty of the Miao people, he still maintains a very proud position regarding the quality of Miao cultural traditions, and the beauty of its land and its people.

Conclusion

The data presented above indicates the presence of central cultural themes and a cohesive cultural value system that is based on the recognition that the Miao lifestyle, in spite of its primitive technology, is of a high spiritual quality. The various themes of responsibility to the Miao collectivity and the various means to express loyalty to the Miao culture will be analyzed in the following chapter in a cross-cultural context.

This study, therefore, in spite of its obvious limitations, will attempt to contribute to a cross-cultural understanding of the processes of empowerment. For example, anthropological research, specifically cultural ecology, represented by Ogbu and others (Ogbu 1974, 1978, 1981, 1987, 1991, 1992; Gibson 1987, 1988) have described caste-like or disempowered groups as those who develop oppositional identities contrasting with mainstream groups; thus, caste-like groups are supposed to reject educational values because mainstream persons adhere to educational values. Miao students seem to retain their affiliation with the Miao people, while accepting the importance of education, and see no conflict in being both educated and Miao; yet they are aware that sometimes they are treated as an underclass. These students know that their village life, their language and cultural traditions, in contrast with the language and traditions of the Han people, are considered primitive and of low status. Most Miao students had to acquire Mandarin as a second language and did not become totally fluent in reading, writing and speaking until they reached the university. In fact, Miao students have different levels of oral and written language fluency. Some have become fully bilingual, while others are still struggling with meaning, grammar and phonetics. The process of empowerment among the Miao people seems to be rooted in their commitment to help their villages. The logical means to help their villages is to acquire knowledge, and through knowledge, prestige, status, honor and power to make changes. Looking at some of the recent research on immigrants in Europe and the United States, there seem to be promising comparisons if we adopt more flexible theoretical models of adaptation and adjustment (as well as models for academic success).

While in the empowerment research a great deal has been discussed regarding the role of education and intellectual development in the empowerment of racial or ethnic minorities, China offers a unique case that can assist researchers in their study of the role of education in empowerment. Education, virtue and knowledge are intertwined in Chinese philosophy and Chinese cultural traditions that cross-cut nationalities. Both Paulo Freire (1973), and many centuries before, Confucius, speak of the need to understand one's role in society, one's dignity and one's truth. At the base of critical pedagogy and the curriculum reform it inspires, is this same assumption, that education, whether formal or informal, is the means to understand the common bond uniting humankind and the fundamental rights afforded to all human beings.

The ethnic and racial crises affecting world order today, the denial of human rights to many individuals, and the inter-ethnic conflicts that surface in many places on earth today, suggest that the study of minority education and minority leadership in China is significant. China has rapidly become one of the most powerful economies of the world. The disproportionate allocation of economic and political power among peoples, especially among members of many nationalities, such as the Miao, whose annual family incomes continue to be extremely low, suggests the need to understand the role of education in the empowerment of these groups. Given the demographics of China and its global role in the world economy, the investment in education is a price that China must pay to avoid additional revolutions and to open participation of all groups in the national social, political and economic structures of the country.

The role of education will be of such importance that the Chinese government will invest millions of dollars in training teachers, local educational leaders and technical experts to raise the educational level of its citizens even in the most remote villages. Educational policies will have to be formulated clearly grounded on studies of nationality groups and low-income or minority populations. Much of recent educational research in the US and Europe has attempted to deal with the achievement motivation of students seeking academic excellence, as well as the lack of motivation for students failing in the classroom. The work of educational anthropologists has raised the issue of increasing marginalization of minority groups who do poorly in school and feel, as a result of their poor academic performance, neglected, unwanted and isolated. Some of the feelings of isolation and the bitter experience of failure is reflected in the letters from the Miao students. The analysis of the poor performance of minorities in the United States has been examined by cultural ecologists and other educational researchers. Their attempt to examine the dynamics of culture in the development of motivation to achieve academically, or in the development of resistance to achieve, is based on the impact of large macro-sociological and psychological structures of society: discrimination, oppression, poverty, history of slavery, etc. The data collected in this study would indicate that, beyond cultural ecological factors affecting most nationality groups in China, there are important family and community factors that serve to motivate low-income and other minority students to achieve highly in schools. Furthermore, the research conducted by Russian and American scholars on the social and cultural context of cognitive development alludes to factors that are important also among Chinese students. The work of Vygotsky and Bakhtin, as interpreted by Wertsch, for example, indicates that language and culture (the home languages and cultures of oppressed nationalities in China, for example) play a very important role in mediating the acquisition of knowledge and in fostering academic development of ethnic or racial minority groups.

This study opens the door to the discussion of new theoretical frameworks that may partially explain the unprecedented outcome of high achievement among the members of the Miao group of students, despite their humble origins and their parents' relative low level of education. The results of interviews and questionnaires, the analysis of their university learning environments, the analysis of their life accounts, and the text analysis of some of their most eloquent statements, lead to the realization that education is seen by parents of the Miao as the most congruent activity in the context of Confucian philosophy, as an effective instrument of empowerment for the entire family, and the hope for the future careers of these young men and women.

References

DeVos, G. (1992) *Social Cohesion and Alienation: Minorities in the United States and Japan*, San Francisco, CA: Westview.
DeVos, G. (1993a) Psychological anthropology: A professional Odyssey. Unpublished manuscript, Berkeley, CA: University of California, Berkeley.
DeVos, G. (1993b) Scoring manual for basic interpersonal concerns. Unpublished manuscript, Berkeley, CA: University of California, Berkeley.

DeVos, G. and Suárez-Orozco, M.M. (1990) *Status Inequality: The Self in Culture*, Newbury, CA: Sage Publications.

Freire, P. (1973) *Pedagogy of the Oppressed*, New York, NY: Seabury.

Gibson, M. (1987) 'Punjabi immigrants in an American high school', in Spindler, G. and Spindler, L. (Eds) *Interpretive Ethnography of Education: At Home and Abroad*, Hillsdale, NJ: Lawrence Erlbaum Associates, Publishers, pp. 281–310.

Gibson, M. (1988) *Accommodation Without Assimilation: Sikh Immigrants in an American High School*, Ithaca, NY: Cornell University Press.

Ogbu, J. (1974) *The Next Generation: An Ethnography of Education in an Urban Neighborhood*, New York, NY: Academic Press.

Ogbu, J. (1978) *Minority Education and Caste: The American System in Cross-cultural Perspective*, New York, NY: Academic Press.

Ogbu, J. (1981) 'Origins of human competence: A cultural-ecological perspective', *Child Development*, **52**, pp. 413–29.

Ogbu, J. (1987) 'Variability in minority school performance: A problem in search of an explanation', *Anthropology and Education Quarterly*, **18**, pp. 312–34.

Ogbu, J. (1991) 'Immigrant and involuntary minorities in comparative perspective', in Gibson, M. and Ogbu, J. (Eds) *Minority Status and Schooling: A Comparative Study of Immigrant and Involuntary Minorities*, New York, NY: Garland Publishing, Inc., pp. 3–33.

Ogbu, J. (1992) 'Understanding cultural diversity', *Educational Researcher*, **21**(8), pp. 5–24.

Chapter 7

Early Socialization, Social Identification and Empowerment

This and the next chapter deal with the theoretical implications of the data presented in the previous chapters. The recurrent discussion of the impact that early home socialization had on the lives of Miao students, especially on their achievement motivation and the overall sense of empowerment to succeed, deserves discussion, especially in light of the work by cultural ecologists. What is the role of early socialization in the process of social-identification and the acquisition of cultural values? How do youngsters handle the apparent conflicts between home socialization with its specific values, and school socialization? What can we learn from the study of Miao students in China that can help us reformulate a theory of early socialization and social identification for empowerment?

Immigrant, refugee and ethnic minority children go through a complicated process of new social identification as they become exposed to new social, cultural and linguistic norms, and they often have to uproot and leave friends, family and a familiar environment. Additionally, in some settings, immigrant children must face the psychological assaults of being perceived as less valuable than other children, of being judged as incompetent linguistically, socially and culturally. This chapter raises a number of questions that set the stage for the central discussion of the nature of early socialization of minority children in China and the United States. The assumption is that early socialization is intimately related to the formation of the processes of self-identification as a member of an ethnic or minority group, and of conscious acquisition of ethnic prejudice and racial awareness. It is during early childhood that we learn how to respond to prejudice and how we select defense mechanisms such as denying the reality that causes pain, selectively learning only those things that are compatible with our ethnic and social identification, acquiring achievement motivation, cognitive skills, and psychological resistance to pain and lack of affection. In the context of early socialization, we must point out the serious consequences of abuse and neglect. What provides children with the incentives and commitment to achieve in school? Under what conditions are children, even those who live in poverty, willing to make great sacrifices in order to obtain knowledge and become empowered to participate in the social,

Early Socialization, Social Identification and Empowerment

economic and political institutions of a society? George Spindler, recognizing that we have dealt primarily with 'minority peoples who have had to operate in what some would describe as an essentially colonial situation' and consequently 'may have the theoretical rights of self-determination and self-regulation, but, in fact, do not and could not exercise these rights' (1987:168) makes this insightful observation:

> There are now strong movements underway towards self-determination. Some are very militant, separatistic, and nationalistic. Others are more accommodative. But all share in striving for self-determination, and regulation of the schools is an important aspect of this determination. These people recognize, perhaps in different terms, what we have said — that education is a process of recruitment and maintenance for the cultural system. For minority people the schools have been experienced as damaging attempts to recruit their children into an alien culture. Their self-images and identities were ignored, or actively attacked.
>
> (Spindler, G. 1987:168)

To some extent the identity of many of the nationality groups in China was attacked or ignored for many years, until the formation of the People's Republic of China in 1949 that resulted in the recognition of all nationalities. The information gathered in China among the Miao for this project leads to some theoretical reflections that are best discussed in a cross-cultural perspective, and along the lines of the work of George and Louise Spindler. Psychological and cultural anthropologists (DeVos 1973, 1982, 1983; DeVos and Suárez-Orozco 1990; Spindler, G. 1987, 1988) have discussed the processes of social identification as part of socialization, a process whereby worldview, norms of behavior and cultural values are transmitted from the senior to the junior generations. George Spindler views early socialization as a crucial mechanism to transfer and restructure culture (Spindler, G. 1974; Spindler and Spindler, with Trueba and Williams 1990). Part of culture is the system of values and traditions that enhance social identification processes by ritually strengthening the sense of belonging in a group. It seems, from the work by George Spindler and his associates, that early socialization can also be an instrument for marginalization; those individuals who are 'unassimilable' or unwanted receive clear messages early in their lives, from the first contacts with social and educational institutions.

While the ultimate outcome for many members of society is to become marginal as a result of the impact of social institutions, it seems that the process of marginalization is not necessarily a terminal state; marginalized individuals can indeed become empowered under certain conditions and with the assistance of more knowledgeable persons. This final process of empowerment that constitutes a drastic change from previous situations (either collective or individual) is of particular importance in the study of immigrant, refugee and minority populations. Can we argue that the Miao people characterize in China one of the most isolated and disenfranchised populations? Yes, we can. Can we argue that the Miao university students of this study became part of the elite of university students who enjoy a high status in Chinese society? Yes, we can. Did all Miao university student internalize the change from peasant villagers to prestigious university students? In different degrees and with different implications all of them realized this change. Did students feel less Miao because they acquired knowledge and status? No, they felt more committed to their people, and more appreciative of their Miao cultural traditions, language and folklore. How did they reconcile the two opposite parts of their social identity: being a Miao peasant boy or girl and a high status university student? Is there a contradiction, a conflict or a discontinuity? To answer this question we need to look at other studies and then come back to the data gathered here.

One of the basic tenets of achievement theories, including cultural ecology, is that the social and cultural context in which a person acquires cultural values plays a major role in determining how that person faces social demands and resolves conflicts, including those conflicts associated with discriminatory practices. To what extent is cultural ecology applicable to the case of the Miao students? Cultural ecologists would want us to believe that the social oppression suffered by certain social groups leads them to the development of a castelike personality which is based on the development of an oppositional self-concept. Ogbu, the most visible scholar identified with this theoretical development, presents a typology of minority groups and an explanation of their differential school achievement (1974, 1978, 1987, 1989, 1991a, 1991b, 1992; Ogbu and Matute-Bianchi 1986; and Gibson and Ogbu 1991).

One of the most controversial features of cultural ecology is this typology of minority groups and the behavioral characteristics attributed to each group:

> I have identified three types of minorities in cross-cultural studies. One is *autonomous minorities*. These are people who are minorities primarily in a numerical sense. They may possess a distinctive ethnic, religious, linguistic, or cultural identity. However, although they are not entirely free from prejudice and discrimination, they are not socially, economically, and politically subordinated. Autonomous minorities do not experience disproportionate and persistent problems in learning to read and to compute, partly because they usually have a cultural frame of reference that demonstrates and encourages school success. This type of minority is typically represented in the United States by Jews and Mormons.
>
> (Ogbu 1987:320)

Essentially, small groups who may or may not have a distinctive ethnic identity and who are successful in school are the autonomous type. Here, as we see, Ogbu considers school success as one of the essential properties of this group's definition. Therefore, their academic success is already taken for granted, and needs no explanation. Ogbu continues:

> *Immigrant minorities* are the second type. These are people who have moved more or less voluntarily to the United States because they believe that this would lead to greater economic well-being, better overall opportunities, and/or greater political freedom. Although the immigrants often experience difficulties due to language and cultural differences, they do not experience lingering disproportionate school failure. The Chinese in Stockton, California (Ogbu 1974) and Punjabi Indians in Valley side, California . . . are representative examples.
> (Ogbu 1987:320–1)

What is understood by *disproportionate academic failure* is not clear. This definition clearly includes refugees who come of their own will seeking political freedom. The substantive differential achievement among Indochinese, Chinese, Japanese and other Asian American groups, and as well as within each of these groups has been recently documented (see Trueba, Cheng and Ima 1993). There is still a definition of the group in terms of what is supposed to be explained with the theory; this group is characterized by academic success, or the lack of *disproportionate academic failure*. Therefore, there will have to be further explanation of the success or failure of these two first groups, and that explanation will have to be other than their being *autonomous* or *immigrant* minorities. How do we distinguish autonomous from immigrant? Is it possible to move from one category to another? It is not clear. For example, are the recently arrived Japanese Americans autonomous or immigrant? Ogbu goes on:

> *Castelike or involuntary minorities* are people who were *originally brought into United States society involuntarily* through slavery, conquest, or colonization. Thereafter, these minorities were relegated to menial positions and denied true assimilation into mainstream society. American Indians, black Americans, and Native Hawaiians are examples. In the case of Mexican Americans, those who later immigrated from Mexico were assigned the status of the original conquered group in the southwestern United States, with whom they came to share a sense of peoplehood or collective identity. The Burakumin in Japan and the Maori in New Zealand are examples outside the United States. It is castelike or involuntary minorities that usually experience more difficulties with social adjustment and school performance.
> (Ogbu 1987:321)

The implied assumption in characterizing this group is that all these minority groups share in common the fact that they are in a mainstream society against their will, and that their castelike status is a direct result from oppression in the form of slavery, conquest or colonization. Subsequently, Ogbu collapsed the first two groups into one called *voluntary* groups, and *involuntary* groups (the castelike). While Ogbu recognizes that there are individual and subgroup differences, he believes that castelike minorities are taxonomically distinct. George DeVos, Ogbu's teacher and intellectual mentor, used the term *caste* and *castelike* to refer to disenfranchised autochthonous groups (such as the Native Americans in the US, the Burakumin in Japan and the Maoris in New Zealand). He explained in psychoanalytic terms their attributes and conflicts, and ultimately their inability to function effectively in society because these groups have suffered persistent degradation and isolation. DeVos and Romanucci-Ross (1982) and DeVos and Suárez-Orozco (1990) argue that beyond social class factors or other social structural elements, there are profound psychological (psychodynamic) forces affecting castelike persons' poor adaptation to society and their school underperformance.

Cultural ecologists also believe that immigrant groups exhibit primary and secondary cultural discontinuities; voluntary groups (autonomous and immigrant) show primary discontinuities (those existing before they came in contact with the mainstream population), but the involuntary groups (castelike) exhibit secondary cultural discontinuities (those resulting from their contact with the mainstream population). The concepts of cultural *continuities* and *discontinuities* was first used by George and Louise Spindler in their acculturation studies of the Menominee (Spindler, G. 1971). I am aware that the original intent of cultural ecologists was to attack the pseudo-scientific genetic or biological determinists on the grounds that determinism does not explain differential academic achievement, because determinism does not take into consideration differential achievement resulting from sociological and psychological factors at different levels of specificity (macro-environmental or sociological factors, in contrast with intra-personality factors), macro-sociological factors such as job ceiling, segregation, oppression, etc., and psychological factors such as individual achievement motivation based on cultural values acquired in the home country.

Following the contributions of DeVos (1967, 1973, 1980, 1982, 1983; DeVos and Wagatsuma 1966; DeVos and Romanucci-Ross 1982; Wagatsuma and DeVos 1984) Ogbu and his associates established specific relationships between the deeper psychodynamic levels of ethnic identification and the macro-sociological levels of the environment in which minorities function. In addition, cultural ecologists showed the differential impact of cultural contact, that is, between one's own cultural values, and the values of the host country, in the context of real life issues such as physical and psychological survival in searching for a job, or in facing racial discrimination, poverty, and low-quality schooling. The questions cultural ecologists kept asking themselves was: What is unique about castelike groups who must acquire secondary discontinuities? What is the significance of secondary discontinuities, and how do they affect the process of social redefinition of immigrant or other groups? Cultural ecologists, Ogbu in particular, think that the answer to these questions lies in the notion of *cultural inversion*:

> Cultural inversion is the tendency for some members of one population, in this case involuntary minorities, to regard certain forms of behavior, certain events, symbols, and meanings as inappropriate for them because they are characteristic of members of another population (e.g., white Americans) at the same time, the minorities claim other (often the opposite) forms of behaviors, events, symbols and meanings as appropriate for them because these are not characteristic of white Americans.
>
> (Ogbu 1987:323)

What is the origin of that tendency? How is that tendency to develop an oppositional identity related to the ethnic or home culture? All that cultural ecologists say is that, through cultural inversion, involuntary minorities develop their oppositional ethnic identity, while voluntary minorities use their home cultural frame as the foundation of their ethnic identity and the source of motivation to succeed. In one of his most recent articles, Ogbu states that involuntary minorities 'use cultural inversion to repudiate negative white stereotypes or derogatory images' or even as 'a strategy to manipulate whites, to get even with whites' (Ogbu 1992:9). In the same article, Ogbu offers some further insights or qualifications in his use of cultural inversion:

> Secondary cultural differences seem to be associated with ambivalent or oppositional social or collective identities vis-a-vis the White American social identity. Voluntary minorities seem to bring to the United States a sense of who they are from their homeland and seem to retain this different but non-oppositional social identity *at least during the first generation.* Involuntary minorities, in contrast, develop a new sense of social or collective identity that is in opposition to the social identity of the dominant group after they have become subordinated. They do so in response to the treatment by white Americans in economic, political, social, psychological, cultural, and language domains.
>
> (Ogbu 1992:9. Emphasis ours)

What happens after the first generation? All these factors (including language domains) are as general a cause of *oppositional identity* as can be. Why would these same factors affect only castelike groups? Do these factors affect them all collectively as a group? Are these groups the ones Ogbu mentioned earlier: African Americans, Mexican Americans, Hawaiians, Maoris, Burakumin, etc? What is the empirical evidence behind these assertions?

Because cultural contacts and their impact on self-identification (via *cultural inversion*) is at the heart of Ogbu's argument we must note with DeVos and Romanucci-Ross (1982) and DeVos (1990) that ethnic identity cannot be measured by examining the cultural content of various groups:

> Ethnic identity cannot be studied through specific attention to objective features of physical differences, territory, language, religion, occupational and economic features, or other specific cultural traits. One cannot be content with any etic approach to ethnicity. Rather, as Barth (1969) saw it, the problem is an emic one of *boundary maintenance* — whatever the contrastive features employed to define a group.
> (DeVos 1990:207)

DeVos (1990:208) contends that ethnicity goes together with social class as 'a central topic of social theory', and that in order to understand group affiliation ('social belonging') it is necessary to look at social behavior; consequently, the most productive approach to the study of ethnicity is to examine the dynamics of conflict in society, rather than the static formal structures or integration of society, because change is 'the reality of human history'. In this context of continuous change, cultural ecology examines the social behavior of minority groups, and contends that voluntary minorities (autonomous and immigrant) develop an independent identity that they retain as the point of reference to their home culture, and thus they can better cope with racism, oppression and other abuses they may suffer in the host society. In contrast, involuntary minorities develop an oppositional ethnic identity, one which defines their cultural characteristics in opposition to mainstream culture. The final outcome of this oppositional ethnic identity is supposed to be that 'castelikes' cannot generate academic achievement motivation to reach the levels of excellence that other groups achieve. Why should oppressed peoples develop oppositional ethnic identities in the first place?

Is Cultural Ecology Applicable to the Miao?

From the data gathered among the Miao in China, it is clear that they form one of the most oppressed groups politically, economically and educationally. Miao families have one of the lowest annual incomes in China and one of the lowest educational levels. The extreme poverty of Miao families makes it very difficult to help their children obtain an education beyond the third grade in elementary school. The history of wars between the Miao and the Han, the dominant society in China, resulting in the conquest of the Miao that ended in their low socio-economic condition, would suggest that the Miao people could be labeled castelike — to use Ogbu's term — for several generations. Yet, as Miao students move through high school and college, and as they pursue their various university degrees (and even university professorships), they do so without developing oppositional identities. Indeed they are proud to be Miao and use their emotional attachment to their ethnic group as a means of reaching high levels of academic excellence, as do other minority student groups, such as the Hui and the Mongols.

Early Socialization, Social Identification and Empowerment

The fundamental difference between China and the United States is that since 1949 China became officially multicultural and, through the leadership of Chairman Mao, it recognized the status of all nationalities as part of China. Thus, it is perfectly normal to belong to a nationality or a minority group, and indeed it carries some privileges. Being a member of a nationality, or marrying into a nationality, can bring opportunities to enter the university and obtain federal support, to have more than one child, to participate in the control of the land and other resources belonging to these nationalities in their own territories, etc. Nothing from the interviews, testimonies of students and faculty, questionnaires, or from the readings done on the Miao would indicate that they feel or act castelike, or that they feel less Chinese because they belong to a nationality. When we asked them directly if they felt they were differently treated by faculty than other students, most replied no, and a couple thought that different treatment happened only once in a while. However, to pretend that nationalities are not rank ordered is unrealistic. There are differences in wealth and status, although these differences are not conspicuous in dressing patterns, or jewelry, and certainly *all* students are treated equally in the store, dining room, classes and recreation facilities.

In his critique of cultural ecology, Trueba argues that the application of the castelike label for entire ethnic groups is questionable. Certainly in the case of the Miao students the label castelike is not appropriate.

In the ultimate analysis the academic failure of disempowered minorities and its significance — that is, as a sign of their total failure to adapt to American society — is predicated not on historical grounds and available documentation, but on assumptions about other peoples' cultures, and their differential response to American culture. These are some of the assumptions in Ogbu's reasoning:

1   Castelike minorities in the US are here against their will.
2   They fail in schools because they feel and are incompetent.
3   They are incompetent because they develop oppositional identities in opposition to white mainstream population.
4   School success is perceived as a white cultural trait.
5   The oppositional identity of castelike minorities is the result of what happened to their ancestors many years ago (perhaps several hundred years ago: slavery, oppression, etc.).
6   Group differences of these castelike, involuntary, or nonimmigrant groups in socio-economic level, exposure to American culture, family literacy level, and first and second language development, are inconsequential for their current academic achievement.
7   Differential quality of schooling prior to arrival this country, as well as the quality of schooling in this country, are clearly irrelevant or secondary to their current academic achievement.

8   The fundamental factor explaining achievement is the intrinsic cultural characteristics of minority groups and their response to that of the host country.
9   There is, therefore, a deterministic element in cultural ecology that forces castelike individuals to exhibit certain behaviors (leading to failure) over which they have no control. Therefore, Ogbu effectively disempowers these groups.
10 In turn, the voluntary minorities (model minorities) must succeed through the same deterministic cultural forces, regardless of personal merit.
11 This determinism absolves policy makers and practitioners from any responsibility to attempt to help castelikes or to play an important role in the success of the others (the model minorities).

Overall, these assumptions may have a weak historical base and a fundamental blindness towards the demonstrable heterogeneity of ethnic and racial groups throughout their various historical periods of adjustment to American society. This is the case of African Americans, Latinos, Hawaiians, American Indians, and others in the United States. European scholars are persuaded that their studies of ethnic minority groups often do not lend themselves to cultural ecological frameworks. More important, ethnic and racial groups exhibit significant collective responses in their ability to use their home cultural institutions in order to adapt successfully to the host country (see Trueba, Rodriguez, Zou and Cintrón 1993; Trueba 1993:10–11).

Poverty and Disempowerment

In the tradition of an ethnography of empowerment outlined by Trueba (in Delgado-Gaitan and Trueba 1991:137–80) this study has attempted to examine the process of *conscientization* discussed by Freire (1973) through the testimonies of the Miao students. The analysis of these testimonies shows drastic changes in the life of Miao students resulting from both macro-sociological and macro-psychological factors associated with the social reform of Mao's regime, as well as internal (intra-personal) factors related to the role of the Miao language and culture in social identification. The analysis of the links between the macro-levels and the intra-personality changes suggests the need to examine intermediate analytical levels of behavior, for example, family and community values, schools and peer group socialization, etc. Indeed, learning environments cut across all analytical levels and are interrelated as demonstrated by DeVos (1990:208–14). In a powerful methodological statement, DeVos proposes the following:

> In any multilevel approach, as discussed in my introduction, ethnicity can be defined in reference to four levels of analysis: first, in respect

to a social structural level; second, as a pattern of social interaction; third, as a subjective experience of identity; and fourth, as expressed in relatively fixed patterns of behavior and expressive emotional styles and how self and nonself (or in-group and out-group process) operate to maintain social distinctions.

(DeVos 1990:210)

Miao university students are socialized to become Chinese citizens first and members of the Miao nationality second. They have chosen to attend high school, college and university in order to improve their lives and those of their own ethnic group. They see no conflict between being a good Miao person and being a good student who achieves high levels of excellence, because academic achievement is viewed as a means to bring honor to their families and communities. They have earned respect and knowledge at a high personal cost, deprived at times of food and sleep. The target of their studies is often their own history, language, cultural traditions and folklore. They display their cultural and linguistic knowledge, their costumes, songs and history with peers and professors. Indeed, they have integrated their present social identification of being successful university students with their family values.

Much of the philosophy behind the social reforms that eventually permitted Miao students to attend the university, and that abolished dynasties, nobility and differential social strata among the working people, is based on Confucius' concept of virtue, knowledge and education. At the very foundations of the empowerment process is the conviction that after Chairman Mao's revolution, all peasants belonged in Chinese society, and nobody should be exploited or mistreated. The castification of peasants in the previous centuries was predicated on an asymmetrical relationship between peasants and nobility. Peasants were supposed to serve their lords (the nobility). Indeed the vast marginalization and disempowerment of peasant groups was ended *de jure* in 1949, although in reality the poverty of many of the groups, including the Miao, placed them at the mercy of more powerful groups. Castification and disempowerment takes place when there is an institutionalized and systematic way of creating oppressive relationships; that is, the underclass does not have neither the same rights nor the same obligations of the upper classes. Oppressive relationships have macro-structural arrangements that ultimately determine people's own self-identification. The conditions in China are such that, given the opportunity, even the poorest peasant can explore social and economic opportunities, and educational development.

The contrast between European countries or the United States and China in the way their minority groups are treated, is enormous. In Europe, the hiring of cheap hand labor (guest workers) to produce economic goods at competitive prices has resulted in the presence of a large permanent immigrant population whose roots are no longer in their country of origin — Eastern Europe, Turkey, Greece, North Africa, Central and South America, Italy, Spain, etc. Given the recent economic problems of Europe, it is no surprise that there are strong right wing movements to expatriate immigrants who, regardless of length of residence or place of origin — even if they are born on European soil, find themselves unemployed. There is legislation in various European countries (Germany, Belgium and France, for example) curtailing the number of immigrants allowed and the conditions for entry. Despite these policies, illegal immigration in Europe is rampant, and the abuse of immigrants of color (especially Moslems) is alarming.

Poverty lines in Europe and the United States follow racial and ethnic lines, especially among recent immigrants. There are 300,000 legal immigrants and refugees allowed to come to the United States annually, and there are 2 to 3 million undocumented immigrants who have entered the country in the last decade. The American Government has little control over the waves of immigration resulting from hunger, economic and political changes around the world. Thousands of immigrants, with or without documents, have continued to come from the South and cross the border every day and night, hoping to find jobs and a better education for their children, in brief a better future out of their ignorance and misery. According to Chavez, a party of twenty-six Salvadorans who had each paid $1,200 to a coyote [a contractor to smuggle illegal aliens from Mexico to the United States, responsible for hiring guides] were left in the desert by the guide without water or food; thirteen of them died (Chavez 1992:58). Often death occurs on Interstate 5 in California, around the San Clemente checkpoint, where migrants, in an effort to avoid detection, hike East through and around the mountains to avoid the border patrol. This means that they have to cross the freeway. Unfortunately, children and older people, not being able to estimate the high speed of passing cars often get killed. For example, from 1987 to 1990 there were thirty-three deaths on the freeway near the San Clemente crossing (Chavez 1992:59) and a number of accidental deaths at the crossing of Interstate Highways 805 and 5 (which go North-South). Other deaths have resulted from abuse of force against undocumented immigrants by law enforcement officers often experiencing extreme frustration and anger and from assaults by vigilantes motivated by hatred of Mexicans; the death rate continues to rise (Chavez 1992:59–60).

The fact that the initial motivation of immigrants and refugees to leave their home country is the love of their children, and that in the US they are willing to sacrifice even their lives in order to help them, is consistent with the support system of the extended family they try to recreate in the US, and the risks they take to open for their families opportunities to get an education and become economically successful. Children are highly valued in the traditions of the Hispanic cultures in Mexico, Central and South America. The extended family is cultivated even across great distances. Migrant families, even after they have established their residences, continue to visit relatives from Texas to California, to Washington and even to Wisconsin. The emotional and financial support is predicated on a system of reciprocity that networks blood-related or adopted kin persons. Critical life events (births, deaths, marriages, incarceration, anniversary celebrations, etc.) gather relatives from far away places. Children learn to depend on a large group of aunts, uncles, cousins, and other relatives. Mexican Americans who have adapted to American society concentrate their political and economic efforts in providing children with a good education, and in improving the instructional quality without losing the home language and culture (Trueba, Rodriguez, Zou and Cintrón 1993). The practice of investing in children and emphasizing in the home strict codes of behavior to insure high school achievement is also universally recognized among many Asian American families (Trueba, Cheng and Ima 1993).

In spite of efforts on the part of the Immigration and Naturalization Service to curtail the flow of immigrants from China and Latin America, the United States continues to be a land of promise for non-English speaking newcomers. Waggoner (1988:79–81) indicates that in 1980 there were 34.6 million persons in the US who speak languages other than English (15 per cent of the total population, or one in seven). Of those, 2.6 million were children under five, and 8 million were school-age children. Many of these children are Hispanic (see the recent work by Chapa and Valencia 1993:165–87). Hispanics number, as of the 1990 Census, 22.4 million (9 per cent of the total US population), an increase of 53 per cent in the last decade. By the year 2010 there will be over 30 million Hispanics, and by the year 2020 the total US youth population (composed of people seventeen years and under) will be 73 million; its composition, however, will change drastically. Hispanic youth will triple between 1982 and the year 2020, and will constitute 19 million (one fourth of the US youth population). Another very fast growing population is that of Asian Americans. Income levels among Spanish-speaking families barely permit them to subsist. As Chapa and Valencia state (1993:165–87) 38 per cent of all Hispanic families have an income of under $10,000; 57 per cent of them have incomes under $15,000, and 77 per cent incomes under $20,000, while at the same time they have more children per family. According to Chapa and Valencia (1993) the Hispanic population has created a demographic explosion that will change the history of the Southwest. Following closer to it is the second fastest growing ethnic population in that part of the United States, the Asian Americans. To the increasing waves of legal and illegal immigration from China, Taiwan and Korea, and Indochina, a new wave of immigrants from the Pacific Islands, the Philippines and Thailand seem to arrive in the Southwest United States in larger numbers every year.

There are a number of important facts about children in poverty in the United States, that clearly contrast with children in China:

1 Among blacks and Hispanics poverty rates are between 2.5 and 3 times higher than among whites (National Center for Children in Poverty (NCCP) 1990:7).
2 Five million children under the age of six lived in families whose incomes were under $10,000, and another 2.7 million children lived in families with incomes of less than $15,000 (NCCP: 8).

Power in Education

> 3   38 per cent of all poor children under six live in inadequate and unsafe housing, have no access to adequate health care, and have parents who are less educated (NCCP:8).
> 4   We would rather pay welfare costs for prisons, teenage mothers and correctional schools for the youth than pay for preventive services, education and job training (NCCP:9–10).

Poverty was defined in 1989 as having a income of less than $9,890 for a family of three, and of $12,675 for a family of four or more. While in 1987 there were thirty-three million people living in poverty, thirteen million of them were children under the age of eighteen, and five million under the age of six. In 1968 only 17 per cent of all children lived in poverty. In 1990, 23 per cent live in poverty (NCCP 1990:16). Children under six tend to be poor more frequently than any other age group: 19 per cent of children six to seventeen are poor, and 11 per cent of adults eighteen to sixty-four are poor. Youngest children suffer poverty more often than any other group. In 1987, out of the 21.9 million children under six living, 3.3 (15 per cent) were black, 2.5 (11 per cent) Hispanic, and 0.8 million (4 per cent) were Asian, Native American, or members of other minority groups. During the same year, 15.3 million (70 per cent) were white. Minority poor children under six, however, were over-represented in 1987: 32 per cent were black children (1.6 million), 21 per cent were Hispanic (1.0 million), 5 per cent were from other minorities (0.3 million), and 42 per cent were white (NCCP 1990:19).

We know that poor children are concentrated in central cities (2.3 million, or 46 per cent), but 54 per cent live outside of central cities (1.4 million, or 28 per cent in suburban areas, and 26 per cent, or 1.3 million in rural areas) (NCCP: 22). It is not a surprise to find that poor children generally live in the most depressed areas. Many of them lack basic civil services and spend much of their meager incomes on rent and utilities. Consequently, food and clothing are inadequate. To the basic question of why poor children are poor, the simple answer given by the National Center for the Children in Poverty is 'because their families are poor'. Consequently, if we want to attack poverty, we must look at the multiple factors causing it. Many of these children live in single-mother homes (about 20 per cent for all children, and 61.4 per cent for children under six years of age). Many of the single mothers never married. In 1987, 67 per cent of black and 70 per cent of Hispanic children living with single mothers were living in poverty (NCCP, 1990:28). While some children move out of their poverty as they grow, the tendency to remain in poverty is higher among those who live with a single-parent.

> The correlation between education and income is consistent over the years: In 1987 the poverty rate was 62 per cent for children under six where the only parent or the better educated parent had not completed high school. The poverty rate was only 19 per cent for children in families where the better-educated parent was a high school graduate.

For children whose better-educated parent had at least some postsecondary education, the poverty rate was only 4 per cent.
(NCCP 1990:33)

The majority of poor children are members of immigrant families and families of color in the United States, and they are also victims of xenophobia and racism. More surprising than to see those statistics and read the papers about children's hardships, is to notice the apathy and indifference shown to children's futures. Children are now becoming parents, and the children of tomorrow find themselves neglected not only by their immediate families but by their parents' parents. The question is why do we all remain silent about such a reality? The ideal of many parents in the past, as well of many immigrant parents today, is to prepare children for the future, to build for them a better life than the one we had ourselves, to sacrifice everything necessary in order to give them peace, freedom, economic prosperity, social status and happiness. We used to think that if we intended to give our children those benefits, education had to be central, indispensable and consequently it deserved every possible sacrifice.

A visit to urban schools in segregated low-income areas is a vivid reminder that if today's education is producing isolated, rough, ignorant and destructive children, their children will be much worse, they will sink into desperation and crime, and form their own underground society with their own survival rules and their own codes of behavior. After all, the gang phenomenon is only a preview of what could happen to our next generation. For many sociopolitical and economic reasons, we became part of a modern technological nation which created its own rules and demands. Prosperity requires hard labor, mobility, independence, and competitiveness. Families, personal relationships, home environments for children and senior adults, traditional cultural values and the personal self-identity (often with its own linguistic and cultural differences) have been crushed in exchange for material goods, promotions and status visibility. Many of the educational functions of the family have been neglected and by default transferred to the schools; and schools cannot function in the absence of home cultural values and support, nor can they provide children with the network of emotional personal relationships and guidance needed to grow up in a difficult world.

The cuts in schools budgets, especially in low-income neighborhoods, have had disastrous consequences with long-term affects. Instruction for children with special needs, such as children of marginalized, drug-culture members, and for children of hard-working immigrant parents whose home language is other than English, has been terminated. In brief, many schools will not be able to offer health and desegregation programs mandated by the state and federal governments (Apple 1992:416). After several decades of decreasing financial support for schools, low-income children and their families have been the ones who have suffered the most. The irreparable damage has become evident in the harm done to children's learning ability, self-confidence and future careers. Families, teachers and law-enforcement agents recognize the rapid deterioration of low-income areas with a segregated school whose budget reflects a fraction of the per capita spent in other schools. Every so often, vivid accounts of the price we will have to pay for this neglect are published. The cycle of poverty and neglect is now taking grotesque turns in low-income schools and neighborhoods.

We hear a great deal about educational reforms, and every so often we label them with fancy names. We talk about new and effective policies, new standards, new curricula, new tests and new results. We speak about teachers for diversity, enrichment education for the learning-disabled, computer literacy, bilingual and bicultural education, multicultural education, outcome based education, etc. Yet, in visiting schools we discover that there are two societies and three totally unrelated school systems, one for the poor, another for the middle class (the good public schools) and another for the rich (the private schools). It is not only the curricular messages that are different in quality, level and sophistication; the overall messages received by children in these three types of schools differ drastically. In the schools for the poor, the message is that the students are incompetent and undeserving of better instruction and are consequently predestined for academic failure and for unskilled jobs (if any become available); that the poor children are inherently different, unprepared cognitively and motivationally to succeed in schools, that their ethnic and cultural heritage and their current life is shameful, and their community is a social disgrace. Middle-class children in public schools may have a range of experiences from very good to not as good, but there is an implied assumption: some of the students can, if they follow the advice of their counselors, reach success and pursue fruitful careers. The rich private schools definitely speak to children's futures, their competence, their intellectual qualities, their moral superiority, and the support system that will pave the way to academic and economic success.

There is no surprise that most of the children in low-income schools drop out and fail, that many of those in middle-class schools drop out and wonder if they belong to mainstream America. Their awareness of a stratified society with differential treatment of students is readily apparent. The public and private institutions that control public resources and offer quality instruction and a strong socialization for academic success are characterized by well-trained instructors, abundance of resources, highly organized reward systems, continuous vigilance on the part of parents, support from public civil and religious authorities, and an aura of self-worth, excellence and patriotism hovering over collective rituals intended to increase social cohesiveness and solidarity among students and instructors. The opposite, lack of resources, incompetent instructors, disorganized rituals, etc., are characteristic of low-income and low-quality public schools.

The study of Miao empowerment is based on the accumulation of facts and the transformation that has occurred in their lives. The evidence shows that prior to their university training (and perhaps even before, by the time they completed high school) Miao students became aware of their own potential. Their awareness of their change and transition into a powerful elite of intellectuals did not occur until they were university students in the company of peers and professors. It is precisely at this point that they are forced to reflect on the vertical structural linkages that cut across the highest levels of the Chinese government (policies about ethnic groups, use of resources for nationalities, etc.) through the bureaucratic layers of regional elementary and secondary schools for Han people, finally to the Central Universities in the capital, the great city of Beijing. As they get closer and closer to their own personal life and become aware of the changes affected in their own social identification (the redefinition of their social identity), they find themselves to be members of a privileged small group of intellectuals, far away from the mentality and lifestyle of the peasant home villages they left behind.

China, having been a closed society that permitted little or no immigration, has not faced the problems facing Europe. The fifty-five nationalities officially recognized in China since 1949 enjoy a special status and are viewed as an integral part of Chinese society. The Manchu, 9.8 million people, and the Zhuang, an even larger group, 15.5 million people, control large portions of Chinese territory that have strategic value for future development (mines and other natural resources). The high economic, political and social status of the Hui, who are Moslems, about 8.6 million people, is quite visible in most major cities, especially in Beijing. One of the main reasons why minorities (or nationalities) have collective power in China, and why individuals from those groups can rise to powerful status (such as the status of university student or professor) is that the New China of 1949 did away with structurally created strata distinguishing Han and non-Han people, and that Mao left the control of territory and its resources to the groups living there. Wealth differences and status differences are not clustered along the lines of ethnic groups necessarily, but respond to differential development of the vast territory of China. Naturally, the most remote regions of the Southwest (Guizhou, Yunnan, Sichuan, etc.) have high concentrations of poor peasants.

Among the nationalities of China there are differences in physical characteristics and in status, but there are no large 'color' populations *per se*. Some groups are clearly identified as physically different, for example, the Uygurs, Mongols, Koreans and others. There is a way to identify peasants by the way they dress, talk and walk, and in cities there are certain feelings of superiority over peasants, but not serious xenophobia. The fear of ethnics documented in Europe among Neo-Nazis and right political groups who organize raids or other conspicuous abuses, do not exist in China, and would be philosophically unacceptable to the general Chinese population. But there is in China a great deal of prejudice against Africans and African Americans, because some Chinese think that they are superior to the Africans intellectually, economically and technically.

In a world increasingly more divided, the experience of racism by Moroccan adolescents documented in Brussels by Hermans (1993:51–76) is alarming. In

Power in Education

1991, there were 114,660 Moroccans officially living in Belgium, over half of them in Brussels (Hermans 1993:53). Moroccan school children reported both systematic experiences of racism on the part of teachers (17 per cent) or occasional experiences (another 17 per cent). A few children said they did not experience open racism. Some of them did not hesitate in stating: 'Yes, there was racism in school and it hurt. In the beginning there was a rejection. I felt the teachers did not like me. But because of my own qualities I made them accept me. However, everybody is a racist and there is not much needed to become one . . .' (Hermans 1993:56). Another child said: 'There was a teacher of whom you could see that he didn't like foreigners. He told you: "You are a Moroccan, you don't belong in this school"' (Hermans 1993:56). School racism, however, is not as vicious as the racism showed by police:

> The Belgians are racists. They don't want us to be well off, to have work or to be well dressed. Then they'll say that 'Moroccan is better off than we are.' But the police are much worse. Inspections, searches, all the people in the street looking at you. They want to see your identification card, you ask why. 'Your card or we will take you to the office!' Or they'll take you and with two, three men they'll beat you up. They'll insult us: 'Sale Marocain, retourne à ton pays.' You can ask all the lads here in school. They search you as if you were a terrorist.
> (Hermans 1993:63)

Immigrants who have worked for over twenty years are denied the right to vote, denied citizenship and even forced to go back to their countries of origin. Hermans says clearly that, 'The majority of the teachers hold negative and stereotyped ideas about the Moroccan immigrants in Belgium' (1993:72), and have very low expectations of the students. In brief, youngsters from immigrant groups, Moroccans, Turks and Spaniards, feel marginalized and unwanted.

In the United States and some European countries, the disempowerment of 'undesirable' children, that is those from low-income, or from ethnic and racial underclass groups does not happen by accident. Poverty, racism, unfair distribution of resources and even conspicuous neglect of children's needs, are the result of a socio-economic system in accord with a power structure. Power structures are embedded in culturally-constructed institutions with values and traditions that permit certain members of society (those of the dominant groups) to retain control of all the social mechanisms related to the production and allocation of resources, mainly access to knowledge, capital and human networks. The neglect of African-American or Chicano children in the form of refusal to allocate resources to their schools and communities, for example, are rationalized as part of the competitive democratic system, and its dogma of supply and demand, performance and merit recognition. Naturally, the judges (gatekeepers) of appropriate competition, adequate performance and merit, must be members of the dominant group. Schools have become the most effective instrument of isolation and social neglect, because they are run by relatively docile persons who follow the judgment of the experts. Educational experts are primarily responsible for classifying and placing children in appropriate pigeon-holes. Testing and evaluation experts deal with children's performance, from the point of entry in schools until graduation, and are at the core of our educational system. Educational psychologists, responsible for the development and use of testing instruments, and curriculum experts, responsible for preparing teachers, are expected to guide schools and open opportunities for all children, especially those who are linguistically, culturally and socially different, and who often find themselves misclassified as incompetent and uneducable, thus become demoralized, marginalized and even hostile to the values inculcated in school. Poverty tends to breed poverty by excluding the poor from opportunities to succeed in school. The American society and its schools are socially and culturally constructed systems for the transmission of knowledge, status and resources.

References

APPLE, M. (1992) 'Do the standards go far enough? Power, policy, and practices in mathematics education', *Journal for Research in Mathematics Education*, **23**(5), pp. 412–31.

BARTH, F. (1969) *Ethnic Groups and Boundaries*, Boston, MA: Little, Brown.

CHAPA, J. and VALENCIA, R. (1993) 'Latino population growth, demographic characteristics, and education stagnation: An examination of recent trends', *Hispanic Journal of Behavioral Sciences*, **15**(2), pp. 165–87.

CHAVEZ, L.R. (1992) *Shadowed Lives: Undocumented Immigrants in American Society: Case Studies in Cultural Anthropology*, SPINDLER, G. and L. (Eds) New York: Harcourt Brace Jovanovich College Publishers.

DELGADO-GAITAN, C. and TRUEBA, H. (1991) *Crossing Cultural Borders: Education for Immigrant Families in America*, London, England: Falmer Press.

DEVOS, G. (1967) 'Essential elements of caste: psychological determinants in structural theory', in DEVOS, A. and WAGATSUMA, H. (Eds) *Japan's Invisible Race: Caste in Culture and Personality*, Berkeley, CA: University of California Press, pp. 332–84.

DEVOS, G. (1973) 'Japan's outcastes: The problem of the Burakumin', in WHITAKER, B. (Ed) *The Fourth World: Victims of Group Oppression*, New York, NY: Schocken Books, pp. 307–27.

DEVOS, G. (1980) 'Ethnic adaptation and minority status', *Journal of Cross-Cultural Psychology*, **11**, pp. 101–24.

DEVOS, G. (1982) 'Adaptive strategies in US minorities', in JONES, E.E. and KORCHIN, S.J. (Eds) *Minority Mental Health*, New York, NY: Praeger, pp. 74–117.

DEVOS, G. (1983) 'Ethnic identity and minority status: Some psycho-cultural considerations', in JACOBSON-WIDDING, A. (Ed) *Identity: Personal and Sociocultural*, Uppsala, Sweden: Almquist & Wiksell Tryckeri AB, pp. 90–113.

DEVOS, G. (1990) 'Conflict and accommodation in ethnic interaction', in DEVOS, G. and SUÁREZ-OROZCO, M.M. (Eds) *Status Inequality: The Self in Culture*, Newbury Park, CA: Sage Publications, pp. 204–45.

DeVos, G. and Romanucci-Ross, L. (Eds) (1982) *Ethnic Identity: Cultural Continuities and Change*, (Second Edition) Chicago, IL: The University of Chicago Press. (First Edition, 1975, by The Wenner-Gren Foundation for Anthropological Research, Inc.).

DeVos, G. and Suárez-Orozco, M.M. (1990) *Status Inequality: The Self in Culture*, Newbury, CA: Sage Publications.

DeVos, G. and Wagatsuma, H. (1966) *Japan's Invisible Race: Caste in Culture and Personality*, Berkeley, CA: University of California Press.

Freire, P. (1973) *Pedagogy of the Oppressed*, New York, NY: Seabury.

Gibson, M. and Ogbu, J. (Eds) (1991) *Minority Status and Schooling: A Comparative Study of Immigrant and Involuntary Minorities*, New York, NY: Garland Publishing Inc.

Hermans, P. (1993) 'The experience of racism by Moroccan adolescents in Brussels', in Roosens, E. (Ed) *The Insertions of Allochthonous Youngsters in Belgian Society*, Special Issue of *Migration*, sponsored by the Verlagsabteilun des Berliner Instituts für Vergleichende Sozialforschung, erscheint vierteljährl. Berlin, Germany: Edition Parabolis, pp. 51–76.

National Center for Children in Poverty (NCCP) (1990) *Five Million Children: A Statistical Profile of our Poorest Young Citizens*, New York, NY: School of Public Health, Columbia University.

Ogbu, J. (1974) *The Next Generation: An Ethnography of Education in an Urban Neighborhood*, New York, NY: Academic Press.

Ogbu, J. (1978) *Minority Education and Caste: The American System in Cross-cultural Perspective*, New York, NY: Academic Press.

Ogbu, J. (1987) 'Variability in minority responses to schooling: Nonimmigrants vs. immigrants', in Spindler, G. and Spindler, L. (Eds) *Interpretive Ethnography of Education: At Home and Abroad*, Hillsdale, NJ: Lawrence Erlbaum Associates, Publishers, pp. 255–78.

Ogbu, J. (1989) 'The individual in collective adaptation: A framework for focusing on academic underperformance and dropping out among involuntary minorities', in Weis, L., Farrar, E. and Petrie, H. (Eds) *Dropouts from School: Issues, Dilemmas, and Solutions*, Albany, NY: State University of New York Press, pp. 181–204.

Ogbu, J. (1991a) 'Immigrant and involuntary minorities in comparative perspective', in Gibson, M. and Ogbu, J. (Eds) *Minority Status and Schooling: A Comparative Study of Immigrant and Involuntary Minorities*, New York, NY: Garland Publishing, Inc., pp. 3–33.

Ogbu, J. (1991b) 'Low school performance as an adaptation: The case of blacks in Stockton, California', in Gibson, M. and Ogbu, J. (Eds) *Minority Status and Schooling: A Comparative Study of Immigrant and Involuntary Minorities*, New York, NY: Garland Publishing, Inc., pp. 249–85.

Ogbu, J. (1992) 'Understanding cultural diversity', *Educational Researcher*, **21**(8), pp. 5–24.

Ogbu, J. and Matute-Bianchi, M.E. (1986) 'Understanding sociocultural factors: Knowledge, identity and school adjustment', in *Beyond Language: Social and Cultural Factors in Schooling Language Minority Students*, Sacramento, CA: Bilingual Education Office, California State Department of Education, pp. 73–142.

Spindler, G. with Spindler, L. (1971) *Dreamers Without Power: The Menomini Indians*, New York, NY: Holt, Rinehart and Winston. Republished by Waveland Press in 1984.

SPINDLER, G. (1974) 'The transmission of American culture', in SPINDLER, G. (Ed) *Education and Culture: Anthropological Approaches*, New York, NY: Holt, Rinehart & Winston, pp. 279–310.

SPINDLER, G. (1987) 'Why have minority groups in North America been disadvantaged by their schools?', in SPINDLER, G. (Ed) *Education and Cultural Process: Anthropological Approaches*, Second Edition. Prospect Heights, IL: Waveland Press, Inc., pp. 160–72.

SPINDLER, G. (Ed) (1988) *Doing the Ethnography of Schooling: Educational Anthropology in Action*, Prospect Heights, IL: Waveland Press, Inc.

SPINDLER, G. and SPINDLER, L., with TRUEBA, H. and WILLIAMS, M. (1990) *The American Cultural Dialogue and its Transmission*, London, England: Falmer Press.

TRUEBA, H.T. (1993) 'Ethnicity and race across cultures: Towards a theory of differential achievement', paper presented at the international conference on 'Educational Reform: Changing Relationships between the State, Civil Society, and the Educational Community', Madison, WI: University of Wisconsin-Madison, June 18–21, 1993.

TRUEBA, H.T., RODRIGUEZ, C., ZOU, Y. and CINTRÓN, J. (1993) *Healing Multicultural America: Mexican Immigrants Rise to Power in Rural California*, London, England: Falmer Press.

TRUEBA, H., CHENG, L. and IMA, K. (1993) *Myth or Reality: Adaptive Strategies of Asian Americans in California*, London, England: Falmer Press.

WAGATSUMA, H. and DEVOS, G. (1984) *Heritage of Endurance: Family Patterns and Delinquency Formation in Urban Japan*, Berkeley, CA: University of California Press.

WAGGONER, D. (1988) 'Language minorities in the United States in the 1980s: The evidence from the 1980 Census', in MCKAY, S.L. and WONG, S.C. (Eds) *Language Diversity, Problem or Resource: A Social and Educational Perspective on Language Minorities in the United States*, New York, NY: Newbury House Publishers, pp. 69–108.

Chapter 8

The Mediating Role of Language and Culture in Social Identification

Cross-cultural research, especially if conducted from various disciplinary vantage points, can help explain the deeper motivation of minority students to achieve. This study has attempted to do linguistic analysis of the testimonies by Chinese students, as well as a content analysis of the themes students pursue in describing their university experiences. The linguistic analysis in anthropological research goes back to the 1960s. According to Hymes, linguistics had not been recognized until 1960 as 'a source of methodological rigor and inspiration', although it was important to anthropology in the United States and historically linked with ethnographic research by Boas and his students, but never 'the only or best source of formal and qualitative methods' (Hymes 1964:10). Hymes suggests that linguistics is not 'a theory of what linguists do, but more importantly, a theory of the nature of language' and consequently it must play a greater role in the study of cognition and cultural behavior (Hymes 1964:11).

Language in Ethnic Identification and Achievement

After recognizing that anthropologists did not fall into the trap of ignoring the significance of speech activity in human development and its relationship to society and culture, Hymes suggests that up to 1964 anthropology played a static role 'repeating platitudes and paeans, stressing that language is important, but without the calibration that would enable one to investigate the importance, either of language in general, or, comparatively, of particular languages'. Clearly, anthropology opposed the misconception that there were 'inferior languages' functionally, and the monolithic conception of homogeneity of language and culture (i.e., the correspondence to one language=one culture). At this point, Hymes makes one of his most visionary statements that redirected much of subsequent ethnographic research:

> Not that the obvious facts of heterogeneity, multilingualism, individual differences in linguistic competence, and the like were denied; they simply did not enter into any anthropological theory of the nature of

language and its cultural role. Hence there are studies of cross-cultural differences in the patterning and importance of behavior having to do with sex, weaning, magic, or almost anything one might care to name, and general theories that try to account for them, in pursuit of what has been described as anthropology's task to account for the similarities and differences in human cultures; but there is none such for language. It stands as one of the most important tasks of anthropology to constitute what might be called a comparative ethnography of communication, concerned in part with the differential role of languages, and of speech behavior, in socialization, personality, interaction and social structure, cultural values, and beliefs (Hymes 1964:12).

As a result of this generation of scholars (to be discussed below, see Sturtevant 1964), ethnoscience and the ethnography of communication developed and produced a substantial number of excellent studies. Ethnoscience was developed partially on the grounds that previous anthropologists were imposing their own cultural biases and cognitive frames upon those of people being studied. Their efforts and contributions went beyond the design of cleaner and more focused ethnographic inquiry into the emic perspectives of the 'others', and discovered the significant role that language plays in the interpretation of observed behavior. Studies such as those by Frake (1961), Berlin and Romney (1964), Metzger and Williams (1963), Sturtevant (1964) and others, were based not only on a very strict process of reconstructed inquiry, but on the assumption that language mediated between actions observed and the interpretation of actions. Another important discovery of ethnoscience (perhaps not altogether explicit) is that the study of other cultures was essentially the study of peoples' actions whose meaning was deciphered through their use of language. Language was used as a means to infer views of the world, expected appropriate behaviors and cognitive taxonomic structures of phenomena, such as the taxonomy of disease by the Subanum of Mindanao (Frake 1961), the numerical classifiers of the Tzeltal (Berlin and Romney 1964) or the organization of wedding ceremonies (Metzger and Williams 1963).

The use of linguistics in specific socio-cultural settings as a means to understand other peoples' behavior and cognitive frames was an important contribution of a parallel field in anthropology called *ethnography of communication* or *sociolinguistics* developed by distinguished scholars such as Gumperz and Hymes (1964, 1972). Since 1964, Hymes recognized the potential contributions of Vygotsky in his *Thought and Language* (1962) to the ethnography of communication because of the connection that Vygotsky saw between language, culture and cognitive development and his recognition of the ideological context of psychological theory (Hymes 1964:11).

Years before the writings of sociolinguists and ethnographers in the United States emphasized the use of linguistic analysis to understand behaviors across cultures, two Soviet scholars, Mikhail Bakhtin and Lev Semonovich Vygotsky, had explored theoretical territories ignored elsewhere. Vygotsky had postulated a sociocultural approach to cognitive development as a mediated action. As the internationally recognized scholar, James V. Wertsch explains:

> Three basic themes run through Vygotsky's writings: 1) a reliance on genetic, or developmental, analysis; 2) the claim that higher mental functioning in the individual derives from social life; 3) the claim that human action, on both the social and individual planes, is mediated by tools and signs. These themes are closely intertwined in Vygotsky's work, and much of their power derives from the ways in which they presupposed one another.
> (Wertsch 1991:19)

The fundamental premise of Vygotsky's approach was that there is a natural unity between sociocultural and cognitive phenomena. Vygotsky was strongly influenced by the work of Darwin and Engels (Wertsch 1991:20) and consequently he saw the transition from primates to humans as a central problem in understanding human cognitive development. He was intrigued by the problem-solving actions of chimpanzees and gorillas and developed the notion of 'tool-mediated' human action which was dependent on specific interactional contexts. As Wertsch observes, for Vygotsky, apes remain slaves of the concrete situation or specific interactional context, while humans have developed 'representational means' to overcome such constraints (Wertsch 1991:20). Vygotsky struggled to translate the inspirational writings of Marx on sociocultural history into a more effective methodological approach to study human development and higher order thinking. With his emphasis on the unique human mental functions (higher order or advanced mental, representational functions, in contrast with rudimentary ones seen in apes) he studied the process of decontextualization. He saw children's cultural development as superimposed on processes of growth, maturation, physical development and inseparable from them, constituting a 'single line of sociobiological formation of the child's personality' (cited in Wertsch 1991:22). While it was clear that for Vygotsky the development of higher order mental functions of the individual was rooted in his/her sociocultural life (a clear influence of Marxist philosophy), what was less clear was the nature of the relationship between the individual and the social group.

The third theoretical construct that helps in exploring the social and cultural context of knowledge acquisition and the learning problems of low-income and underclass students, is Vygotsky's *Mediated Action* (Vygotsky 1962, 1978; Wertsch 1985a, 1985b, 1991). Vygotsky insisted that human action in general was mediated by tools and signs, especially by symbolic sign systems such as language. The relationship between the semiotic level and action was firmly established by Vygotsky in his use of the term *mediated action* which emerged as a result of his research with preschool children in contrast with older children. Wertsch states that:

Vygotsky's account of mediation is a set of assumptions about the nature of particular higher mental functions, more specifically, his view that thinking, voluntary attention, and logical memory form a system of interfunctions relations... He devoted the entire volume [his last, *Thinking and Speech*], in fact, to the issue of how speaking and thinking come to be thoroughly intertwined in human life, a cogent example of the interfunctional relationships that characterize human consciousness.

(Wertsch 1991:30)

The most basic contribution of the Vygotskian tradition, as understood by his own students and modern scholars who have read in the original most of his works (such as Michael Cole and James Wertsch), was the realization that in order to understand conscious human action we must study human existence and behavior in their social and historical dimensions, not in the structure of the grey mass in the human brain or in the isolation of decontextualized psychological phenomena (Wertsch 1991:1–45). It was in the context of these contributions that we can appreciate Bakhtin's own originality and powerful insights.

The Soviet Union of the 1920s was in a political turmoil that resulted in the imprisonment or exile of many intellectuals. The abuse of power by the Stalin regime robbed Bakhtin of his health and freedom in 1929. Bakhtin's research was focused on the nature of language and concrete utterances, rather than on words or sentences. He argued that utterances transcend the individual and reveal specific meanings anchored in concrete sociocultural contexts or situations. Wertsch states that in Bakhtin's view utterance 'is an activity that enacts differences in values ... for instance, the same words can mean different things depending on the particular intonation with which they are uttered in a specific context' (Wertsch 1991:51); that is what Bakhtin called 'different voices' applied both to oral and written communication, voices that exist in the sociocultural environment, not in isolation. Voices are therefore linked to the persons in the act of communicating with each other, to the speaker and the addressee, and language is the dynamic exchange of voices in specific interactional settings that determine meaning.

The significance of Bakhtin's contribution was to find order and meaning where previous linguists saw randomness and chaos. In the past, other linguists had focused on the historical reconstruction of linguistic forms, on syntax and lexicon. Bakhtin emphasized the relationship between discourse and sociocultural milieu, and consequently, the relationship between the speaker and the social group with which he communicates.

What is particularly important for our critique of deconstructionism is that there can be no linguistic meaning or even a trace of mental representation of behavioral phenomena in the isolation of a sociocultural context. The claim that individuals' views are the only valid accounts of social events betrays the intrinsic nature of communicative and mental processes which are anchored in concrete interactional context and therefore subject to a joint interpretation of phenomena. What permits social life and communication between individuals in a social group is precisely that which allows researchers to study other cultures and establish their own interpretation as subjective and as biased as it can be; even the subjectivity and the biases are socially shared, patterned and understandable.

The concept of linguistic and cultural mediation in learning is essential to our understanding of the process of development and early socialization in children, to their differential achievement in school and society and their disempowerment. It is precisely during early socialization, through the mediation of language and culture, that children bond, network and establish the personal, emotional and long-lasting relationships with adults and peers with whom they jointly construct new knowledge.

Determinism (biological, psychological or cultural) does not explain differential development of children; it oversimplifies behavioral phenomena and offers reductionistic explanations of complex processes (especially of the learning processes in environments where intellectual functions and academic outcomes are embedded in power relationships and class structures). On the other hand, resorting to deconstructionism is not the solution. Deconstructionism can destroy even the possibility of exploring explanations of learning behavior and differential outcomes of any kind.

Mediated action theory as applied to cognitive development and learning environments is currently one of the most productive approaches. For example, Luis Moll and associates have been working in Chicano communities, and combining ethnographic approaches in documenting community activities with Neo-Vygotskian theory in their study of interaction patterns within the home and community learning environments. The center of their study is the community, which becomes the repository of the funds of knowledge accumulated or used through networks of family relatives and friends. The reciprocal services provide a strong collective support and an opportunity to learn how to succeed in social institutions. Moll's approach is described in his most recent works (Moll 1990; Moll and Diaz, 1987).

There is a group of scholars who have adopted ethnographic methods as a means to socialize teachers into a reflective mode of teaching. Several scholars have, over at least the last ten years, used ethnographic methods in group settings to assess teaching effectiveness and differential observational skills in future teachers. Their analysis of this inquiry-oriented teacher education has been discussed in the recent literature (Tabachnick and Zeichner 1991; Zeichner 1990, 1991, 1992; Zeichner and Gore 1990). Reflective teaching, meaningful communicative exchanges, and the mediating role of teachers in creating productive learning environment for children are all crucial to this approach.

The mediating role of language and culture are particularly significant in the study of current schools with highly diversified student populations. A genuine understanding of the mediation process has immediate implications for construction of adequate learning environments at home and in school,

Language and Culture in Social Identification

and this understanding brings hope to the ever increasing groups of neglected children. We can no longer hide under the traditional discourse of reform by means of more tests and the enforcement of standards.

Ethnic and linguistic differentiation in modern societies has led to cultural and political conflicts within ethnic groups and between ethnic groups, as well as conflicts between ethnic groups and the white mainstream segment of society. Ethnic group boundaries are a worldwide phenomenon, unfortunately one that frequently brings violence. Castification or disempowerment is an institutionalized process of exploiting members of social groups, such as ethnic, racial, low-income, or other less powerful groups; furthermore, this process reduces such persons to the status of members of a lower caste who can enjoy neither the same rights nor the obligations of mainstream members of society. The conditions under which disempowerment takes place and persists require further study; in turn, the process of empowerment, which is the reverse of disempowerment, requires a systematic and conscious effort to redefine the self, the surrounding interactional settings, the institutional and the macro-sociological environments. Europe and America have retained structures of oppression and disempowerment that seem to perpetuate the abuse of cheap labor by attracting legal and illegal immigrants from third world countries to produce goods and services at competitive prices. These individuals do not receive fair pay and are denied adequate medical care, safety and education for themselves and their families. The acceptance or tolerance of their underclass status in some immigrant and refugee groups produces a profound and lasting personal disempowerment. Continuing economic pressures results in human rights violations and ethnic conflicts around the world. Survival for many groups makes the low status become a lesser evil for many uprooted families. The key question is whether these families and their children can overcome the degradation and exploitation suffered and at what cost they will regain a measure of empowerment in our democratic society.

Educational reforms in this country have been a clear example of what Apple calls *Standards* reaffirmation, as in the context of math education reform. We cannot ignore the crude realities of poverty, neglect, racism and differential power, all of which are an integral of the socio-cultural context of education. The reason is that the 'social construction both of what counts as mathematical literacy and of the problems it should focus on' (Apple 1992:428) are equally important to solve our educational problems. Checking only our standards makes the problems look very easy to resolve:

> it will be all too easy for leadership to be exerted by the most conservative elements in the ideological coalition that is organized under the *Standards*' umbrella. Its lasting impact may give support to the formation of a national curriculum, guided by a national test and largely organized around rightist ideological and educational policies... Yet there are very important elements in the volumes that could help us counter parts of the conservative agenda. A broadened definition of

mathematical literacy, one that is used in *critical* ways to support open and honest questioning of our society's means and ends, is clearly better than a definition that stresses workplace skills and values that largely benefit those with existing power. A vision of assessment that is more humane and guided by broader goals is clearly miles away from those proposals that would impose industrial models of artificial and reductive evaluation standards and procedures. A nation is not a firm and schools are not factories.

(Apple 1992:428–29)

Apple's most recent analysis of the social constraints coming from the powers exercised by central institutions is discussed in his recent book, *Official Knowledge* (1993). The response of ethnic and racial minority and low-income children to the experience of social neglect — felt through both personal day-to-day encounters in schools and other institutions, as well as vicariously through interactions with other children and adults around them — often cuts through the redtape and places the truth in front of our eyes. In his discussion of social degradation and adaptation of minority persons, DeVos distinguishes adaptation from 'adjustment' as follows:

> They can refer both to the internal structures which we assume under the concept of personality, or in many instances, to mutually adaptive human processes of communication and interaction that occur in social role relationships. It is most helpful . . . to remember the clear distinction between *internal structuring of personality*, related to concepts of adjustment or maladjustment, and *social-behavioral responses* which are interpreted as socially adaptive or maladaptive for the individual within his social nexus.
>
> (DeVos 1992:206)

Effective adaptation assumes a general consensus of what a successful adult looks like. Judgments on effective interaction of a person in a social environment, especially with persons with whom the self has primary relationships, imply judgments about both adaptation and adjustment:

> When examining the adaptive strategies of blacks and various ethnic minorities from a problem orientation point of view, we must consider maladjustment as well as maladaptation, to some degree at least, to understand how an individual responds to, or is influenced by, the major values of the dominant society.
>
> (DeVos 1992:207)

Another important factor in our understanding of adaptation and adjustment mechanisms, is to understand the nature of the socialization process during childhood which determines how a social self-identity is internalized, how the ethnic origin plays a role in self-development, in response to discrimination, oppression or degradation:

> But identity formation itself is not simply a conscious process. It is influenced by unconscious psychological processes. Why is a particular minority group successful or unsuccessful in status adaptations within a given society? Explanations are often attempted in purely economic or political forms of analysis. I myself find such analysis rather insufficient because there are, in all cases, some intermediary psychocultural considerations which are crucial. Between the economic circumstances and the adaptive response are significant cultural and personal differences of a psychological nature.
> (DeVos 1992:208)

The discussion of successful adaptation and the criteria to judge success are still highly controversial. Is a black man well adjusted and adapted if he accepts abuse, segregation and a menial job well under his potential and capabilities? Is a black man maladjusted and maladapted if he fights an oppressive system and shows anger? Was Richard Rodriguez (1982) an example of good adaptation because he rejected his language and culture and embraced a new language and culture? The price of the latter may have resulted in a profound personality structural change and may have injured his self-esteem so deeply that self-rejection is symbolized by rejecting his family, his parents' language and cultural traditions. In other words, judgments about successful adaptation may be made from the oppressor's point of view, and may ignore the need for anger and rejection of the status quo in certain societies. Are youths associated with gangs maladapted or maladjusted? From the standpoint of mainstream society, they seem to be both maladapted and maladjusted because they reject conventional social norms, and they break codes of behavior (use physical force, resort to violence, reject mainstream values, etc.). On the other hand, from the perspective of the youth with needs for protection, for belonging, for cultural continuity, for acceptance, for a better economic life, and most of all for survival, the gangs may seem like the most rational solution. Their adaptive behavior, at least in some instances, may not be adaptive to a mainstream lifestyle which is certainly inaccessible to these youth but to the real day-to-day life of violent encounters and death in the ghetto.

As low-income families have become fragmented and lose their capacity to handle the important function of children's socialization — enculturation in home cultural values, working ethic, creating a sense of belonging to a community, etc. — especially in situations of rapid socio-cultural change (as happens with many ethnic groups), gang organizations become surrogate families and provide youth with some emotional and physical security; in some instances, gangs provide some sort of economic support through illegal activities as well.

Peer Socialization through Gangs

Diego Vigil and his colleagues have been studying black, Chicano and Vietnamese gangs in Southern California. The disintegration of families and the pressure on minority children to cope with the social abuse and indifference they perceive in their surroundings, prepares many youngsters to enter gangs and seek alternative ways to the status and lifestyle they cannot have through conventional means. Among the Vietnamese youth gangs (in contrast with the hard-core adult Vietnamese in organized crime units), car theft, house robberies and extortion are frequent methods used to obtain substantial amounts of money:

> The victims are without exception other Vietnamese, and the crime usually occurs within the victims' home. As mentioned previously, many Vietnamese-Americans tend to keep large amounts of cash and gold within their homes. Knowing this, the youth gangs will survey a residence and in small groups (usually four or five persons) will enter the home armed with handguns. Victims are beaten and coerced into revealing the location of their valuables. Sometimes extremely cruel measures are used: One informant had threatened to drown the victim's infant son in the toilet. As victims themselves of communist soldiers who robbed their homes in Vietnam, these youths have few compunctions in using violence. Their methods are efficient and effective. Almost without exception, they are able to extract $15,000 to $20,000 per residence ... Although (or because) they have been academic failures, these youths soon find themselves living a grossly exaggerated version of the American dream. The extensive Vietnamese community provides an abundant supply of victims. The stolen money is then spent in Vietnamese restaurants, nightclubs, and car dealerships.
>
> (Vigil and Chong Yun 1990:157)

In contrast with Chicano and African American gangs, Vietnamese gangs do not fight over turf (they think this is stupid), nor do they pick a particular dress code that distinguishes them from other Vietnamese. They prefer to be inconspicuous. Ultimately, they value gang affiliation because it enables them to enjoy life and have a feeling of group attachment:

> Despite the mobility and independence offered by the youth gangs, intense personal bonds are formed and maintained. One 20-year-old informant said, 'We have a lot of respect and love for each other. We really with together [sic]. We live with each other. We're real close to each other.' Another informant emphatically declared, 'They were family to me ... I love'em. Something come down, I'll be there for them ... I'd die for my homeboys'. Affection is declared by calling their homeboys

ahn (the Vietnamese word for brother) or by using personal nicknames (e.g., one informant was referred to as 'Co', which means flamingo). Thus the structural and geographical fluidity of the youth gangs further hinders the attempts of law enforcement agencies to combat the problem. This fluidity, however, does not diminish the intensity of the personal bonds formed within the gang, which becomes their adopted 'family'.

(Vigil and Chong Yun 1990:161)

In the opinion of these researchers, Vietnamese gangs stem from racism in schools, economic problems, war traumas, family stress, and the students' failure to achieve academic success. These factors are intimately related to the psychodynamics of self-identification processes studied in Korean and Japanese groups by DeVos (1973, 1983), DeVos and Wagatsuma (1966) and DeVos and Suárez-Orozco (1990). The fundamental premise in the work of DeVos, especially in looking at oppressed groups who have been subjected to systematic degradation incidents, is that all human behavior in any form, even if viewed as primarily structured by political, economic or other social institutions, is influenced by personality variables that are culturally transmitted from one generation to another (DeVos 1973:1; cited by Suárez-Orozco, 1993). What many social scientists view as incompatible approaches to explaining human behavior (the social structural and personality characteristics) were combined in multiple levels of analysis by DeVos. This kind of analysis allows us to examine the differential cultural response to similar social demands and stresses placed on immigrant groups.

In the case of Mexican gangs in Southern California, for example, gang members search for self-identity and the mending of school and family relationships in the gangs. Both Chicano (male) and Chicana (female) gang organization is associated with stressful family relationships (Vigil 1988:425). As young children, gang members usually lived in poverty, often in single-mother families, often exposed to physical violence and feel socially disenfranchised; at age ten they may look to the streets (veterans) and *carnales* (brothers — blood brothers or adopted brothers) for their role models (Vigil 1988:425–6). As one of the gang members in Los Angeles said: 'I was born into my barrio. It was either get your ass kicked every day or join a gang and get your ass kicked occasionally by rival gangs. Besides, it was fun and I belonged' (Vigil 1988:427).

Most [gang] members refer to themselves as *cholos*, the Chicano street youth style, and a term also used in some parts of Latin America to describe those who are intermediate, culturally, between the metropolitan and indigenous Indian cultures. Much of the gang subculture reflects a mixture of patterns, combining the usual youth peer cohort friendship and emotional support activities, such as in the Mexican *palomilla* (cohorting) traditions, with the more renowned gang violence

179

and antisocial features also found in most American urban gangs . . . The distorted viewpoint often leads to the public impression that all or most low-income barrio youth are gang members.

(Vigil 1988:422)

The gang members may see their lifestyle as adaptive and even successful. They get what they want through methods that are criminal and undemocratic in the eyes of mainstream society. Mainstream society, largely the cultural descendants of colonial oppressors, viewed as adaptive the behavior of American Japanese families who during World War II were treated like enemies, denied naturalized citizenship, displaced from their homes, detained in relocation centers, forced to lose all their properties, and abused by the public. By 1947, about 17,000 of these Japanese chose to resettle in the Chicago area:

> They were moving into a new urban environment after what we presumed was a traumatic disruption of their previous lives. Instead of finding among the Japanese Americans various symptoms of social and personal dislocation, we found, by and large, a quick, seemingly positive adaptation by them and a surprising degree of social acceptance by midwestern Americans, given the previous wartime climate. The Japanese Americans were able to find new jobs and continue their interest in educational advancement despite their previous lack of job opportunities in California and other states where discrimination against Asians had been very severe.
>
> (DeVos 1992:210)

Why did the Japanese American youth not respond to abuse and segregation by organizing gangs? Why were they submissive and quiet in the face of clear injustices? What cultural factors determined their collective response? These are questions that require an understanding of the role culture plays in shaping personality structures and behavioral mechanisms in the face of adversity. Second- and third-generation Japanese Americans have been less quiet, and, as successful economically and educationally as their ancestors. However, they have drastically changed their social behavior and have even demanded an apology and economic reparations from the US Government for the injustices done to their ancestors.

Social scientists had not been able to listen to gang and ex-gang members who have had the opportunity to reflect why the gangs continue to exist, and what is required in order to leave the gangs, stay away from them and become a productive citizen. For the first time in American history many gang and ex-gang members went public and joined efforts to negotiate a truce. Los Angeles, seen as the gang capital of America, organized a series of meetings in the ballroom of the Westin Hotel: 'The main idea is to show the world that there is a truce, to build mutual relationships with corporate America and with city officials to help us resolve the economic problems of the city', said Malik

Spellman, a member of the *Hands Across Watts*, a group of former gang members that organized the conference. The participants agreed that 'trucing' would permit them to protect their own families, that they were tired of the killings, and wanted peace (Mydans 1993).

If we assume that one of the main reasons for gangs to exist is to provide certain youth with a sense of collective respect, with a sense of belonging, or with mechanisms to handle isolation, deprivation and exclusion from mainstream America, then we need to look at our historical roots and how we have handled marginality and poverty, especially among unwanted groups.

Self-Concept and Prejudice in American Schools and Society

The gang problem, the oppression of minorities, their educational and social neglect, the alienation and isolation of racial, ethnic and low-income children and their families, all have a long history whose roots are well established in the colonial system imposed by Europe in the Americas and elsewhere. But what specific cultural and structural factors in Western societies, especially in America have led to the present condition of racism and mistreatment of minorities? To what extent can we really separate ourselves from our colonial history and our culturally-inculcated prejudices that have resulted in social and economic structures of American society? Why do such structures result in the neglect of certain children today? A young and angry scholar wrote recently:

> Rape, mutilation, employing attack dogs, and burning alive were favorite tactics of my Spanish ancestors. Columbus wrote to Queen Isabella 'Let us in the Name of the Holy Trinity go on sending all the slaves that can be sold'... Our traditional school curriculum regarding Columbus teaches school children to regard as heroes the Spanish purveyors of genocide, slavery, rape and exploitation. This aggression was carried out in the interests of capitalism, with the concept of private property underlying these actions.
>
> (Nieto 1993:3)

African Americans and American Indians have suffered the indignities of European conquest and oppression and the consequences of families being broken up, women being used as objects and raped without mercy, and children used for labor as beasts has left its marks on our current democracies, and on our current social sciences. According to Lapon (1986; cited by Nieto 1993:4), Dr. Samuel A. Cartwright invented in the mid-nineteenth century a mental disease called *drapetomania* which affected only slaves seeking emancipation. To cure such disease, he prescribed that slaves should be recaptured, rubbed with oil, and beat into submission. I wonder if all those great figures in American and British history who had defended slavery, such as Edmund Burke, Thomas Carlyle, Edgar Allen Poe, Brigham Young, David Hume, John Locke, President

Thomas Jefferson, Vice President John C. Calhoun, President James Garfield, President Andrew Johnson, General Robert E. Lee and President Abraham Lincoln (Fikes, Jr. 1992), would have hesitated in using Dr. Cartwright's prescription. Is it a wonder that oppressed people who have been subjected to degradation, suffer today from low self-esteem, insecurity, and alienation? Prejudice about their intellectual capability and moral integrity continue to be a part of the myth that many whites hold about the intrinsic (almost genetic) superiority of whites over people of color (African Americans, American Indians, Asians, Latinos and others).

Immigration policies in the United States have often been designed by people with clear racial and ethnic prejudices. Southern and Eastern Europeans arrived in this country in the last decade of last century and the first three decades of this century. The public anti-immigrant feelings were met with policies of degradation and abuse. The myth of racial superiority of whites and the eugenic policies of the authors of the SAT (Carl Brigham) and Stanford Binet I.Q. tests (Lewis Terman) were explicit: Mexican, Indian and African American people should not be permitted to reproduce, and standardize testing 'was largely developed by psychologists who were sexists, classist, and believed in the racial and genetic superiority of the Aryans' (Nieto 1993:6).

Ethnic prejudice and ethnocentrism are closely connected and can be understood as defense mechanisms. Racial hatred, acted out in the form of systematic discrimination, violence, deprivation of civil rights, overt verbal and emotional abuse, and any other rituals of degradation imaginable, is rooted in a sort of rationalization that effectively denies the fundamental unity of mankind as a single species and the vilification of the 'other' who is victimized. Because racial and ethnic boundaries (the marking lines to distinguish who is and who is not that undesirable 'other') are mutable as a function of changing interactional contexts, a single person can be for some the object of disdain and deserving degradation, and for others an acceptable human being and a member of a common social group (social class, occupational group, cultural group, etc.). Ethnic and racial boundaries are movable also in the sense that a single ethnic group may consist of physically identifiable distinct types (for example, people of color who range from very dark to very light). For example, some European groups (Italians, Spaniards, Greeks, *et al.*) and many immigrant groups in Europe, are physically so diverse that in certain interactional contexts they may pass for white Europeans. In the United States many persons from Puerto Rican and Cuban ancestry are taken for African Americans because of their physical characteristics (dark skin, etc.), while many others are presumed to be European because they are very light.

What have the Jewish Holocaust, or the 'ethnic cleansing' of Eastern Europe or of the former Soviet Union, the terrorism in Spain and Ireland, the assass-ination of *desaparecidos* in Argentina, or the organization of death squads in Brazil taught us about race and ethnicity, about hatred and prejudice? Perhaps one important lesson is that human beings are extremely skilful at rationalizing even their worst actions against their own species. Ethnic hatred and

Language and Culture in Social Identification

racism are intimately related to the ethnocentrism discussed by Barth (1969), DeVos (1990) and Suárez-Orozco (1993). Suárez-Orozco, for example, points out, that at some point in the history of Europe, various groups began to claim a blood relationship with the Aryans:

> The debate over the Indo-European connection went well beyond the scientific realm and fueled competitive nationalistic projects in Europe. At one point various European groups claimed close kinship with the 'Aryan', the upper-caste speakers of an Indo-European dialect who migrated into the northern part of India. Nazism was the most perverse form of such concern over alleged evolutionary superiority founded in a peculiarly mythical link to the noble conquerors of the Indic subcontinent.
>
> (Suárez-Orozco 1993:31)

The cultural myths invented to rationalize abuse of power are not new in history. The Europeans who conquered the new world attempted for centuries to defend the notion that natives from the American continent did not have the same human value (human soul) comparable to those of the Europeans. Slavery, rape and forced labor become permissible on the grounds of the fundamental 'spiritual difference' between Europeans and non-Europeans, as well as on the grounds that civilization and redemption (cultural and religious beliefs) would eventually result from European conquest and domination. The current racial and ethnic problems and debates in Europe and in America seem to repeat history. Prejudice against ethnic groups in Europe, whose intellectual capacity is presumed to be lower, still persists in Belgium, Germany, Holland and England, and the idea that some groups are 'unassimilable' (as the mainstream Americans thought of some ethnic groups at the turn of the century) still is voiced in public circles (see Roosens 1989; Boos-Nunning and Hohmann 1989; Tomlinson 1989, 1991; Eldering and Kloprogge 1989; Suárez-Orozco 1991a). As Suárez-Orozco reminds us, that lack of equal opportunity results:

> in higher unemployment and underemployment rates (particularly among youths) . . . conditions of domestic poverty, disparagement from the majority population, generational conflict, the emergence of peer reference groups fostering a countercultural identity among youths, high minority dropout rates from school, high grade 'retention' rates . . . and delinquency rates.
>
> (Suárez-Orozco 1991a:103)

Anthropologists are aware of the waves of hatred in Europe and the myths of racial superiority among certain Europeans. The roots of the myth of Aryan superiority that eventually produced the Jewish Holocaust of Hitler's Germany, are found in the 'unilineal cultural evolution' that also can be seen in the work of racist European anthropologists. Suárez-Orozco presents a historical analysis of anthropological thought:

> The basic theme in the narratives of the nineteenth-century social evolutionary theories was the notion that social change is directional, unilinear, non-reversible and continuous. According to this model social evolution proceeds in a teleological fashion, evidently from 'good' to 'better' into 'best'. Lewis H. Morgan, whose writing on 'primitive' social organization deeply impressed Marx and Engels, summarized the development of humankind into a single sequence of social evolution from a state of 'savagery' (pre-pottery period) through an epoch of 'barbarism' (the ceramic stage), into 'civilization' (the age of cities and writing).
>
> Such reasoning resulted in an arbitrary hierarchical ordering of cultures according to increasing technological complexity. The structural ordering of cultures usually placed the British, German and French elites on top of the hierarchy (civilized), the peoples of native America, Oceania, and tribal Africa at the opposite (savage) end, typically leaving the peasants of Europe, the Middle and Far East (barbarian), somewhere in between the civilized and savage states.
>
> (Suárez-Orozco 1993:32)

Obviously, as Suárez-Orozco points out, the political advantages of advancing this view of unilineal cultural evolution was to justify the colonial domination by nineteenth-century European countries. This repugnant theoretical ethnocentric pseudo-scientific opinion of last century anthropologists reminds us of the power of ideas, including ideas clearly loaded with racial prejudice and unwarranted claims.

Most of the poor in the United States are also victims of xenophobia which has many expressions and reflects the profound racism of white America. The fear of ethnics has motivated Neo-Nazis to organize vigilante raids, conservatives to advocate monolingualism and monocultural policies (through the English Only Movement), Ku-Klux-Klan members to infiltrate political parties which exclude certain individuals on the basis of color or race, members of the Moral Majority to impose moral codes and protect them through political organizations, and other radical movements of the right to restrict speech and freedom of expression viewed as offensive to some, and to sponsor a highly militant organized membership to restrict public services to ethnics on the grounds that ethnic groups do not contribute their fair share to the cost of such services. In their view, the funding of education in the home languages of ethnic groups who do not speak English is unjustified. Also, in the view of right radicals ('conservatives'), the use of affirmative action criteria to implement fair employment policies (policies that reflect the ethnic composition of the labor force), or to provide remedial mechanisms for ethnic students, is equally unacceptable. There are many other instances of ethnic (often racially motivated) hatred. Kozol, voicing the stereotypic remarks of racist Americans, states:

Language and Culture in Social Identification

> When they hear of all these murders, all these men in prison, all these women pregnant with no husbands, they don't buy the explanation that it's poverty, or public schools, or racial segregation. They say, 'We didn't have much money when we started out, but we led clean and decent lives. We did it. Why can't they?' . . . 'They don't have it.' What they mean is lack of brains, or lack of drive, or lack of willingness to work. 'This is what they have become, for lots of complicated reasons. Slavery, injustice or whatever.' . . . And they don't believe that better schools or social changes will affect it very much. So it comes down to an explanation that is so intrinsic, so immutable, that it might as well be called genetic.
>
> (Kozol 1991:192)

The flat and direct statement 'They don't have it' is an emphatic return to a biological determinism, perhaps under the cover of a new cultural determinism. This is important to consider in the light of the most popular literature regarding low achievement of minority groups, groups described as castelike. I contend that there is a return to another type of determinism. Following the refutation of last century's biological determinism (based on 'unilineal cultural evolution') which was led by Boas (1916) and his colleagues, anthropology saw a kind of psychological determinism creep in and then be refuted. Is a new cultural determinism creeping once more into our theoretical discussions of differential minority achievement?

Pockets of poverty seem to hide from the public eye. Jonathan Kozol, in his search for schools in need, and in an attempt to break the silence that has characterized the politics of unequal education, went to Camden, New Jersey (1991:133–74) the fourth-poorest city of more than 50,000 people and the poorest children in the country; with about a quarter of the families living on an income of less than $5,000 per year, and about two-thirds of them on welfare:

> The city has 200 liquor stores and bars and 180 gambling establishments, no movie theater, one chain supermarket, no new-car dealership, few restaurants other than some fast-food places. City blocks are filled with burnt-out buildings. Of the city's 2,200 public housing units, 500 are boarded up, although there is a three-year waiting list of homeless families. As the city's aged sewers crumble and collapse, streets cave in, but there are no funds to make repairs.
>
> (Kozol 1991:137)

What Kozol was asking was: what is it like to be a child in this city? To find some answers he spent part of the Spring of 1990 in a city nearby (the closest to Camden with hotel facilities). Here is a story reflecting some of the answers:

> Luis speaks about the guidance system at the school. 'This what it's like', he says. 'You go in to your counselor. He's under pressure so he acts impatient: "What do you need?"' You ask for help on college credits. They don't know. You end up choosing on your own . . . We need people who can tell you what we do not know, or what we need to know . . . Chilly, which is the nickname of a young Cambodian girl, speaks up for the first time: 'I'll give you an example. I went to my counselor. He said, "What do you want?" I said, "I want to be a lawyer." I said, "Why?" He said, "Your English isn't good." I'm seventeen. I've been here in American four years. I want to be a lawyer. He said, "No. You cannot be a lawyer. Look for something else. Look for an easier job."'
>
> (Kozol 1991:155)

How do we explain the counselor's answer? How does he understand the standards of academic performance, and how does he assess the ability of Luis or Chilly to pursue an academic career? What seems to occur is that these two children are perceived as members of the underclass which is presumed to be unable to perform at the level of mainstream society. Indeed the question is why and how underclass communities perpetuate their low status in society? In different language, McDermott has raised this issue in a cross-cultural perspective. He states that, 'Even in the presence of efforts by modern states to subdue the arbitrary and oppressive standards of host groups and to accommodate minority behavior patterns by programs of rationalization and equalization, pariah groups endure' (McDermott 1987:175). He goes on to mention the Koreans and Burakumin in Japan, the Lapps in Norway (and in Sweden), the African Americans, Hispanic and American Indians in the United States, the Catholics in Ireland, *et al.* Then he asks the question: How does this happen?

During the early socialization process, children acquire cultural values and social mores, as well as the appropriate language skills to function effectively in their own sociocultural environments. These knowledge, values and skills are often in contrast with those taught in schools, and therefore earn these children the low status ascribed to them by school personnel and other children (McDermott 1987:175). The genesis of the low status as outlined by McDermott starts when the teacher treats a child as inadequate, and the child finds the teacher oppressive:

> It is neither ascribed to the child [the low status] nor naturally acquired by him in the sense that puberty is acquired. First, some form of miscommunication between a child and his teacher must take place. If this is not repaired quickly, a mutually destructive or regressive one-to-one relationship will be established between the teacher and the child . . . The teacher's role as administrator in charge of failure becomes dominant. And the children's revolt grows . . . Teachers do not simply ascribe minority children to failure. Nor do minority children

simply drag failure along, either genetically or socially, from the previous generation. Rather, it must be worked out in every classroom, every day, by every teacher and every child in their own peculiar ways. Viewing school failure as an achievement implies that school failure can be understood as a rational adaptation by children to human relations in host schools.

(McDermott 1987:178)

The essence of the explanation presented by McDermott is described in the context of interpersonal interaction and the politics of everyday life. The content of the messages communicated in the classroom involve not only the obvious explicit material (math, science, English, etc.), but the quality of the relationship between the participants in the interaction, as well as a label corresponding to the status of the persons involved. Therefore, it stands to reason that:

If the wrong messages of relationship are communicated, reading, writing, and arithmetic may take on very different meanings than they do for the child who is more successful in getting good feelings from the politics of a classroom. The wrong messages of relationship can result in learning disabilities.

(McDermott 1987:181)

In summary, for McDermott low status is jointly constructed by children and teachers in efforts to assign meaning to social acts, and to act appropriately. Children's patterns of selective attention — which represent a rational adaptation to the politics of everyday life in school, helps understand the acquisition of children's abilities, statuses and identities, and determine their institutional biography and future academic achievement:

School failure and delinquency often represent highly motivated and intelligent attempts to develop the abilities, statuses, and identities that will best equip the child to maximize his utilities in the politics of everyday life.

(McDermott 1987:204)

This analysis is consistent with the work of Vigil, DeVos, Suárez-Orozco, and Apple. But it leaves open for discussion a number of issues related to the reasons why some minority children are more likely to fail and others to succeed, as well as issues of macro-sociological organization structures leading to failure in certain groups and not in others (factors well above interactional patterns and communication of messages in the classroom).

Theoretical discourse on children's abuse and neglect, their suffering, their inability to face roles and challenges imposed on them by the previous generations, and their overall disenfranchisement and despair is a reflection of societies run by adults who have been hardened with experiences of isolation

Power in Education

and brutality and have lost sensitivity for children's needs. To conceptualize the impact of early socialization on children born in a world of war, economic crises, political turmoil, poverty and emotional isolation, one must resort to various disciplines in the social sciences. One of the reasons why the work of anthropologists, sociologists, sociolinguists and psychologists seems often redundant and complementary, is that those disciplines have been affected by the philosophical currents and international crises affecting all sciences. The fundamental principle argued by DeVos (in most of his work, especially the most recent ones, DeVos and Suárez-Orozco 1990; DeVos 1992) is that in order to understand behavior we must first recognize the intimate relationship between the sociocultural contexts of behavior and the psychodynamics of personality structure. DeVos goes further in his explanation of human behavior, particularly in his discussion of differential achievement motivation, by suggesting that the early socialization process may create mechanisms that screen out both perceptions and interpretations of behaviors related to learning; that is what he calls 'selective permeability' which he explains as follows:

> Relevant to the continuity of social class or caste, there are psychological coping mechanisms, or if you will, defensive mechanisms related to ego functioning that induce the selective perception and execution of behavior related to particularized learning experiences. Let me, very briefly, consider problems of relative 'non-learning' evidenced in particular ethnic minorities as well as in men and women of majority culture. To do so, one cannot escape some psychological examination of how the self is selectively defined, progressively. By the time individuals are collectively exposed to formal education, they are not perceiving the same stimuli in the school situation. They are not equally ready to internalize the same educational materials. Depending on the degree to which internalization is threatening to one's social identity, they are 'selectively permeable' to school experiences.
> (DeVos 1992:241)

DeVos' example of this principle at work is in the comparison between the Japanese and the Mexican immigrants:

> in the Confucian tradition, the family supports learning from mentors. The Japanese peer group mutually supports learning within the classroom. The child is psychologically ready to be receptive to teachers. In other instances in American culture, the peer group, especially Mexican and black groups, can buttress a pattern of learning resistance on the part of the child. I hasten to add that such lack of learning is not necessarily consciously controlled. Individuals 'freeze up' when asked to learn something that might threaten an 'incompetence' that is a protective part of one's identity, be it sexually or socially defined.

For example, many boys and men 'cannot cook', women or scholars cannot learn to replace a rubber gasket in a leaking faucet.
(DeVos 1992:242)

DeVos has made a case to examine the significance of psychological forces in facilitating or impeding the acquisition of new knowledge. It is not only in the process of developing achievement motivation where the emotional needs of children demand a stable relationship with an adult, but more so in the actual process of knowledge acquisition that this relationship plays a key role. If learning is not consciously controlled and if incompetence is part of a defense mechanism, then the creation of pleasant, peaceful and comfortable learning environments for children is most important both at home and in schools.

References

APPLE, M. (1992) 'Do the standards go far enough? Power, policy, and practices in mathematics education', *Journal for Research in Mathematics Education*, **23**(5), pp. 412–31.
APPLE, M. (1993) *Official Knowledge: Democratic Education in a Conservative Age*, New York and London, England: Routledge.
BARTH, F. (1969) *Ethnic Groups and Boundaries*, Boston, MA: Little, Brown.
BERLIN, B. and ROMNEY, A.K. (1964) 'Descriptive semantics of Tzeltal numeral classifiers', *American Anthropologist*, **66**(3), Special Issue: Transcultural Studies, Part 2, pp. 79–98.
BOAS, F. (1916) *The Mind of Primitive Man*, New York, NY: Macmillan.
BOOS-NUNNING, U. and HOHMANN, M. (1989) 'The educational situation of migrant workers' children in the Federal Republic of Germany', in ELDERING, L. and KLOPROGGE, J. (Eds) *Different Cultures Same School: Ethnic Minority Children in Europe*, Amsterdam, The Netherlands: Swets & Zeitlinger, pp. 39–59.
DEVOS, G. (1973) 'Japan's outcastes: The problem of the Burakumin', in WHITAKER, B. (Ed) *The Fourth World: Victims of Group Oppression*, New York, NY: Schocken Books, pp. 307–27.
DEVOS, G. (1983) 'Ethnic identity and minority status: Some psycho-cultural considerations', in JACOBSON-WIDDING, A. (Ed) *Identity: Personal and Socio-cultural*, Uppsala, Sweden: Almquist & Wiksell Tryckeri AB, pp. 90–113.
DEVOS, G. (1990) 'Conflict and accommodation in ethnic interaction', in DEVOS, G. and SUÁREZ-OROZCO, M.M. (Eds) *Status Inequality: The Self in Culture*, Newbury Park, CA: Sage Publications, pp. 204–45.
DEVOS, G. (1992) *Social Cohesion and Alienation: Minorities in the United States and Japan*, San Francisco, CA: Westview Press.
DEVOS, G. and SUÁREZ-OROZCO, M.M. (1990) *Status Inequality: The Self in Culture*, Newbury, CA: Sage Publications.
DEVOS, G. and WAGATSUMA, H. (1966) *Japan's Invisible Race: Caste in Culture and Personality*, Berkeley, CA: University of California Press.
ELDERING, L. and KLOPROGGE, J. (Eds) (1989) *Different Cultures Same School: Ethnic Minority Children in Europe*, Amsterdam, The Netherlands: Swets & Zeitlinger.

FIKES, JR. R. (1992) *Racist and Sexist Quotations: 'Some of the Most Outrageous Things Ever Said'*, Saratoga, CA: R&E Publishers.

FRAKE, C. (1961) 'The diagnosis of disease among the Subanum of Mindanao', *American Anthropologist*, **63**, pp. 113–32.

GUMPERZ, J. and HYMES, D. (Eds) (1964) 'The ethnography of communication', *American Anthropologists*, **66**, p. 6.

GUMPERZ, J. and HYMES, D. (1972) *Directions in Sociolinguistics: The Ethnography of Communication*, New York, NY: Holt, Rinehart & Winston.

HYMES, D. (1964) 'Directions in (ethno-) linguistic theory', *American Anthropologist*, **66**(3) Special Issue: Transcultural Studies, Part 2, pp. 6–56.

KOZOL, J. (1991) *Savage Inequalities: Children in America's Schools*, New York, NY: Crown Publishers, Inc.

LAPON, L. (1986) *Mass Murderers in White Coats*, Psychiatric Genocide Research Institute.

MCDERMOTT, R. (1987) 'Achieving school failure: An anthropological approach to illiteracy and social stratification', in SPINDLER, G. (Ed) *Education and Cultural Process: Anthropological Approaches*, Second Edition. Prospects Heights, IL: Waveland Press, Inc., pp. 173–209.

METZGER, D. and WILLIAMS, G. (1963) 'A formal ethnographic analysis of Tenejapa Ladino weddings', *American Anthropologists*, **65**(5), pp. 1076–101.

MOLL, L. (1990) *Vygotsky and Education: Instructional Implications and Applications of Sociohistorical Psychology*, Cambridge, MA: Cambridge University Press.

MOLL, L. and DIAZ, E. (1987) 'Change as the goal of educational research', *Anthropology and Education Quarterly*, **18**(4), pp. 300–11.

MYDANS, S. (1993) 'Gangs go public in new fight for respect', *Los Angeles Times*, May 1, 1993, p. 1.

NIETO, J. (1993) 'From Christopher Columbus to Rodney King: Power and inequality in the United States', presented at the Third Annual Conference of the National Association for Multicultural Education, Los Angeles, CA, February 12, 1993.

RODRIGUEZ, R. (1982) *Hunger of Memory: The Education of Richard Rodriguez: An Autobiography*, Boston, MA: David R. Godine.

ROOSENS, E. (1989) *Creating Ethnicity: The Process of Ethnogenesis*, in BERNARD, H.B. (Series Editor) *Frontiers of Anthropology*, **5**, Newbury Park, CA: Sage Publications.

STURTEVANT, W.C. (1964) 'Studies in ethnoscience', *Transcultural Studies in Cognition*, Special Issue of the *American Anthropologist*, **66**(3), Part 2, pp. 99–131.

SUÁREZ-OROZCO, M.M. (1991a) 'Dialogue and the transmission of culture: The Spindlers and the making of American anthropology', *Anthropology and Education Quarterly*, **22**(3), pp. 281–91.

SUÁREZ-OROZCO, M.M. (1993) 'Remaking psychological anthropology', unpublished manuscript, Center for Advanced Study in the Behavioral Sciences. Stanford, CA.

TABACHNICK, R. and ZEICHNER, K. (Eds) (1991) *Issues and Practices in Inquiry-oriented Teacher Education*, (The Wisconsin Series of Teacher Education), London, England: Falmer Press.

TOMLINSON, S. (1989) 'Ethnicity and educational achievement in Britain', in ELDERING, L. and KLOPROGGE, J. (Eds) *Different Cultures Same School: Ethnic and Minority Children in Europe*, Amsterdam: Swets & Zeitlinger, pp. 15–37.

TOMLINSON, S. (1991) 'Ethnicity and educational attainment in England — An overview', *Anthropology and Education Quarterly*, **22**(2), pp. 121–39.

VIGIL, D. (1988) 'Group processes and street identity: Adolescent Chicago gang members', *Journal for the Society for Psychological Anthropology, ETHOS*, **16**(4), pp. 421–44.

VIGIL, D. and CHONG YUN, S. (1990) 'Vietnamese youth gangs in Southern California', in HUFF, C.R. (Ed) *Gangas in America*, Newbury Park, CA: Sage Publications, pp. 146–62.
VYGOTSKY, L.S. (1962) *Thought and Language*, Cambridge, MA: Massachusetts Institute of Technology Press.
VYGOTSKY, L.S. (1978) *Mind in Society: The Development of Higher Psychological Processes*, COLE, M., JOHN-TEINER, V., SCRIBNER, S. and SOUBERMAN, E. (Eds) Cambridge, MA: Harvard University Press.
WERTSCH, J. (1985a) *Vygotsky and the Social Formation of Mind*, Cambridge, MA: Harvard University Press.
WERTSCH, J. (Ed) (1985b) *Culture, Communication and Cognition: Vygotskian Perspectives*, Cambridge, MA: Cambridge University Press.
WERTSCH, J.V. (1991) *Voices of the Mind: Sociocultural Approaches to Mediated Action*, Cambridge, MA: Harvard University Press.
ZEICHNER, K. (1990) 'Preparing teachers for democratic schools', *Action in Teacher Education*, **11**(1), pp. 5–10.
ZEICHNER, K. (1991) 'Contradictions and tensions in the professionalization of teaching and the democratization of schools', *Teachers College Record*, **92**(2), pp. 363–79.
ZEICHNER, K. (1992) 'Educating teachers for cultural diversity', unpublished manuscript, Madison, WI: Wisconsin Center for Educational Research, School of Education, University of Wisconsin-Madison.
ZEICHNER, K. and GORE, J. (1990) 'Teacher socialization', in HOUSTON, W.R. (Ed) *Handbook of Research on Teacher Education*, New York, NY: Macmillan, pp. 329–48.

Chapter 9

The Basis of Empowerment: Cultural Therapy and Critical Theory

Empowerment as a transition from a subordinate position of oppression and lack of control of one's destiny to a position of conscious decision-making to demand respect for one's rights and to control one's destiny, is a complex process that has both psychological dimensions (discussed earlier) and a number of sociocultural requirements. Empowerment does not occur in a vacuum, but it presumes specific sociocultural contexts that define opportunities for change. Knowledge of one's rights does not constitute an opportunity to change a status of oppression and misery. The conditions that permit change from the status of oppression to that of control of one's life are socially and culturally guided. In the same way as racial or ethnic prejudice and self-rejection are socially constructed through the media or other people's opinions, the redefinition of the self is conditioned to a new social reality, or at least the hope of creating one. Paulo Freire's discussion of the pedagogy of hope (1993) is based on this fundamental assumption that change is possible only if we accept the possibility that we can be agents of change. This chapter argues that the theoretical foundations to understand the nature of empowerment are cultural therapy and critical theory. Cultural therapy, as an emerging area in educational anthropology, deals with the conditions for healing from psychological wounds suffered in childhood and young adulthood, especially in a world saturated with trauma, racism and intolerance. Critical theory demands a conscious effort to examine the epistemological roots of educational research and practice as a means to understand the world and to provide all peoples with a genuine opportunity to learn in order to enjoy full human rights and become truly empowered. The relationship between these theoretical areas of cultural therapy and critical pedagogy is predicated on the fact that both require consciousness, awareness, and action; furthermore, both see education as a political process that permits individuals to participate in societal institutions; finally, both areas assume that the transition from disempowerment to empowerment is possible only if both collective social construction of a new set of relationships is created, and if the individuals can internalize these new relationships. In this chapter, cultural therapy is the first and most fundamental step in setting the conditions for the individuals to reconstruct a social

Cultural Therapy and Critical Theory

and cultural environment in which oppression is eliminated. Without understanding what racism, oppression and abuse can do to a person, it is impossible to conceive a life of freedom and self-confidence. The relationship between cultural therapy and critical pedagogy is also predicated on the grounds that in order to help children establish an ethnic and social identity that empowers them to participate fully in a democratic society, they must know who they are and understand that learning, education and critical reflection is needed to understand oneself in a given historical context.

Oppressive environments are heavily controlled by the media and public images of minority or disenfranchised groups. For example, the biased views of Africans and African Americans makes us believe that there is a relationship between African American culture and violence:

> In essence, in the absence of alternative protrayals of, say, Africans and African Americans, the news seems to indicate that violence is 'endemic to black culture' . . . and is somehow a 'natural' occurrence. Blacks *are* mentioned, but what counts as 'black' is incorporated into hegemonic discourse, just as in the textbooks . . .
>
> It is the discourse of 'tribalism' that seems to dominate news accounts. Thus, in treatments of Africa, conflict 'appears' as seemingly incomprehensible self-destruction. It is irrational and primitive — in a word, 'tribal'. This is not limited to the treatment of conflict in, say, South Africa. A similar repertoire of visual and linguistic codes have often been employed to represent black youth actions in Britain and the United States.
>
> Rather than addressing violence as part of South Africa's political struggle, it is reduced to the discourse of political and cultural underdevelopment. It is the black population that is irrational, not yet ready for democracy. The dominant white South African government is the 'rational peace keeper', the group that is engaged in serious compromises in the face of an uncertain, yet surely violent future. In essence, it is the white capitalist West — ultimately rational and willing to be fair — that is the 'keeper of the flame' against the persistent crisis caused by irrational native people. Yet, if this is the case of Africa, it is not only the case for Africa.
>
> (Apple 1993:107)

The major point made by Apple, and recognized by many other social scientists, especially those in sociolinguistics and anthropology — the ethnographers of communication, for example, such as Gumperz and Hymes (1964, 1972; Gumperz 1982, 1986) and others mentioned in Chapter 2, is that racial and ethnic bias are socially and culturally constructed in the very process of communication, especially through the 'official' channels of communication. The consequences for empowerment are clear. We cannot preach empowerment without a serious consideration of the social and cultural changes required for a new social and cultural understanding of people's values and ethnic identities. The media reflects common values, but it also reinforces common biases. These biases transcend public life and enter the classroom and the interpersonal life of students:

> As a number of people remind us, students are engaged in constant attempts to make sense out of their social experience. Television plays no small part in that sense-making struggle. Thus, students seeing television dramas about prisons often exploit the potential for multiple meanings by actively comparing their own experiences of powerlessness in schools with those of prisoners. Aboriginal children in Australia when 'reading' television shows that portray African Americans and Native Americans as being defeated or misunderstood, actively construct a category which includes blacks, (North American) Indians, and themselves in opposition to dominant meanings. 'Reading' television in this way provided them with a means of articulating their own powerlessness in a white dominated society.
> (Apple 1993:111–12)

The media, therefore, can also serve as an instrument of sociocultural change and help oppressed peoples to articulate their status and need for emancipation. These points are particularly relevant to the content of this chapter and the case of China. The awareness of the outside world that occurred in an intensified fashion since the foundation of the New China in 1949 has profoundly affected all minorities, but especially those most isolated, like the Miao. Knowing that the past deprived many Miao people from participating in mainstream societal institutions (political and economic), Miao university students have been forced to search their collective historical accounts in order to redefine their new self-images as university students and empowered individuals within the New China, the China that is now competing for a global market and modern technology, and attempting to build a new socio-political structure in which all minorities can indeed excel and participate with equal rights and obligations. Consequently, the social and cultural changes that started in 1949 have logically led to possibilities and opportunities for Miao people that were never imagined before. A village boy from Guizhou can think about travelling abroad and developing ambitious economic plans. The transition from a closed village environment to that of a powerful position is possible thanks both to cultural therapy and critical pedagogy. Cultural therapy in the form of a Freiran understanding of the historical moment in which Miao people live, and the role of education in their lives (education as an instrument for becoming active change agents within mainstream Chinese society), is essential for Miao students to succeed in the university. Their entire motivation hinges upon the premise that education will open doors so they can participate as full citizens, indeed as privileged citizens, in the process of constructing modern China. An essential component of this therapy is critical thinking and critical pedagogy.

Cultural Therapy and Critical Theory

The concept that Freire has shared with the English speaking world of *conscientização* is viewed by Gadotti (1992) as intimately related to popular culture, to the social construction of social relations and images that Apple was talking about earlier. Gadotti explains Freire as follows:

> O pensamento de Paulo Freire tem suas raízes mais profundas no debate político-cultural do final dos anos 50. Tratava-se do debate em torno da construçâo na estrutura do ensino da extensâ da educaçâo para todos. Um projeto de emancipaçâo construçâo de uma nova naçâo brasileira passava pela assunçâo de sus characterísticas de naçâo latino-americana e terceiro-mundista, ao contrário do que as elites dominantes pensavam, que era criar, no Brasil, uma 'nova Europa' ou uma 'nova Amêrica'. Daí Paulo Freire insistir na questâo da 'invasâo cultural', da 'dependência' e da 'consciência alienada'. Denunciando essa 'realidade Nacional', ele estava anunciando, dialeticament, o seu fim e inaugurando, entre nós, um vigororoso movimento em torno de un pensamento pedagogico autônomo. Paulo Freire reintroduz a reflexâo sobre o social no pensamento educational brasileiro, compromento-se com ideas socialistas e democráticos.
>
> Cultural popular, portanto, é sinonimo de 'conscientizaçâo', ou seja, de tomada de consciência da realidade national, para transformá-la e criar novas formas de relaçôes sociais e políticas; significa consciência de direitos, possibilidade de criar novos direitos e capacidade de defendê-los contra o autoritarismo, a violência (simbólica ou nâo) e o arbítrio. Enfim, cultura popular significa cultura da cidadania.
>
> (Gadotti, 1992:36–7)

The thinking of Paulo Freire has its most profound roots in the politico-cultural debate of the late 50s. It was a debate about the construction of an educational structure that would extend education to all. An emancipation project to construct a new Brazilian nation was based on the assumption that its characteristics would be those of a Latin American third-world nation, in contrast to what the dominant elites thought, that is to create not a Brazil, but a 'new Europe' or a 'new America'. Therefore, Paulo Freire insisted on the question of 'cultural invasion', of 'dependence' and of 'alienated conscience'. Denouncing that 'national reality', he was announcing dialectically its end, and inaugurating, among ourselves, a vigorous movement around an autonomous pedagogical concept. Paulo Freire reintroduced a reflection on the Brazilian social concept, committing himself to socialist and democratic ideas. Popular culture, therefore, is synonymous with *conscientizaçâo* (conscientization), that is, of becoming aware of the national reality in order to transform it and create new forms of social and political relationships; it means awareness of rights, possibilities of creating new rights and capabilities to defend them against authoritarianism, violence (symbolic or not) and arbitrary decisions. In brief, popular culture means culture of citizenship.

(Gadotti 1992:36–7; translation by Henry T. Trueba)

The need for cultural therapy is clearly established by Apple, Freire and Gadotti (as we have seen), because the very thought of emancipation requires the recognition of the legitimate popular or ethnic cultures represented by the individuals seeking empowerment. The relationship of culture and politics, and of both to education is essential. A pedagogy that does not recognize the fundamental rights people have to their language and culture cannot lead to empowerment. Cultural therapy deals with a deeper understanding of the consequences of cultural hegemony which result from imposing a dominant culture on peoples conquered or oppressed, and it advocates the need to recognize ethnic and popular cultures.

Cultural Therapy

Personality changes over time, often triggered by cultural conflicts arising from changes in the social and cultural environment, can be understood in terms of the distance between the original ethnic and social identity resulting from early socialization in the home and community, and the successive redefinitions of the self resulting from adaptation to new socio-cultural environments. To use George Spindler's concepts, the *enduring self*, which is the individual's perception of self anchored to the set of values and cultural norms acquired during early socialization, is in clear contrast to the *situated self*, that is, the perception of self as successively adapted new sets of cultural values and norms demanded by, and congruent with, new environments. These concepts were presented by George and Louise Spindler in their early work (Spindler, G. 1959); Spindler, G. and Spindler, L. *Native North American Cultures: Four Cases* (1977); Spindler, G. *Dreamers Without Power: The Menomini Indians* (1971); Spindler, G. *Education and Cultural Process* (first edition in 1974, we use here the 2nd edition, 1987); *The Making of Psychological Anthropology*, (1978, a 2nd edition is in preparation); the 'Roger Harker' study (Spindler, G. and Spindler, L. 1982); as well as their more recent work in the *Doing the Ethnography of Schooling: Educational Anthropology in Action* (original edition in 1982, 2nd edition used here, 1988); *Interpretive Ethnography of Education* (1987a); *What do Anthropologists Have to Say About Dropouts?* (Trueba H. and Spindler, G. and Spindler, L. 1989); and Spindler, G. and Spindler, L. with Trueba, H. and Williams, M. *The American Cultural Dialogue and Its Transmission* (1990). More recently, George and Louise Spindler discuss these concepts in the context of cultural continuities and discontinuities associated with multiculturalism in *Pathways to Cultural Awareness: Cultural Therapy for Teachers and Students* (Spindler, G. and Spindler, L. 1994).

Cultural therapy is a process of cultural reflection on one's own ethnicity, race, class and status in a historical context (as Freire suggests 1973, 1993) and an effort to come to terms with one's reality in the surrounding cultural context. The purpose of cultural therapy is to heal. Healing is here understood as a process of conscious awareness and acceptance of one's cultural reality. The assumption is that by knowing one's roots and cultural reality in its various dimensions, one will be able to accept or rationalize the distance between the enduring self and the situated self, or in simpler terms, the cultural continuities and discontinuities in one's values, perspectives and lifestyle. The need for healing is not the same in all groups and segments of the population. The ethnohistory of some groups, their traumas and psychological scars are a function of the degree and nature of the discontinuities they face in their lives. Children in western societies, especially children of immigrants, must face serious cultural conflicts as they contrast their early childhood experiences at home, where they felt safe and competent, with their experience in the host country's schools where they feel stupid, traumatized and rejected. The degree of trauma and degradation and the adaptive strategies they borrowed from adults of their ethnic/racial group and social class can lead to serious intra- and inter-personal conflicts as they grow between two cultural worlds. Cultural discontinuities do not necessarily occur in transnational immigration movements. The case of China is here relevant. Within a single country, a child can go from being a peasant, ignorant and isolated villager, to being a gifted university student in a city like Beijing or Hong Kong. The distance between the enduring self as a peasant and the situated self as a university student is perhaps greater than the distance between being a poor child on the outskirts of Beijing and becoming a student at the Beijing Normal University. In the former case, the peasant child has to acquire Mandarin as a second language, and compete through a series of difficult examinations with nationally selected peers for a university opening; the peasant child then has to get food money and emotional support to withstand difficulties and isolation away from his/her family thousands of miles away from home. The latter case demands changes in social status and adaptation to a new lifestyle within the same city and through the same language.

Cultural therapy, as presented by the Spindlers, is not linked to the political process, but it certainly is to the educational process. Cultural therapy, regardless of the degree of cultural discontinuities, consists of facing individuals with the painful issues of cultural misunderstandings involved in interaction across class, race, cultures and ethnicities. There is a great deal of ethnocentrism in all of us, and as we interact with persons who are different from us, we tend to project and superimpose values onto their behaviors and our perceptions of their values; often we go as far as rejecting them as we perceive them. Human responses to xenophobia, or the fear of diversity, spread over a continuum from single dislike or indifference to profound hatred with intent to destroy those who are different from us. Often these perceptions and evaluations of other peoples are grounded in life experiences and early socialization that transmits prejudice and misunderstandings from generation

197

to generation. But these perceptions and misunderstandings are often rooted in interactional events and experiences shared to some degree with those people who are different. Historical hostilities, superficial assessment of peoples' lifestyles, physical appearances, behavior and cultural rituals are often enough to persuade us that those people are 'undesirable'.

One of the purposes of cultural therapy is to bring about an understanding of the nature of differences between other peoples and our own people. At the heart of cultural therapy is a deeper understanding of the process of early socialization we underwent, and a better understanding of how our enduring self was constructed — the fundamental premises and assumptions about others, about ourselves, and about the differences in belief systems and values. To consciously understand racial prejudice requires a profound reflection on the type of traumas we suffered as children because of our race. Humans need to understand how to share the earth on which we all live and to recognize the basic commonalities of all members of the single human species existing on earth. Therefore, looking at the role of early socialization, with a focus on the process of social identification, as we have done in this study, can bring about a better understanding of how cultural therapy can help heal the wounds opened up by prejudice and insensitivity.

Awareness of our early childhood socialization and the self-concept developed during those years may be so drastically different than the self-concept we have today, that the problem in healing is to understand how and why these two social identities are so far apart. In other words, part of the fruit of cultural therapy can be to establish a bridge of understanding between the enduring self and the situated self, thus creating needed harmony. In the case of Miao students, for example, the cultural values of love for parents, family and community that were grounded in their childhoods in the small villages are fundamentally unchanged; but their lifestyle, status and current knowledge are no longer similar to their peers' in the village. Their explanations of the world, sense of citizenship in China and in the world, their ambitions, and scholarship have become more worldly and so has their view of themselves. Tolerance of small abuses in the junior high school when they began to learn Mandarin, the humiliation suffered because of their accents, smell, clothing, etc., is gone and will never be repeated. Those students are respected people both in their villages and in the large city; they are members of an educated elite, with security of employment, the use of several languages, the ability to speak and write, a substantial knowledge of subject matter, and a much broader view of life than most other people in China. Deep down, however, there are hurts, and during the interview process, students cried remembering the tough times and the ridicule they suffered. Their commitment to their ethnic group, their families and their home values stands strong, but is viewed as the foundation for their new values and achievements. They reached personality integration by obtaining an understanding of their own change, and in doing so, with each others' help and the help of their mentors (Miao professors); that integration is the fruit of cultural therapy. The ultimate result is that they did not reject their enduring self, but modified it to adjust to the new cultural environment; they established a bridge between their enduring self and their situated self.

As the new generations of social scientists examine the contributions of the second half of the twentieth-century anthropologists, they may well look at cultural therapy as one of the most important. This century has been the theater of the most vicious attacks against humanity: the Holocaust of Jewish, Gypsies and other racially segregated individuals in the 1930s and 40s, the systematic extermination of Moslems in Croatia and Serbia, the terrorism in the Middle East, in South Africa, in Europe (Spain, Ireland, etc.) and Central and South America (especially in Argentina and Colombia). Humankind is more than ever in desperate need to heal from the injuries some persons have inflicted on others. Children, the ultimate victims of these excesses, need, more than any others, the chance to heal and the opportunity to live a life without abuse or neglect. We believe that the process of empowerment cannot take place until healing has occurred. Cultural therapy is one of the necessary conditions for empowerment. In their *Pathways to Cultural Awareness*, George and Louise Spindler deal with empowerment for children and the role of schools and suggest the application of cultural therapy in the curriculum of ethnically diversified school settings. Their intuition about the need for the human race to heal from its multiple wounds and contradictions through a better understanding of inter-ethnic relations and of culture is a timely and important statement from the founders of educational anthropology. Who could really question the need for healing? Daily stories about hatred, cruelty, war and conflict dividing nations, states, cities and neighborhoods are an impressive demonstration of the open wounds and emotional injuries that result in loss of self-esteem and positive social identity. The Spindlers advanced the concepts of the enduring self and situated self in an effort to explain the complexity of modern people to arrive at an integrated self-concept as they go through the process of social identification. The question, 'Who am I?' cannot be simply answered by, 'I am an American', or 'I am a Chinese'. As we adapt to new living environments we leave behind our initial social identity and the values acquired during childhood. The painful route that many people have been forced to take, from their infancy to their present adult life, has resulted in a very confused notion of self-identity. The increasing marginalization of children results in lack of self-confidence and lack of hope; indeed, it results at times in bitterness about society, especially about people in power.

The assumption that is at the heart of a strong and positive social identity is a conscious reflection on one's own cultural reality (a truly healing process of understanding oneself and others) and leads to practices of acceptance of the self, of one's family, ethnicity, race, and background (social, linguistic, religious, etc.). Conflict in human interaction does not have to result in destruction and hatred, if only we can learn about ourselves and others through the culture of therapy. The empowerment of many (those from low status, low income, especially those from 'undesirable' racial/ethnic backgrounds) depends on their ability to learn, reflect and contextualize in a socio-historical frame the events that have hurt them the most. For many persons hurt by racism, prejudice and bigotry, the necessary (though not sufficient) condition to heal cannot come from the outside, it must come from within, and it must be based on a deep cultural knowledge and understanding of the nature of human behavior analyzed from the perspective of the mediating role of language and culture in the acquisition of all knowledge and values. The ethnocentrism of social groups who learn to hate, dehumanize and destroy others — often with the intent of gaining power — is truly a pest that can contaminate the entire human race. Unfortunately, academic disciplines, including the social sciences, have reflected the biases of peoples in power, and have contributed to the demise of people of color and other 'undesirables' or 'unmeltables'. The pseudo-theories postulating unilineal cultural evolution which exalted the genetic/biological superiority of Aryan groups in Europe and the need to assess presumed mental deficiencies in immigrants (especially those deemed undesirable) have not died as yet; they remain in the unconscious and conscious prejudice exhibited by those in power. It is refreshing to see how some Chinese nationalities, especially university students, explore new avenues to reach new democratic structures, and attempt to link their efforts to Chinese political history, while at the same time they take advantage of Government financial support policies.

The process of empowerment among the Miao students studied in this project is linked through its most intimate intra-personal roots with the process of social identification that took place in early childhood and continued by the ongoing support of family and community through adolescence and young adulthood. One of the important lessons we learned from the Miao is that it takes courage and candor to support children through their education, and it takes great personal sacrifice to make it possible for a child to climb the tough ladder of academic success. In contrast, the structural neglect of children in western societies, the selfish destruction of learning environments caused by lack of financial support for low-income children, the continued oppression of families of color, the disregard for their desperate efforts to get out of their ignorance and disempowerment, may in the ultimate analysis hurt all of us through the erosion of the quality of life in western society.

With a keen sense of history and honest minds, George and Louise Spindler have looked carefully into the phenomenon of low achievement of minorities in the context of cultural discontinuities and change that requires a major cognitive and cultural reorganization of learning categories and strategies in children. The Spindlers have compared American society with others in the world, and have used this comparison to prepare educators to understand themselves better, to heal, and to enter American institutions as active participants so they can commit and belong in society. The Spindlers see academia in many western societies (including the United States) as excluding some ethnics from the benefits enjoyed by mainstream members and as using academic institutions as a mechanism to marginalize the poor, unwanted students coming from ethnic and low-status backgrounds. The psychological and cultural mechanisms that lead to the marginalization of many students have been central to the theoretical concerns of George and Louise Spindler. Therefore, their most recent contribution to the intellectual and practical daily lives of many teachers and social scientists is cultural therapy. George and Louise Spindler, as did Paulo Freire (1973), feel that in order to come to terms with the meaning of being human (members of the same species) and with our cultural diversity in schools and society, we must first understand better our cultures and ethnicities, and their interdependency. Their use of cross-cultural research and reflective cultural analysis is a powerful instrument to create positive inter-ethnic relations. This research provides a historically-grounded and rich comparative analysis of the process of self-identification and adaptation to new human environments.

Critical Theory

Critical theory is part of a general epistemological movement to re-examine the most fundamental philosophical foundations of theory, empirical research and practice. Critical theory, as applied to the educational process, has been called critical pedagogy. Critical pedagogy is an integral part of the process of empowerment, because it is aimed at allowing all people to become active participants in the political process (Freire 1973, 1993; Gadotti 1992). This is consistent with the work of Apple (1982, 1989, 1992, 1993). Critical pedagogy focuses on the basic principles of sound teaching and learning. There are different types of critical theory, such as 'libertarian', 'radical', and 'liberationist' (according to McLaren 1989; Giroux and McLaren 1989) which are different nuances of the same position. The writings of Henry Giroux and Peter McLaren are not only two of the best examples of critical theory applied to the struggle for education in American society, but also forceful expressions of two scientists who speak for many educators. Other critical thinkers such as Apple 1978, 1982, 1989, 1992, 1993; Aronowitz and Giroux 1991; Freire 1973; Popkewitz 1991, 1993; Giroux 1991; 1992 have also profoundly influenced modern social theory and critical pedagogy.

The relationship between critical theory and critical pedagogy is examined by Gadotti (1992) who interprets Freire as creating a new ideology and a vigorous movement that links popular culture to critical pedagogy. In other words, in order to conceptualize a new social reality, it is necessary first to become aware of the consequences of oppression and violence, of the hegemony of dominant cultures and of the need for social and political change. Critical theory departs from this basic realization or *conscientização* that oppressed people have the right to their culture and should have the power to defend those rights (Gadotti 1992:30–8). For Aronowitz and Giroux the concept of critical theory has a particular meaning:

> Critical theory, left and right, bemoans the 'eclipse of reason', the 'closing of the American mind', 'the culture of narcissism'; and it assails contemporary culture from the point of view of a discourse referring to an anterior state of affairs that, even if suffused with suffering, is alleged to have put high value on the search for Truth.
> (Aronowitz and Giroux 1991:136)

These authors discuss critical pedagogy in postmodern times and provide a broad context for the conflicting views about education. Postmodern education is — for some — in a chaotic state of affairs, hopelessly entangled in the politics of class and culture of recent years, clearly resulting in conspicuous neglect of all children's intellectual growth and political socialization, especially children of color. Is this a fair assessment? Scholars, to a lesser or greater measure, have also pointed out the benefits of postmodern education, one in which people have the freedom to denounce social class evils, to discuss openly difficult issues on race relations and ethnic affiliation, and a period in which a new understanding of social, cultural and economic reproduction is possible (Apple 1988).

What does this view suggest for the way we look at the issue of school reform? Specifically, what is the role of critical pedagogy in school reform? What is its role in the preparation of teachers for ethnically and economically diverse industrial societies, such as the United States?

In an attempt to answer the above questions, McLaren redefines critical pedagogy as:

> a variety of important counterlogics to the positivistic, ahistorical, and depoliticized analysis employed by both liberal and conservative critics of schooling-an analysis all too readily visible in the training programs in our colleges of education.
> (McLaren 1989:159)

McLaren's counterview can be considered a political compromise between the negative and the positive postmodern critical pedagogues. In his mind, critical theory can help educators and researchers to develop a pedagogy (critical pedagogy) that permits them to create a new ideological orientation, better grounded in real life problems. When McLaren talks about the foundational principles of critical pedagogy, he feels that critical pedagogy resonates with the symbolic and powerful sensibility of the Hebrew word *Tikkun*, which means to heal, repair, and transform the world. In his mind, critical pedagogy offers a sociohistorical and political direction to educators who seek hope. McLaren is profoundly committed to a critical pedagogy for the oppressed (in the sense expressed by Freire) (McLaren 1989:160–1). In some sense, critical pedagogy is a quasi-declaration of independence, a peak in historical liberation of radical thinking (McLaren 1989:160–5). Thus, McLaren describes critical pedagogy as follows:

Cultural Therapy and Critical Theory

> A critical pedagogy situates itself in the intersection of language, culture, and history — the nexus in which the students' subjectivities are formed, contested, and played out. The struggle is one that involves their history, their language, and their culture and the pedagogical implications are such that students are given access to a critical discourse or are conditioned to accept the familiar as the inevitable. Worse still, they are denied a voice with which to be present in the world; they are made invisible to history and rendered powerless to shape it.
>
> (McLaren 1989:233)

This tells us that critical theory challenges the canons of knowledge and encourages ethnic and racial minorities and women to reclaim their histories in such a way that they feel empowered to play a key role in building a new social, economic and political order. As McLaren points out, 'A major task of critical pedagogy has been to disclose and challenge the role that schools play in our political and cultural life' (McLaren 1989:160).

Today education faces challenges and crises of unexpected magnitude. For example, McLaren describes these challenges as follows:

> Rampant illiteracy, growing dropout rates among the poor, and a dramatic increase in classroom violence and despair exemplify the plight of today's students and teachers. As we fail to consider the possibility of practical political action or to exercise our abilities to intervene in the world, our dreams glide over the domain of ethics and continue to be manufactured in a culture of unchallenged consumer hype and moral destruction. Today more than ever before we need a pedagogical theory that is able to counter the New Right's excoriating attack on schooling, which argues that the moral vocabulary of critical pedagogy must be expunged as leftist or socialistic... As the dark and ambivalent wings of history beat about the stage of our present era, where hope is held hostage, where justice is lashed to the altar of capital accumulation, and where the good works of our collective citizenry have been effaced by despair, we desperately need a new vision of what education should mean.
>
> (McLaren 1989:21)

He then points out that teachers must begin to examine critically our society's complicity in maintaining structures of inequality and injustice, and that teachers must face their own responsibility in the reproduction of inequality. The solution, according to McLaren, is critical pedagogy, that is, resistance to the intellectual and moral oppression coming from all corners of society (McLaren 1989:21–3).

Since the late 1950s, as a result of the Civil Rights movement, many American scholars have addressed issues related to multiculturalism or cultural pluralism in American and European societies. However, different people have different interpretations of multicultural education (Sleeter and Grant 1987:436; Trueba, 1993). Yet, most educators share the view that multicultural education has the purpose of enhancing the education of all people, including those of color. Trueba argues that:

> Multicultural education is not only the education of minority groups, but of all Americans to learn to respect and appreciate each group and their collective richness in languages, cultures and traditions. Equally important is the inculcation of the principle of responsibility of all citizens to treat all persons, regardless of their diverse background, with the same respect. To accomplish this end, much has been written about ethnic and racial hatred, and about the need to heal; hatred hurts not only the victims, but also all of us who are members of this democratic, pluralistic society.
>
> (Trueba, 1993:9–87)

According to Banks, multicultural education is, first of all, an ideal whereby everyone should have an equal opportunity to get an education and learn effectively in school, regardless of gender, social class, ethnicity, race, or culture. Second, multicultural education is also a reform movement that attempts to make schools more responsive to the needs of all students from diverse socio-economic, racial, and ethnic backgrounds. Third, multicultural education is an ongoing process, a movement whose goals can never be completely achieved, yet one which requires that both teachers and students be enriched through a continuous interactional process of cultural sharing (Banks and McGee-Banks 1989:2–23).

The concern of American educators to prepare teachers for culturally diverse classrooms and for a multicultural America brings back issues discussed above about the early socialization for academic achievement, and the trauma suffered by certain children who come from low-income and ethnic minority groups. There has been no mention in the literature about cultural pluralism in China, nor any educational studies of minority students in China. What can we learn from multicultural China? And what can China learn from multicultural America? How does the concept of critical pedagogy relate to early socialization, ethnic and social identification processes and empowerment? Is Chinese multiculturalism comparable to that of America? America is a multicultural society which is made up of subgroups that differ from each other on the basis of social class, ethnicity, race, culture and gender. In contrast, Chinese minority groups (or nationalities) have territorial control of the lands they have occupied for centuries and have a recognized social status that gives them certain privileges. As in America, some of the more isolated minority societies (or nationalities) have schools of inferior quality if compared with the schools of mainstream populations. The questions raised by American teachers are also relevant in China. For example, what should teachers who work in a culturally diverse setting know? Or, as Zeichner (1991, 1992) puts it, multicultural teacher education deals with 'what teachers need to be like, know, and be able to do, to work successfully with diverse students' (Zeichner 1992:2). Multicultural teacher education is intended to help develop a better understanding of the strategies needed to function effectively in ethnically, culturally and linguistically diversified schools. Sleeter also emphasizes the need for teachers to 'develop and amplify the school's power to validate students' experiences and identities, to promote democratic values and critical thought, and to empower young people' (Sleeter 1991:9). Multicultural education is seen by many scholars as a means to raise critical thinking skills in culturally different children, and thus become empowered. Consequently, in this sense, critical pedagogy can be very instrumental to teachers.

Critical pedagogy provides educators with the philosophical foundations for multicultural education and a theoretical framework in which we can redefine the relationships between teachers and schools administrators, between the center of power and the margins of power. Critical pedagogy not only calls into question certain forms of subordination that generate injustices in school settings among teachers responsible for teaching low-income, minority and other children of disempowered families, but it also challenges institutional reforms and ideological positions that 'have historically masked their own relations of power behind complex forms of distinction and privilege' (Giroux 1991:194). Consequently, multicultural teacher education based on critical pedagogy must raise questions about the social order and the status of teachers and minorities in the current educational system, and it must also advocate compliance with equity and democratic participation in social institutions by all persons.

Critical theory is an essential component of multicultural teacher education and calls for a profound commitment to the type of society in which racial prejudice and abuse of power are unacceptable. While there has been a substantial amount of literature discussing the philosophical and political dimensions of critical theory, there are relatively few applied models for teacher education which use as foundations the principles of critical pedagogy and critical theory. Merino, Minnis and Quintanar have produced (1989) one of the most solid theoretically and practical assessment models, Models for Training Student Teachers in Multicultural Education. This model presents three different approaches to work in culturally and linguistically diverse settings. One approach is the traditional course, which is the *competency model*, focused on teaching about minority cultures in the US with emphasis placed on learning styles, values, customs and traditions of a few major ethnic groups. The second approach is the *Teacher as Ethnographer Model*, which emphasizes the importance of training teachers to conduct systematic observations and ethnographic studies in order to gain deeper insights and understandings of minority groups. The third approach is the *Selective Eclectic Introspective Model* which intends to use a large and diverse body of knowledge of effective ways of integrating culture with the teaching process as well as providing means for investigating the background of students. It may include a number of features from other approaches in specific settings.

There have been other practical attempts to develop pragmatic approaches to preparing teachers for diversity using critical theory principles, or, as some refer to it, conscious reflectivity. One of these examples is the teacher preparation programs for diversity developed at the University of Wisconsin-Madison, School of Education, under the leadership of professors Robert Tabachnick and Kenneth Zeichner (see Tabachnick and Zeichner 1991). These scholars and their associates have developed what they called 'reflective teaching', which has as its basic theoretical foundation the importance of thinking reflectively about teaching. This program, organized primarily for mainstream students, consists of field-based experiences in schools with low-income and minority students (especially blacks). Students are given guidance and support in their activities and perform their duties under very close supervision from school and university faculty personnel. One of the strategies taught to these students is 'teaching story-telling' through which student teachers learn about their underlying assumptions, presuppositions and interpretive frames as they confront minority classrooms. Students in the teacher education program are encouraged to rethink their views and to write ethnographic journals about their daily experiences. This program was extremely successful and helped a great deal in preparing white students to work in minority schools. The program also developed a unique sense of *esprit de corps* among the cohort of students.

Conclusion

Implicit in this process called 'norm-centered' is the important notion of socialization or enculturation, that is, a process of culture acquisition (see Spindler, G. 1988 and Spindler, G. and L. 1987a and 1987b). This concept is also used by DeVos (1973) and is an integral part of the process of ethnic identification discussed in the previous chapters. Both of these anthropological approaches emphasize the acquisition of knowledge and values necessary to function effectively as an adult in society; and both stress the need for conscious, organized and intentional tasks children voluntarily engage in, experience and live through as a means to acquire the knowledge necessary to function effectively in a given society. Anthropology assumes the existence of an intimate relationship between the social or cultural world and the cognitive world, and both require an intimate link between learning and experiencing. Most importantly, both propose as an outcome of the education/socialization process the acquisition of knowledge, norms, values and skills by children, so they can function in the world of adults as productive members of society. In other words, the child is socialized through his/her higher mental functions to understand and internalize cultural norms, values and symbols through the assisted performance and mentoring of an adult (in the sense articulated by Vygotsky 1962, 1978). It should also be noted here that the anthropological concept of socialization is very closely related to the principles of cognitive development stated by Soviet socio-historical school of psychology as represented by Vygotsky (1962, 1978) and Wertsch (1985a, 1985b, 1991); that is, the relationship between learning and experience, and the inseparability between the social and the cognitive in the learning process are clearly congruent with anthropological thinking and critical pedagogy.

Another important connection between anthropology and the Soviet socio-historical school of psychology is the idea that action (or activities demonstrating cognitive performance) are mediated by culture and embedded in the cultural value system that provides the rationale and motivation for acting. Furthermore, there seems to be a symbiotic relationship between acting and thinking, between social and cognitive levels of activity and between the cultural values embedded in action and the willingness to act. George and Louise Spindler in their *American Cultural Dialogue and its Transmission* (1990) discuss the nature of American culture and the notion of culture as leading to action in ways deemed to enhance social values and norms. The global view of the many relationships between educating or socializing children to become Americans and the kind of schooling designed for them are better grasped if we assume the basic premises of Vygotskian psychology. The study presented here on the Miao from China lends substantial support to these premises. Peasant Miao children retain a profound commitment to hard work, willingness to sacrifice personal comfort, and high academic achievement motivation based on the assumption that such achievement is a means to repay the kindness of parents. For example, the premise that learning is experiencing is part of the Confucian philosophy; virtue in action is related to wisdom and scholarship. Schools provide a number of activities (often called the hidden curriculum) directed to create a set of values unique to a given culture. The messages that the hidden curriculum can bring are sometimes positive and sometimes negative. At times, the hidden curriculum can be an instrument of upward mobility and positive adaptation to change, or it can perpetuate social strata, oppressive relationships and pain.

Educational anthropology can help us understand better the social, cultural and psychological mechanisms for achievement motivation and empowerment of children who come from very humble origins, such as the Miao in this study. These disciplines can help us become aware that the value of equity, justice and democracy in American and other societies is ignored when we neglect children because they are members of unwanted groups and suffer social stereotypes. Critical theory and critical pedagogy are intimately related with the central assumption of cultural therapy that demands cultural awareness, (*conscientização*) in order to discover the impact of oppression and the way to empowerment. Understanding the role of culture in determining racial or ethnic prejudice, and the impact of such prejudice on the formation of the self-concept, requires critical pedagogy. The internalization of the cultural values grounded on ethnic identities, and the recognition that these values are legitimate and worthwhile is only one step towards empowerment. Action must follow. Awareness is only part of *conscientizaçâo*, because *conscientizaçâo* or conscientization demands willingness to engage in political action in order to change the social relationships that have deprived individuals from enjoying their rights and the power to defend such rights. Acting upon this knowledge is essential.

In conclusion, cultural therapy can create a climate in which critical analysis of our lives, as well as our theories and practices on teaching and learning becomes possible. It provides stimulating avenues for comparison and for increasing our understanding of the relationship of culture to learning and empowerment. Embedded in the concept of cultural therapy is the struggle against cultural ethnocentrism but not the commitment to pursue cultural diversity with political action. Critical pedagogy, however, requires such a commitment and the concept of conscientization is seen as the first step in the active involvement for social and cultural change.

References

APPLE, M. (1978) *The New Sociology of Education: Analyzing Cultural and Economic Reproduction*,

APPLE, M. (1982) *Cultural and Economic Reproduction in Education*, New York: Macmillan.

APPLE, M. (1989) *Teachers and Texts: A Political Economy of Class and Gender Relations in Education*, New York: Routledge. (First published in 1986).

APPLE, M. (1992) 'Do the standards go far enough? Power, policy, and practices in mathematics education', *Journal for Research in Mathematics Education*, **23**(5), pp. 412–31.

APPLE, M. (1993) *Official Knowledge: Democratic Education in a Conservative Age*, New York, NY: Routledge.

ARONOWITZ, S. and GIROUX, H. (1991) *Postmodern Education: Politics, Culture and Social Criticism*, Minneapolis, MN: University of Minnesota Press.

BANKS, J.A. and MCGEE-BANKS, C.A. (Eds) (1989) *Multicultural Education: Issues and Perspectives*, London, England: Allyn and Bacon Publishers.

DEVOS, G. (Ed) (1973) *Socialization for Achievement: Essays on the Cultural Psychology of the Japanese*, Berkeley, CA: University of California Press.

FREIRE, P. (1973) *Pedagogy of the Oppressed*, New York, NY: Seabury.

FREIRE, P. (1993) *Pedagogia da Esperança: Um reencontro com a pedagogia do oprimido*, Sâo Paulo, Brazil: Editora Paz e Terra, S.A.

GADOTTI, M. (1992) *Escola Cidada: Uma Aula Sobre Autonomia da Escola*, Cortez Editora/ Editores Asociados, Sâo Paulo: Brazil.

GIROUX, H. (Ed) (1991) *Postmodernism, Feminism and Cultural Politics*, Albany, NY: State University of New York Press.

GIROUX, H. (1992) 'Educational leadership and the crisis of democratic government', *Educational Researcher*, **21**(4), pp. 4–11.

GIROUX, H. and MCLAREN, P. (Eds) (1989) *Critical Pedagogy, the State and Cultural Struggle*, New York, NY: State University of New York Press.

GUMPERZ, J. (Ed) (1982) *Language and Social Identity*, Cambridge, MA: Cambridge University Press.

GUMPERZ, J. (1986) 'Interactional sociolinguistics in the study of schooling', in COOK-GUMPERZ, J. (Ed) *The Social Construction of Literacy*, Cambridge, MA: Cambridge University Press, pp. 45–68.
GUMPERZ, J. and HYMES, D. (Eds) (1964) 'The ethnography of communication', *American Anthropologists*, **66**, p. 6.
GUMPERZ, J. and HYMES, D. (1972) *Directions in Socio-linguistics: The Ethnography of Communication*, New York, NY: Holt, Rinehart, and Winston.
MCLAREN, P. (1989) *Life in Schools*, New York, NY: Longman.
MCLAREN, P. (Ed) (1991) *Postmodernism, Postcolonialism and Pedagogy*, Victoria, Australia: James Nicholas Publishers.
MERINO, B., MINNIS, D. and QUINTANAR, R. (1989) 'Models for training student teachers in multicultural education', paper presented at the Commission for Preparing Teachers for Cultural Diversity, Davis, CA: University of California.
POPKEWITZ, T.S. (1991) *A Political Sociology of Educational Reform: Power/Knowledge in Teaching, Teacher Education and Research*, New York, NY: Teachers College, Columbia University.
POPKEWITZ, T.S. (Ed) (1993) *Changing Patterns of Power: Social Regulation and Teacher Education Reform*, New York, NY: State University of New York Press.
SLEETER, C. (Ed) (1991) *Empowerment Through Multicultural Education*, Albany, NY: State University of New York Press.
SLEETER, C. and GRANT, C. (1987) 'An analysis of multicultural education in the US', *Harvard Educational Review*, **57**(4), pp. 421–44.
SPINDLER, G. (1959) *Transmission of American Culture*, The Third Burton Lecture. Cambridge, MA: Harvard University Press.
SPINDLER, G. with SPINDLER, L. (1971) *Dreamers Without Power: The Menomini Indians*, New York, NY: Holt, Rinehart and Winston, republished by Waveland Press in 1984.
SPINDLER, G. (Ed) (1978) *The Making of Psychological Anthropology*, Berkeley, CA: University of California Press.
SPINDLER, G. (Ed) (1987) *Education and Cultural Process: Anthropological Approaches*, Second Edition, Prospect Heights, IL: Waveland Press, Inc.
SPINDLER, G. (Ed) (1988) *Doing the Ethnography of Schooling: Educational Anthropology in Action*, Prospect Heights, IL: Waveland Press, Inc.
SPINDLER, G. and SPINDLER, L. (Eds) (1977) *Native North American Cultures: Four Cases*, New York, NY: Holt, Rinehart & Winston.
SPINDLER, G. and SPINDLER, L. (1982) 'Roger Harker and Schönhausen: From the familiar to the strange and back again', in SPINDLER, G. (Ed) *Doing the Ethnography of schooling*, New York, NY: Holt, Rinehart & Winston, pp. 20–47.
SPINDLER, G. and SPINDLER, L. (Eds) (1987a) *The Interpretive Ethnography of Education: At Home and Abroad*, Hillsdale, NJ: Lawrence Erlbaum Assoc.
SPINDLER, G. and SPINDLER, L. (Eds) (1987b) 'Cultural dialogue and schooling in Schoenhausen and Roseville: A comparative analysis', *Anthropology and Education Quarterly*, **18**(1), pp. 3–16.
SPINDLER, G. and SPINDLER, L. with TRUEBA, H. and WILLIAMS, M. (1990) *The American Cultural Dialogue and its Transmission*, London, England: Falmer Press.
SPINDLER, G. and SPINDLER, L. (Eds) (1994) *Pathways to Cultural Awareness: Cultural Therapy for Teachers and Students*, Newbury Park, CA: Corwin Press.
TABACHNICK, R. and ZEICHNER, K. (Eds) (1991) *Issues and Practices in Inquiry-oriented Teacher Education*, (The Wisconsin Series of Teacher Education), London, England: Falmer Press.

TRUEBA, H.T. (1993) 'Many groups, one people: The meaning and significance of multicultural education in modern America', *Bilingual Research Journal*, **16**(3) and (4), pp. 83–107.
TRUEBA, H.T., SPINDLER, G. and SPINDLER, L. (Eds) (1989) *What do Anthropologists have to Say about Dropouts?*, London, England: Falmer Press.
VYGOTSKY, L.S. (1962) *Thought and language*, Cambridge, MA: Massachusetts Institute of Technology Press.
VYGOTSKY, L.S. (1978) *Mind in society: The Development of Higher Psychological Processes*, in COLE, M., JOHN-TEINER, V., SCRIBNER, S. and SOUBERMAN, E. (Eds) Cambridge: Harvard University Press.
WERTSCH, J. (1985a) *Vygotsky and the Social Formation of Mind*, Cambridge, MA: Harvard University Press.
WERTSCH, J. (Ed) (1985b) *Culture, Communication and Cognition: Vygotskian Perspectives*, Cambridge, MA: Cambridge University Press.
WERTSCH, J. (1991) *Voices of the Mind: A Sociolcultural Approach to Mediated Action*, Cambridge, MA: Harvard University Press.
ZEICHNER, K. (1990) 'Preparing teachers for democratic schools', *Action in Teacher Education*, **11**(1), pp. 5–10.
ZEICHNER, K. (1991) 'Contradictions and tensions in the professionalization of teaching and the democratization of schools', *Teachers College Record*, **92**(2), pp. 363–79.
ZEICHNER, K. (1992) 'Educating teachers for cultural diversity', unpublished manuscript, Madison, WI: Wisconsin Center for Educational Research. School of Education, University of Wisconsin-Madison.

Chapter 10

Implications for Research and Educational Reform in the United States

Educational reform is believed to be anchored in social reform. Yet, very often social reform starts in the universities, and flows from the powerful discourse that intellectuals generate. Often it is linked to critical thinking associated with cultural therapy, or critical theory. Reform follows educational philosophy and cultural values. In the United States the wave of university protests against the Vietnam War finally brought a drastic change in government policy that ended the war. Civil rights activism in the universities since the 1960s resulted in the hirings of blacks and Hispanics in government, industry, business and public service sectors. In China, the courageous student revolt in Tiananmen Square, the deaths of hundreds of them, and the underground revolt of students seeking democratization and modernization in their country, started a new trend that will change the political structure of China in very significant ways. Thus, the role of universities is powerful, far beyond the current simplistic assumption that scholars are harmless and isolated individuals. Ideas are powerful and universities generate many of them. Mao knew this, and he wanted to change the intellectual climate of universities by exposing them to the life of the peasantry, and consequently, breaking the elitist and exclusivist life of many higher education institutions in China. The reality that has followed Mao's Revolution is modern China, not far from what he envisioned; a country in which peasants could have access to education and thus are capable of moving up the ladder.

New Intellectual Leaders and Educational Reform

Mao's Revolution resulted in a magna carta emancipating minority groups who had been conquered and oppressed and gave each of them the status of nationality (parallel status with the Han nationality). However, the actual consequences of Mao's Revolution did not have its full impact until the last decade when the new generations of the recognized nationalities began to climb the socio-economic ladder and to occupy positions of power. The most

211

important social mechanism that opened the door to previously marginal groups, such as the Miao, was the commitment of the Central Government to invest in the education of young representatives of those nationalities. The 7.3 million Miao in China as of 1990, had grown considerably from the previous decades. In 1953, a few years after their official recognition as a nationality, the Miao numbered 2.5 million, and ten years later, in 1964, 2.7 million. Their rapid growth from 1964 to 1982, when they reached a population of over 5 million, is explained by scholars as a response to reprisals for representing their true ethnic identity. For many years the Miao had been fighting the central government, run by a majority of the Han people, by not responding to the census or refusing to identify themselves as Miao until the early 1980s. The establishment of the New China in 1949 came with special respect given to all nationalities and special care in the form of subsidies for children's education. The largest number of Miao people remained in the Southwest provinces of Guizhou (3.7 million), Hunan (1.6 million) and Yunnan (near 1 million). Other Miao were scattered in Hubei, Hainan and Guangxi.

With the New China, generations of Miao children and their families began to discover the benefits of education in the form of secure government jobs and upward mobility in the private sector. Educational institutions remain relatively powerless without the approval and support of the government. But the convergence of both institutional initiatives and government support is now producing outstanding minority intellectual leaders. Contrary to what has happened in Western societies, which have focused their energy on regulatory aspects of teacher education reform that 'are partly obscured by a public discourse that focuses attention on formal responses to socioeconomic events and tends to divert critical attention away from the power that is exercised — and the interests that are served' (Popkewitz 1993:vii), Chinese educational reform focused on attracting members of the various ethnic groups to central universities for special training. The essence of the Chinese reform had been the liberation of the peasantry, especially the poorest segments of it, and the poor peasantry overrepresented by certain ethnic groups, such as the Miao.

Because this project is probably the first of its kind, and because it is limited in scope, the lessons to be learned from it for future research are modest and tentative. There are no efforts at gaining insight into the major fifteen or twenty major nationalities (out of the fifty-five, not counting the Han) through ethnographic, historical and cultural studies. The materials available in Chinese are not accessible in the United States, and there are no available translations in English or other European languages. This research project was limited for a number of reasons — lack of time and resources for lengthy personal interviews with all university students, and/or lengthy visits to their villages of origin. The interviews with selected students, and the visit to the Guizhou Province provided interesting information, but not enough to generalize for other Miao populations. The scope of the project had to center around what we suspected was the most productive approach to the understanding of high achievement among the 'peasant' children who were known by their humble origins and low status.

While national forces and diverse socio-political movements have different affects on educational institutions of each country, there is an increasing realization that a world educational system is emerging and that it exhibits similar characteristics, tensions and trends. Comparative education seems to be based on this premise (see Schriewer 1993.) How uniform the standardization of educational structures and policies, the research paradigms, the methodologies and the findings, is not clear; what seems to be clear is that in a greater or lesser measure all countries are being impacted by similar universal phenomena such as the integration of women in the labor force, the awareness of the educational rights of all individuals, the impact of information technologies, the changes in roles of teachers and the regulatory controls of state governments over educational institutions. More subtle is the increasing world-wide acceptance of ideological accountability beyond national borders and the international control of production and dissemination of knowledge via publication of journals, textbooks and other documents. The preparation of experts and their control of various fields, especially in the sciences (medical sciences, genetics, molecular biology, biochemistry, physics and mathematics) are seen as increasingly more relevant to national economic development and consequently more deserving of investment, protection and monitoring.

In spite of the recognized limitations of the present study, there are important lessons we learned for the planning of future research in China and other countries. First, regarding our research methodologies, we are aware that it is important to expand gathering data efforts and to make them more systematic. It is not enough to interview students of the same ethnic group, either individually or collectively. It is essential to visit their home villages and to assess their credibility and local recognition in order to gauge their possible impact as educational reformers. Furthermore, within the university setting, it is desirable to expand the sources of information about the process of intellectual development and the role of the mentoring relationship between professors and students. Researchers should pursue as many professors who work with minority students as possible, to investigate the role of administrators, to study the network of relationships of students across ethnic groups within the same institution, and thus assess the formation of support groups for new intellectuals who come from humble origins. Furthermore, one needs to understand these university students in their thinking patterns, and to study their written compositions for subjects outside their ethnic languages and cultures.

Another lesson from this modest study is that one cannot understand minority students and universities in China without first understanding the organizational structure of the university, the lines of authority, the distribution of labor, budget control, surveillance patterns, and role of government officials in monitoring the ideological and political matters that arise within the university. In order to obtain quality information one needs to develop very close relationships with trusting administrators and have access to the documents that cross their desks every day. There is a great deal more that is never committed to paper and reflects traditional protocol, implied obligations, reciprocal agreements, and just plain *modus operandi* that differs from Western universities. All these dimensions provide the necessary social and political context for understanding student intellectual development and their potential as future educational reformers.

Selective Approaches to Educational Reform

Educational reform that holds the promise of increasing national economic productivity and opening new avenues of modernization, information technology and international communication, are of primary concern to all governments, including the Chinese. Issues about democratization of educational opportunities to all ethnic, social and cultural groups, are most controversial in Europe, the United States, and Japan, and least controversial in China, for the historical reasons alluded to earlier (the impact of Mao's Revolution and the emancipation of all oppressed nationalities). Therefore, educational research that is related to economic development (especially basic research on the natural sciences — including medical and genetic research) is immediately impacted through international channels. On the other hand, applied educational research with some relevance to policy and reform, emphasizes from time to time central themes with presumed import for educational reform cross-culturally. These themes respond to concerns that cut across Western countries (particularly Europe and the United States) and other nations such as China, Japan and Korea. In England, for example, these themes are: quality, diversity, parental choice, school autonomy and accountability (Whitty 1993:2). In the United States, the 'new' school initiatives of 1990 and 1991 emphasized fiscal accountability, drug-free environment, parental choice, and quality. Similar themes and concerns are mentioned in Belgium, Germany, France and Spain. The rhetoric in Chinese public schools emphasizes strict discipline and accountability of students to teachers and parents. The criticism from pedagogues in the United States is that the focus of educational reform and concern statements is too narrow, centered around schools, and mostly schools in which principals and teachers have little power to change anything. The explosiveness of ethnic issues and unemployment has serious implications for educational policy affecting ethnic minority immigrants. The main concern of many European countries is diversity, 'cultural purity', and the economy. The threat of documented and undocumented immigrants has risen to a level of hysteria and has resulted in violent public responses against innocent victims of bigotry.

In order to discuss the implications of this study for research and educational reform, we should outline some of the specific educational assumptions that guided the study:

Implications for Research and Reform in the US

1. Much of the disparity and problem facing education, and much of the resulting despair among educators is intimately connected with the ineffective role of federal organizations, policies and practices. Therefore, a great deal can be accomplished towards the improvement of educational practice if federal institutions and policies became instrumental forces to streamline bureaucracies and to create clear lines of accountability in state and national organizations responsible for educational outputs.
2. The outcomes of schooling are intimately related to the social and cultural setting in which students live, the community, peer organizations, and especially the outside forces (violence, drugs, lawlessness, etc.), which poison the school learning environment and oppose instructional effectiveness.
3. Ethnic, linguistic, and socio-economic diversity can become a positive force in the construction of democratic societies, provided that schools, universities, businesses, industry and the federal government work jointly with local communities to develop adequate learning environments for students, provide support to teachers, and demand accountability from school personnel to the communities.
4. The infrastructure of the US economy, and its ultimate survival as a model democracy in the world, are contingent upon the successful pursuit of the American dream of opening educational opportunities for all peoples, particularly for low-income, handicapped, ethnic, linguistic and other minority students who are underrepresented in colleges and universities.

Educational research focused on issues of diversity and equality is bound to explore the need for structural reforms in educational systems and to ask questions such as the following:

1. Have schools become warehouses for minority children? Do they have a chance to get an education? Are schools, as learning centers, the prerogative of the middle and upper classes? If so, what are the consequences for our democracy, social order and correctional system?
2. Are the schools doing a good job? Are they preparing our children to meet the demands of life, industries, businesses, professional careers, and positions of responsibility? Are they reaching most students?

The recognition that *all* children can be educated and that their linguistic, cultural and socioeconomic differences can enhance the educational experience of all children in a democratic society is now questioned and new advocacy for resegregated schools has resulted in the neglect of many children whose only fault is being different and/or poor. An integral part of American education has been the inter-ethnic rich experience of its pluralistic society. The diversity of that cultural heritage and the significant contributions of many members of ethnic and linguistic groups have enriched American science and technology, and have defended the US democracy against the waves of hatred and racism around the world. Schools have an important role in creating a pluralistic society in a climate of respect and appreciation for other cultures, languages, traditions and life styles. We know that effective schools are few and are often those supported by elite communities. Illiteracy, violence, drugs and teacher frustration have been on the increase consistently over the last twenty years. Teachers, principals and superintendents candidly confess that they feel unprepared to make schools effective educational institutions.

Adults seeking retention, or retraining for new employment, are often deprived of the means to pay for their education and lack orientation to search for the right educational opportunities. Indeed school effectiveness is pervasive even beyond K–12 and ignores the technical demands of modern industrial conglomerates and businesses. School authorities and teachers are not able to search for the appropriate technological assistance to upgrade the professional skills of their educational personnel.

Finally, communities, especially those in metropolitan or urban centers, are often no longer functional units within the support system that maintained school effectiveness and high morale among students and teachers. As these communities have become dysfunctional, so have their schools. Accountability in these schools for successful outcomes is no longer realistic or possible. Survival (in the short-term) is the top priority of teachers and students; teaching or learning is secondary.

Educational research, including studies focused on minority groups, will ask questions addressing the comparability and competitiveness of educational training across countries, such as the following: In comparison with other industrial societies, is our students' school performance competitive? Are the levels of achievement in specific subjects, especially in math and science, considered inferior to that of some European and Asian countries? Western democratic societies, for example in Europe and in Latin America, have chosen not to support policies of educational opportunity for all. Indeed, while the performance of students at certain levels and in certain disciplines seems to be higher than that of American students, the participation of members in some segments and social strata of those societies is indeed curtailed; in fact, many higher education institutions become elite organizations closed to low-income individuals, immigrants and minorities. America has chosen to maintain an educational system open to all, but at the same time, America wants to maintain the quality of its schools along with their ethnic and economic diversity. Is this possible, and at what cost and under what conditions?

We are not going to abandon our educational democratic ideals, but we must pursue quality through strategic planning and selected investment of federal resources. We have confidence that all children can learn if they receive adequate support and assistance. The use of their home languages and cultures as a means to maximize their motivation to achieve and to embrace the English language and American values is still the best alternative and the most effective path to quality education. Educational outreach activities are intended to include ethnic and low-income communities, to offer them educational alternatives, to assist families of immigrants and refugees in their adjustment to this country, to reward excellence wherever it is found (even amongst the poorest) and to use the rich multicultural resources of America in promoting excellence and academic achievement for all children.

Basic Reform in Academia

Beyond issues of equity and diversity, as developing countries improve their postsecondary education, they need to create more effective school organizations in order to pursue and evaluate goals of instructional effectiveness. Schools in Europe and the United States are at the mercy of complex federal, state and local bureaucracies, and there is no simple way of reorganizing them without first attempting to coordinate all federal agencies involved with the schools. In contrast, China's system is more centralized and monolithic, and financial and ideological matters are closely monitored. There is an increase at the national level in the accountability of school personnel, and incentives exist to improve the performance of teachers, teacher trainers, and personnel from school districts, state departments of education, colleges and universities. Consequently, the need for a major simplification of the gatekeeping operations on the part of federal institutions relative to regional institutions is becoming urgent. The amount of time and paperwork teachers, principals and other school personnel must face to receive central government funds is often multiplied by the lack of coordination between the layers of offices, institutions and programs and within central departments of education. The amount of waste of resources, time and money involved in handling educational matters from central government offices is becoming a nightmare and is compounded by bureaucratic idiosyncrasies, thus raising everybody's level of frustration.

In brief, the global questions facing educational research, especially applied research with implications for equity and reform, revolve around the following concerns:

1. How to energize bureaucracies and create accountability to the public?
2. How to use technology to facilitate instruction and communication in educational institutions?
3. How to conduct strategic planning and develop realistic implementation steps.
4. Whether to focus on teacher education reform emphasizing field-based activities, support groups, in-service activities, or other vital areas of education.
5. How to develop and maintain instructional partnerships with industries, businesses, and other interested parties?
6. Whether to redefine the school mission and the purpose of education.

Role of Universities in Democratic Reform of Schools

Public universities in western countries are rightly viewed as the foundations of democracies, as the institutions par excellence responsible for opening the doors of social participation to *all* peoples — especially those who have been oppressed; thus, institutions supported with state and federal monies are expected to help build and maintain the economic, social and technological infrastructure of society. In China, public universities are tightly controlled by the government in order to prevent 'destructive' ideologies from 'poisoning' students' minds. Universities have no business dealing with politics in China. On the other hand, universities, as in western societies, are expected to serve *all* citizens, and to pursue equity policies in favor of equal service and opportunity to *all* students regardless of origin, ethnicity and religious differences. Furthermore, both western and Chinese public universities have the responsibility for preparing school personnel responsible for instruction — teachers, principals, superintendents and curriculum experts. Additionally, Chinese and western universities have also been charged with the responsibility of preparing public health professionals, physicians and scientists in charge of the health system. In western societies, health and education are required conditions for competent participation of citizens in democratic institutions; in Chinese universities, health and education are required for dedication and obedience congruent with good citizenship. Investments in the health and education of children and their families is still viewed in China and in America as the necessary price for maintaining a strong and well-trained labor force, a strong economic growth, a competitive edge in technological development, and an adequate military power.

Educational Problems in North America

Many attacks against urban American elementary and secondary schools are justified and reflect social neglect, racial and ethnic biases, disorganization and lack of financial support. In contrast, the American system of higher education continues to be perceived as the strongest and best funded in the world. Research and development in all fields, especially in communication technologies, medical fields and the social sciences, continues to excel in comparison with European and Asian universities, and are often recognized as the best in some fields. However, the recent decline in many higher education institutions, notably the California system of higher education, although it is a part of the slow economic recovery of the 1980s and 90s, has shown the vulnerability of the entire American university system and the speed of academic erosion in the educational values of the American people. There is an increasing lack of commitment to the long-term education of the new generation of children. The unwillingness to invest in the next generation is a mystery, especially if the economic consequences — for example in the retirement system, health services and overall quality of life — will be felt by today's taxpayers.

The increasing trend of research universities to pursue adequate funding from private and federal sources is a response to the lack of state support on the part of the legislature; the lack of support from the state is a reaction to the perceived indifference of universities to the interests of local constituencies. This phenomenon is called 'the privatization of public institutions of learning'. As the trend to withdraw state support increases, so does the struggle to tailor research priorities to the highest bidders and to increase the percentage of extramural monies to maintain the quality of university functions. These problems face not only American universities, but also European universities. The consequences of this trend to underfund research institutions are many and extremely pernicious. Public universities are been redefined as 'publicly assisted' not 'publicly supported' institutions, consequently they have less commitment to local constituencies and closer ties to outsider sources of funding. The revolt of faculties whose salaries have remained low over the last decade, while the demands on their time and the pressures have escalated, is perfectly understandable. Rapid inter-institutional mobility and low morale are two immediate results of this trend.

There is another more pernicious trend that has accompanied the withdrawal of state support: the demand for compliance with regulatory demands from state and federal organizations whose role consists primarily of policing the performance of university personnel. The assumption is that an increase in the quality of instruction and services for students will follow an increase in compliance with regulatory policies from the state. A great many resources and much time is spent in checking compliance and studying non-compliance. This has been accentuated during the most recent budget cuts in state support.

In this climate of distrust and lack of morale, the commitment of universities to the education of school children and youth is put to a serious test. There is not only a consistent lack of resources to expand university activities in partnership with schools, and to pursue innovative interdisciplinary approaches to help schools cope with their problems, but there is consistent harassment by state authorities, regents and central administrators to monitor the academic production of faculty: credit hours, office hours, use of budget resources, increased amount of paper work to participate in school activities, lack of flexibility and monies to allow faculty to work in schools, etc. The continuous reviews — within the university, across universities to cover entire university systems — mandated by diverse authorities, are used as a means to target budget cuts and distribution of support for competing programs (teacher education programs, health programs, etc.).

One should add that a visit to universities around the country and the simple reading of educational journals and nationally respected newspapers are enough to persuade anybody that many universities lack visionary leaders, genuinely committed to the education of *all* children and especially individuals with the backbone necessary to face the anarchy in which faculty have learned to live. The lack of incentives for faculty to serve the public, and the lack of vision to inspire them to do so result in conflicting entrepreneurship of individuals who seek their personal welfare at the expense of the common welfare of the institution and of the students they are supposed to serve. Petty politics, rivalry, lack of decency in dealing with each other, sheer hatred and racism, petty abuse of university resources, negligence of academic ideals, refusal to serve as good citizens in the governance of the institution, abuse of power in university committees, self-righteousness and arrogance in judging faculty performance (especially the performance of women and young faculty), lack of respect for students' rights and needs, refusal to cooperate with colleagues across departments and even within departments, and ultimately sterility resulting from self-perpetuation and intellectual self-cloning, are problems that become accentuated during periods of consistent stress and lack of support from state and central administration authorities.

Because the performance of faculty and staff under stress and with low morale is lowered by the lack of investment and incentives on the part of the central administration, there is a vicious circle of poor performance and decreased support. Ultimately, faculty have the need to search for incentives outside the university, either within their professional fields or totally outside of academia. One of the elements that speeds the demoralization of faculties is the lack of mechanisms for the faculty to voice their concerns and obtain responses from the administration. The frequent departure of the best faculty and the lack of quality replacements (when there are funds to replace them) gradually results in the acceptance of institutional mediocrity and the colonization by professional dilettantes who can no longer advance knowledge, but retain a thin layer of disciplinary knowledge to teach routine courses with the least possible effort.

Survival and Elitism in North America and China

Higher education institutions that have managed to retain their high status as research institutions and thus their fiscal resources and faculty, have often used a dual standard a rhetoric of openness and a practice of restricted acceptance of outsiders; openness in rhetoric means liberal discourse and written communication on issues of educational philosophy and academic policies, as well as liberal policies in the pursuit of students and faculty from other countries. Openness in rhetoric is exemplified by discussions or written discourse on philosophical and disciplinary matters, as well as openness in the pursuit of students and faculty from multicultural and international backgrounds. The actual selection of underrepresented students and their retention reflect selective patterns of gradual incorporation of outsiders with conditions. These institutions have managed to remain fairly well-supported by their constituencies, by the legislature, regents, departments of public instruction, etc. The role of the central administration is to maintain both the rhetoric of liberalism and the practice of rigid selection of faculty and students. The overall balance and trends remain unchanged over the years in terms of the social, ethnic and economic composition of faculty and students.

These organizations function in a relatively unchanged rigid culture that constrains new administrators in the amount of change they can make. The infinite number of mechanisms to prevent deans, vice chancellors and chancellors from making changes, reflect the strength of the departmental governance traditions of discourse, gatekeeping and lip-service to liberal causes. In truth, the curriculum may remain untouched for decades, the process of hiring, promoting or denying tenure and promotion might continue for decades, regardless of the obvious inequities, abuse of power and the changes in disciplines and new fields of inquiry around the country. Change is avoided until the end, because the investment in the status quo is long-term and very high.

It is precisely in this context that the rhetoric of acceptance of African American, Latinos, Native Americans, and other underrepresented students is contradicted by the little effort invested in preparing them to face traditional hurdles in day-to-day management, and to achieve at the level of white students. By the same token, some African American, Latino and Native Americans faculty are attracted to the junior ranks, and as they approach tenure they are discouraged and turned down, rather than assisted, coached and promoted to the higher ranks. The same, although to a lesser extent, is happening in the hiring and promotion of women.

The survival of predominantly white institutions with white faculties and traditional structures is perfectly compatible with the rhetoric of liberalism and the myth of being an open institution, because few token minorities are retained in lower level positions and in some disciplines where they look less dangerous, (politically, as well as from the standpoint of the disciplines they represent) minorities are seen as incompetent to lead a discipline through new trends. In brief, elitism and protectionism of traditional disciplines are perfectly compatible with the appearance of openness. These elitist institutions become revolving doors for faculty and students who are trapped, or have no other choice. In the end, working in these institutions discloses to many underrepresented minorities and women the hypocrisy and viciousness of racism protected by the cloak of 'academic excellence' and the semblance of 'disciplinary purity'. Righteous senior faculty can very easily spread doubts about the likelihood that a junior minority faculty may ever make it to the rank of associate professor with tenure. The consensus of those in power remains the norm of 'quality' scholarly work, regardless of the authorities outside the institution that respect the work of the faculty in probation. The arrogance of members of divisional committees or faculty committees, whose judgment is defended by these committees, against authorities in the same field outside the institution, leads to numerous grievances and erroneous decisions.

In this context of university turmoil and disarray, where faculty are engaged in cannibalistic exchanges and displays of insane arrogance, where faculty are confused and demoralized, where key administrators lack vision, integrity and leadership skills, and where public opinion, the legislature and the public in general are unwilling to continue to support traditional institutions giving the appearance of being less and less willing to serve students, and less and less accountable, it is not a surprise that the overall commitment of universities to the education and welfare of children has suffered a great deal. The above struggles are key factors in demoralizing institutions from investing in future generations. Their energies are invested in survival and self-preservation.

What can Chinese universities learn from the problems faced by Western universities? How can these problems be avoided? In the first place, Chinese universities are clearly underfunded, they are relatively very few, and they are under strict surveillance. Academic freedom, research and development projects, international exchanges, and in the natural and medical sciences, adequate equipment, appropriate training of personnel and incentives to stay, are practically nonexistent. The rapid brain drain of Chinese universities is being felt these days. In America alone, in July of 1993, about 46,000 Chinese students and visiting scholars (including Ph.Ds and MDs) received their 'green cards' or residents' status. The development of higher education institutions takes many years, consistent and generous support from stable sources, and acceptable policies dictating state–university relations. It is not enough to bring to the university in greater numbers children of peasants, representatives of ethnic groups so far marginalized, and other individuals committed to equity principles and a liberal philosophy of education. Much more will be needed in order to fully develop the talents of Chinese youngsters who attend universities. In some respects, the American university system, which is indeed totally foreign to Chinese culture, may be used to design the cultural equivalent in China, a type of university that is well-funded and has incentives to retain the brightest. Ultimately, university professors must be committed to the education of the next generation.

Our contention is that this commitment to children and the future generations can be precisely the missing element that can help redirect institutions of higher education and help focus the many misguided efforts to regain public support and momentum in the difficult fiscal recovery facing many of those institutions. The fundamental *raison d'etre* of universities must be related to the overall welfare of society, and consequently, the welfare of children and families. Not only some families, those with the means to pay high tuition costs, or those who can make the highest grades, but also the children that tend to be neglected by the school system and never reach the university. Universities have a vested interest in retaining their public character and service commitment to *all* citizens, because without this character, the financial support to these universities will be (and has been) removed. Private institutions have the prerogative of maintaining elite populations and select their student bodies. Yet, paradoxically, many private institutions, such as Stanford, Harvard, Yale, Cornell, Syracuse, and many other outstanding institutions, have been more open to students of color and have supported a genuine balance of both incomes and diverse ethnic, racial and cultural backgrounds, than public institutions. They have been more successful in diversifying faculty and student bodies than many public universities.

Why would the commitment to *all* children be desirable as a central focus to attract public support and diversify public institutions? The reorganization of the curriculum, the selection of diverse faculty (representing underrepresented minority groups), the adoption of admission and instructional policies encouraging minorities to enter and graduate from the university, cannot as of themselves solve the serious lack of prepared underrepresented student populations to compete well with mainstream populations. The work of universities needs to start much earlier. Faculty from all disciplines and fields must join forces and take ownership in efforts to prepare children to do well in elementary and secondary school, to be guided wisely into all academic and non-academic professions, to accept the values required to succeed in the university (high literacy level, commitment to study). For as long as the university remains isolated from the schools and communities, waiting for low-income and underrepresented minority students to apply, it will remain an institution for the mainstream only, and will continue to increase the gap between persons of color and those who enter universities and pursue degrees. Ultimately, the very survival of our democratic system will depend on the success of the universities to recognize their responsibility to help educate *all* children and to actively pursue this commitment in collaboration with schools and community organizations.

References

POPKEWITZ, T.S. (Ed) (1993) *Changing Patterns of Power: Social Regulation and Teacher Education Reform*, New York, NY: State University of New York Press.

SCHRIEWER, J. (1993) 'Comparative education in the emerging world society', paper presented at the international conference on 'Educational Reform: Changing Relationships between the State, Civil Society and the Educational Community' Madison, WI: University of Wisconsin-Madison, June 18–21, 1993.

WHITTY, G. (1993) 'New schools for new times? Education reform in a global context', paper presented at the international conference on 'Educational Reform: Changing Relationships between the State, Civil Society and the Educational Community' Madison, WI: University of Wisconsin-Madison, June 18–21, 1993.

Index

acculturation 32
achievement motivation 109, 115, 150, 189, 207
  across cultures 131
  and behaviour 188
  and honor 159
  and language and culture 170–89
  resistance to 148
achievement theories 152
adaptive strategies 109, 197
  effective 176–7, 180
adjustment strategies 176
African American culture: and violence 193
agriculture: in China 60
  by Miao 84
ambitions: of students 128–9
American culture: holistic model 33
  multiculture of 204–5, 216
Anshun, Guizhou 99
anthropological ethnography 36
Asian Americans 161
autonomous regions, of China 54, 62, **63**, 64
  differences with provinces 65
  power of 58, 65

Bakhtin, Mikhail 171, 173
Bakhtinians 24, 36
behaviour: and achievement motivation 188
  changes in 137, 138
  holistic description of 37
  interpretation and study of 35
  and language 38
  in pluralistic societies 37
  rigidification of 141
  in social context 37, 156

Beijing 61, 113
boundaries: and ethnic identity 141, 156
Bouyei 66–8 *passim*
Britain: and opium trade 56–7
Burakumin: social oppression of 17–18

castelike concept 19, 153–8
  passim, 185
castification 43, 159, 175
Central University for Nationalities (CUN), Beijing 84, 105, 113–14
  student testimonies 88–98
Chahua, Yunnan 101
change: agents of 192
  by students 123–7, 135, 158, 165
  in universities 220–1
Chen Yongling **Plate 7**
children: educational commitment to 222–3
  immigrant 150, 160
  labour 102
  marginalization of 199
  poverty of, in US 161–4
  see also socialization, early
China: African prejudice 165
  autonomous regions 54, 58, 61, 62, **63**, 64
  brain drain 222
  census, 1982 60
  closed society 56
  economic reforms in 61
  educational reform 212
  ethnic groups 3
  minority empowerment 23, 62, 64, 147–8
  modern political organization 61–71
  multiculture of 157, 204–5
  national unity 61–2

224

Index

open economy 60
population 53–4, 59, 61, 133
provinces 62, **63**
racial differences 53
social change, and culture 41, 54
universities in 109–10, 165, 200
Chinese identity 58
class: and schooling 14, 15
clothing style: of Miao 81, 86, **Plate 4**
colonial system, and racism 181
commitment, of Miao: to children 222–3
students, to education 83–108, 110, 112, 119, 139, 207
to people 134, 147
communication: in China 121–2
between nationalities 94
with parents 119–20, 121–2
community: sharing in 92
conscientization: process of 158, 195, 201, 207–8
critical theory 5, 20, 21, 192–6, 201–6
cross-cultural: comparison 37, 38, 40
research 12, 48
culture: acquisition 33, 40
and action 41
and behaviour 38
concept of 39–42
definition 39
and economy 14
and educational ethnography 31–48
and empowerment 21, 24, 148
and ethnicity 42–5
Miao 80–1, 100, 108
role in social identification 170–89
and schooling 14, 16
and social change in China 41
see also American culture
cultural: characteristics, of Miao 4, 5, 11, 13, 19
conflict 32
discontinuities 197
ecology 17, 20, 152, 156–8
heritage 94
inversion 18, 154–5
myths 23
pluralism 204
reality 199
therapy 5, 20–1, 192–201
transmission 33, 40, 41
unilineal evolution 24
values system 22, 86, 123–5, 140, 150, 197, 207
curriculum: hidden 22
and inequality 15, 22

data: analysis 37, 47
collection 37, 45, 47, 213
deconstructionism 173–4
decontextualization 172
Dekun Wu 84
democratization: and education 131
Deng Xiaoping 59, 60
determinism 154, 158
biological 185
cultural 185
psychological 185
Dingzhi Pan 84
discontinuities: cultural inversion 18
primary and secondary 154, 155
disempowerment 20, 21, 23, 24, 159, 166
and ethnography 44
of minority children 21, 174, 175
and poverty 158–67
disproportionate academic failure 153
Dong 66–8 *passim*
drapetomania 181
drop outs: from school 164
Du Xiaobo 93–4, 104, 111, 112, 117, 119–23 *passim*, 125, 127, 128, 134

economy: and culture 14
education, and Miao 1–3, 77–80, 86–108, 194, 203
benefits of 212
commitment to, and honor 37–8, 103, 159
comparative 213, 216
and cultural system 151
and democratization 131
and empowerment 13, 147, 148, 192
for all 195, 215, 216
higher 79–80, 110
and income 162–3
investment in 212
and modernization of rural communities 130
multicultural 204–5
payment for 216
postmodern 202
and poverty 79, 88–91, 92, 95–7
socio-cultural change through 137
world system 213
educational ethnography 32
research design 31–48
educational reform 164, 211–23
emancipation 196
empowerment, and Miao 1–3, 133, 164–5, 207

225

Index

and critical theory 192–6, 201–6
and cultural therapy 192–20
and education 13, 147, 148, 192
and ethnography 43–4, 130
and language 106–7
and minorities 133
processes 20–5, 131, 132, 146, 147, 151, 159, 175, 200
enculturation 206
equality: between cultures 104
ethnic: cleansing 23
  conflict 42
  hatred 184
  identity 155–6
    and education 1–3, 11, 13, 139, 143
    and empowerment 3, 132
    and language 170–89
    process of 4, 17–20
    and self-identification 18
  minorities 3, 4, 11
    in China 3, 12, 13–17, 62, 66–71
    empowerment 13, 48, 64
    group boundaries 23, 42, 182
  pluralism 39, 42, 43
  prejudice 182
ethnocentrism 23, 24, 182, 183, 197, 200, 208
ethnographic: analysis 5
  research 35, 36–8
ethnography, modern 34–6, 43–4, 171
Europe: education for all 217
  immigrants 159–61, 183

family: Miao 84, 163
  students' bond with 115, 117–19, 134
  disintegration of 178
feelings: and Chinese 134
  of Miao students 137
food: lack of 120–1, 135

gangs: youth, and socialization 178–91
gender: inequality of 87
government: grants from 6, 112
  gratitude to 105
grants: education 6, 112
Guangxi Zhuang, China **63**, 64, 72, 74
guestworkers 159
Guizhou 105, 144
Guizhou Institute for Nationalities (GIN) **Plates 1, 5,** 46–7, 79, 84, 105, 114–15
  student testimonies 98–102
Gu Jiehua **Plate 6**
Gu She (Jiang Lue) 85

Han 66, 70
  hegemony 57–8, 61, 64, 133
  language: *see* Mandarin
Hanren 58
hardship: of Miao families 102, 104
  see also under education: poverty
Hispanic: in US 161, 162
Hmong 1, 131
  in US 11, 107–8
  achievement motivation 115
holistic: description, of human behaviour 37
  model, of American culture 33
Hong Kong 57, 60
honor, for parents 134, 139, 159
  and education 37–8, 103
  obligation of 104, 139, 140
housing 84, 85
Hua Guofeng 59, 60
Huangguoshu Pubu, Guizhou **ix**
Huang Xiuyi **Plate 6**
Huaqiao, Yunnan 102
Hui 4, 59, 66–8 *passim,* 71, 73, 133, 156

illiteracy rate: of Miao 78, 102
immigrants: assimilation of 42, 175, 179
  children 150
  European 159–60
  success of 131
  in US 182
income: average annual, of Miao families 112, 133, 156
  and education 162–3
inequality: and critical pedagogy 203
Inner Mongolia, China 62, **63**, 70
inquiry-oriented teacher education 24
institutes for nationalities 79
instrumental statements 142
internalization: process of 141
interviews: in research 45–7
introception 141
Islam 73

Japanese Americans 180, 188
Jesuit missionaries: in China 56
Jewish Holocaust 23, 183, 199
Jilin City, China 7, 8

knowledge: acquisition of 189
  and power 105
Koreans: in China 59
  language of 65

226

language, local: and dialects 67, 100, 144
  diversity of 67
  and education 11, 13, 16
  and empowerment 21, 24, 106–7, 148
  and ethnic minorities 3, 70
  importance of 22
  mediating role, in social identification 170–89
  Miao 67, 80, 93–5 *passim*, 97, 99, 100, 102, 105, 108, 144, 146
  oral 106
  role, in culture and behaviour 38
  and social identification 5
  use of 65
language, regional 71
Latin America: ethnic pluralism in 43
learning: and experience 22
letters: importance of, for students 119–20
Li Liao 85
Li Maohong 101, 108, 111, 118–22 *passim*, 124, 126–7, 129, 134
Lin Yaohua **Plate** 7
Long Jianhua 92–3, 111, 117, 119–23 *passim*, 125, 127, 128, 135, 136

Manchu 4, 66–8 *passim*, 71, 72, 165
Manchu-Tungus 59
Mandarin language 70, 71, 89, 93–5 *passim*, 104, 105, 107, 112, 133, 147
Mao Zedong 54, 59, 60, 102
  Revolution 1949 12, 23, 59, 159
    and education for all 211
  social reforms 158
marginalization 151
  of children 199
marriage: arranged 87–8, 122, 123
  choice of partner 122–3, 135
  costs of 87–8, 123
  laws 65
  and Miao 81, 84, 87
Mashan, school 78–9
media: and sociocultural change 194
mediated action theory 24, 172, 174
methodology research 4, 34–5
Mexican: culture 39
  youth gangs, in California 179–80, 188
Miao 4, 42, 66–8 *passim*, 71, 74–81
  aspirations 137
  clothing **ix**, 81
  commitment to education 37–8, 103
  culture 80–1
  disenfranchised 152
  distribution 74, 107–8, 144, 212
  emancipation 106
  empowerment 133, 164–5
    as example of equality 134
  history 4, 75–7
  inner self 140–3
  isolation 152
  languages 67, 80
  lifestyle 146
  marriage 81, 84, 87–8
  migrations 75–6, 146
  oppression 76–7
  patrilineal clans 81, 84, 85
  population 74, 144, 212
  school education 45, 77–80, 88–102
  self-sufficiency 108
  uprisings 78
  and US Hmong 1, 107–8
  see also under language, local; students, Miao
migration, by Miao 3, 4, 146
minorities 53, 152, 153
  castelike 153, 154, 156, 157–8
  immigrant 153
  involuntary 154–6 *passim*
  voluntary 153–6 *passim*
  see also ethnic: minorities
modernization: and ethnic identity 132
Mongolians 59, 73, 156
  language 65
Moroccan immigrants: to Belgium 165–6
motivation: of Miao 2, 148
  see also achievement motivation
multiculturalism 5, 39, 157, 204–5, 216
multilingualism 39

nationalities: and ethnic groups, in China 3
Na Yong, Guizhou 94
Neo-Vygotskians 22, 24, 34, 36, 174
Ningxia Hui, China **63**, 64, 73

obligation: sense of 104, 139, 140
opium: trade 56–7
  war 1839 56
oppositional self-concept 152, 155, 156
oppression, of Miao 3, 19, 156, 159, 193, 207
  and self-esteem 182
  and status 192
oral evidence: in research 46

parents: respect for 119
patrilineal clans 81, 84, 85
personal experiences: of Miao students 140

Index

personality integrity: of Miao 197
pluralistic societies: behaviour in 37
population: of China 53–4, 59, 61
  of ethnic minorities 66–8
  of Miao 74, 144, 212
poverty: cycle of 164
  and disempowerment 158–67
  and education 88–91, 92, 95, 96, 106
  of Miao 77, 156
  and US children 161–4
  in US 159–61, 167, 185
power: and knowledge 105
  structures 166
provinces: of China 62, **63**, 64
  and autonomous regions 65
psychological: anthropology 32
  ethnography 36
psychopedagogics 22

qualitative research methods 31, 32, 35
questionnaires 47, 110–29

racial purity 23
racism 197
  in Europe 183
  in US 163, 181, 182
reflective teaching 24, 174, 206
relationships, personal: of Miao students 134
research design 4, 12
  of educational ethnography 31, 45–8
  qualitative methods in 31, 32, 35
responsibility: sense of 140
rigidification: of behaviour 141
role models: for Miao students 138
Russians: in China 59

sacrifices: of parents 139
  by Miao students 118, 143
Santou economic zone 60
schooling: dynamic mechanisms of 14
schools: effective 216
  failure of 34, 187
  function of 14
  funding, and effect on poor children 163–4
  quality of 216–17
  role, in creating and maintaining social strata 14–15, 203
secret societies: in China 54–5
selective permeability 188
self: enduring 196, 197, 199
  situated 196, 197, 199
self-concept: children's 22, 197
  of Miao 138
  oppositional 152, 155, 156
self-determination 151
self-esteem: sources of 138–9
self-identification 2, 38, 110, 179
  inner Miao 140–3
  process of 18, 192
self-pity 104
sexual codes: at university 113
sexual relations: and marriage 88
Shanghai: population density 61
Shangshui, Guizhou 96
Shenzen economic zone 60
social: change, and culture, in China 41
  epistemology 14
  identification 17–20, 200
    for achievement 130–7
    contradiction in 152
    and family values 159
    theory of 137–40
  neglect 176
  status, change for students 125–7
socialization, early 20, 84, 150–67
  passim, 206–7
  abuse and neglect 150
  and cultural change 21
  and cultural therapy 197
  home 150
  and low status 186
  process 143
  and rigidification of behaviour 141
  role of language and culture in, 170–89
  school 150
  and social identification 150, 151
  through gangs 178–81
society: conflict in 156
sociocultural change: and media 194
socioeconomic change: in China 54
sociolinguistics 171
Sogdian script 73
Solomon Islands: schooling and status 16
Special Economic Zones, China 60
standards reaffirmation 175
status: low, and early socialization 186
  of Miao, and education 132, 136, 147
students, Miao: biographies of 47
  change in values 123–5
  characteristics 109, 110–15
  as Chinese citizens 159
  early years of training 88–102, 109, 110

Index

expectations of 123
goals of 128–9
instructors' treatment of 127–8
role as educational leaders 143
sacrifices by 118, 143, 200
social status, change in 125–7, 135, 158, 165
success: measurement of 139
Sushen 72

Taijing County: Miao in 78
Taiping rebellion 55–6
Taiwan: and China 60
Tajiks 59
Tao Wencen 101–2, 111, 118–22 *passim*, 124, 126, 127, 129, 135
Tao Xiaoping 98, 111, 112, 117, 119–22 *passim*, 124, 126–8 *passim*, 135, 136
terrorism: and ethnography 43
Tiananmen Square demonstration 1989 59, 211
Tianjin: population density 61
Tian Zhenmin 94–5, 105–6, 111, 117, 119–23 *passim*, 125, 127, 128
Tibetans 66–8 *passim*
Tibet, China **63**, 64, 65, 70
transcultural comparative perspectives 35
transfer culture 151
transport: problems of, for Miao 94, 96
Triads 55
Trueba, Henry **ix**, 34, **Plates 2**, **6**, **8**, 158
life history 9–11
Tujia 66–8 *passim*
Turkic 59
language 73

university: in China 109–10
commitment of 219, 222–3
demoralization in 220, 222
education, commitment of Miao students 83–108, 110, 112, 119, 139, 207
experiences at 109–29, 119–22, 152
life 112–13, 136
organizational structure 213
private, in US 223
rewards from 103, 119, 212
role of 211, 218, 220
underfunding 219, 220, 222
US: castelike minorities in 157–8
and education for all 217
educational problems 218–20
elitism in 220–2

immigrants 159–61, 167, 182
self-concept and prejudice in 181–9
Uygur 4, 66–8 *passim*, 71, 73–4
language 65
population 73
Uygur: *see* Xinjiang Uygur, China

values: change in students' 123–5, 136, 137
of Chinese families 139
value system: in culture 39
hierarchy of 103–4
Vietnamese youth gangs 178–9
village head 85
village life: equalitarianism 85
among Miao 84–8
organizational structure 84, 85
Vygotsky, Lev S. 171–3

Wang Bingzhong 100, 111, 118–22 *passim*, 124, 126–8 *passim*, 136
Wang Daqing 88–91, 103, 111, 115–17, 119–23 *passim*, 125, 127, 128, 134–6 *passim*
Wang Zhongmin 95–6, 106, 111, 112, 117, 119–22 *passim*, 124, 125, 127, 128
Weining, Yunnan 84
western societies: and ethnics 200
White Lotus Sect 55
witch doctors 86
work ethic written evidence: in research 45, 46
Wu Dekun, Professor: life history of 143–5, 146
Wu Zhiguo, President, Guizhou Institute for Nationalities **Plate 8**

xenophobia 163, 165, 184, 197
Xiamen economic zone 60
Xinjiang Uygur, China **63**, 64, 65, 70, 74
Xiong Jinliang 99–100, 111, 118–22 *passim*, 124, 126–8 *passim*, 135
Xiong Qiang 97–8, 107, 111, 112, 117, 119–22 *passim*, 124, 126–8 *passim*, 134–6 *passim*

Yali Zou **ix**, **Plates 7**, **8**
life history 7–9
Yang Dexin 96–7, 107, 111, 117, 119–22 *passim*, 124, 126–8 *passim*, 134–6 *passim*

Index

Yang Li 99, 104, 105, 111, 117, 119–22 *passim*, 124, 126–8 *passim*, 136
Yang Yuxi 100–1, 111, 118–22 *passim*, 124, 126–8 *passim*, 134
Yan Yingjun **Plate 6**
Yi 66–8 *passim*

Yi Lang 85
You Fang 86

Zhuang 4, 66–8 *passim*, 70–2 *passim*, 165
Zhuhai economic zone 60